UFO HUNTERS

UFO HUNTERS

BOOK ONE

WILLIAM J. BIRNES

TOR®

A TOM DOHERTY ASSOCIATES BOOK
NEW YORK

UFO HUNTERS: BOOK ONE

Copyright © 2013 by A&E Television Network

All photographs used with the permission of A&E.

A Tor Book
Published by Tom Doherty Associates, LLC
175 Fifth Avenue
New York, NY 10010

www.tor-forge.com

Tor® is a registered trademark of Tom Doherty Associates, LLC.

ISBN 978-0-7653-2520-4 (hardcover)
ISBN 978-1-4299-8799-8 (e-book)

Tor books may be purchased for educational, business, or promotional use. For information on bulk purchases, please contact Macmillan Corporate and Premium Sales Department at 1-800-221-7945 extension 5442 or write specialmarkets@macmillan.com.

First Edition: September 2013

Printed in the United States of America

0 9 8 7 6 5 4 3 2 1

Dedicated to the initial originator of the idea for *UFO Hunters*, my wife, Nancy Hayfield Birnes, the editor-in-chief of *UFO Magazine* and the cohost of Future Theater radio, who watched her idea for a series about hunting for the truth of the UFO phenomenon take shape on television. Even during the series, she stepped in to guide the show, first toward Leslie Kean's National Press Club Conference, and then to Stephenville, where we had boots on the ground even as the UFO flap continued. Nancy was the show's inspiration. Her coconspirator in this venture was Pat Uskert, who took to the road without any network backing to bring back footage and interviews that eventually became the demo reel for what would become *UFO Hunters*.

CONTENTS

ACKNOWLEDGMENTS

First to Pat Uskert, Ted Acworth, and Jeff Tomlinson, the cast of *UFO Hunters,* who put their own lives and jobs aside to join the search for UFOs. We all came from different backgrounds, had different belief systems and life experiences, but had to mesh together in front of a camera where we argued cogently and intelligently about how facts can support speculation and what happens when two and two doesn't equal four.

Next, of course, to Jon Alon Walz, our executive producer and head of the production company Motion Picture Productions, whose vision about a unique show with four guys from different backgrounds on an impossible quest that ultimately paid off, made the show possible. Our senior producer Dave Pavoni, who was the beating-heart center of the setup for each episode by turning the impossible into reality, and our coexec producers, show runners, and directors Alan LaGarde and Steve Nigg, both of whom were unflappable in the face of unimaginable difficulties with schedules and travel and last-minute conflicts. Both Alan and Steve had very special talents that went way beyond telling the camera which way to shoot. Both individuals knew how to harmonize a crew, get the best out of everyone, and all the while deal with daily demands from the production office and the network. When we almost missed our flight in Mexico City and had to get all the way across the airport while carrying our bags, it was Alan LaGarde who commandeered an electric golf cart, piled us all on top, leaned on the horn, and, in a scene from *The Great Race,* got us to the jetway just in time for the flight, while proclaiming to all, "This is what makes us a family."

Jeff Tober, the coexecutive producer and later executive producer, was in charge of all the editing and postproduction. You can watch hundreds of other UFO- and paranormal-themed reality shows but you won't find one that even comes close to the look, feel, continuity, and intelligence of *UFO Hunters.* And that's because of Jeff Tober, one of the most skilled heads of editing and postproduction in the business.

Our line producers were John Duffy and Jeremy Gardiner, assisted by coproducer and field coordinator Dan Zarenkiewicz, all of whom kept the daily production schedule flowing and coordinated the production office with the field crew.

Our writer/producers for individual episodes in Season 1 were Kevin Cummins, Tracy Chaplin, Autumn Humphreys, and Chad Horning, and also Stu Chait. Stu also served as story editor and was probably single-handedly responsible for our getting picked up for Season 2 when he was in the editing bay at the Santa Monica production office, saw my "you are a hybrid" conversation with Terrell Copeland—that was only a suggestion, by the way, not an accusation—and just as the film editor was about to cut that scene out, told him to leave it in. Stu's instincts were that good. When our new exec at History, Mike Stiller, saw the scene, he said that was the reason for the Season 2 pickup. Thanks, Stu.

In the second season we were joined by Kevin Barry, Rob Bluemthal, John Greenwald, Scott Goldie, and Dave Story, all of whom pushed us to do better, think harder, and not to cop out.

John Tindall was our FX producer, the guy who set off explosions in his lab, demonstrated what type of electrical failure brought down the B-25 over Kelso, Washington, and, with Ted Acworth, debunked the debunkers of the Rendlesham forest story by proving with his magical GPS equations that the light the U.S. Air Force personnel saw floating above the forest floor could not have been the lighthouse at Orford Ness. So much for the debunkers.

Our director of photography was Kevin Graves, probably one of the most gifted DPs in the business, who had the ability to size up a shot in an instant and pull it off quickly even as the sun was uncooperatively sneaking behind a cloud. Our B-camera operator was Brian Garrity, who could hang upside-down from rock overlooking the North Sea one day, wiggle himself into a crevasse outside of Roswell on another day, go caving while still wielding a large Varicam on another day, and still go back to L.A. to compete in a triathlon and keep up with the best and the fastest. Finally, our assistant camera, Linh Nguyen, was the support that kept the cameras rolling. He could take apart a camera and reassemble it in 110-degree Arizona desert heat and do it so quickly that the sun didn't have time to set.

Our sound mixer was my friend Shah Martinez for season 1, who worked with electrician, gaffer, and swing man Stan Eng, who never met an Asian fusion buffet he didn't like. While Shah could get sound out of a rock, Stan had the ability to create and strike a set in minutes, even as the vans were getting loaded. During season 1, on our way back to the United States from the UK after the Bentwaters episode, we discovered at the airport, to our chagrin, that the British airport baggage handlers wouldn't move our equipment because it was overweight. Brian Garrity, Kevin Graves, Linh Nguyen, Shah Martinez, and Stan Eng broke down all the equipment and repacked it while Alan LaGarde and Dan Zarenkiewicz negotiated with the airline to allow our equipment to fly home with us. It was an amazing display of competence.

I have to acknowledge all of our associate producers and production assistants, our editors and assistant editors, and all the help we received on the road.

Finally, of course, to Dolores Gavin at History, who picked us up as a series after our pilot episode and never stopped prodding us to do better, and to our exec at History, Mike Stiller, who inspired us and stood up for us the entire time.

It would be churlish and ungrateful of me not to thank my most patient publisher, Tom Doherty, and even more patient editor, Bob

Gleason, as well as editor Eric Raab and assistant editors Whitney Ross and Kelly Quinn for steering this manuscript through.

Thanks, guys, thanks to everyone, the best crew and best editors ever, for making *UFO Hunters* one of the top reality shows on television and a piece of our cultural zeitgeist. We hunted for, and eventually found and caught on camera, a UFO. It was a magnificent experience, the best three seasons of my life.

UFO HUNTERS

UFO ROAD TRIP

Al I could do was stand there, incredulous and dumbstruck, watching a metal disk in the sky as solid and substantial as a frying pan."

Pat Uskert had looked up and just stopped and stared. He truly didn't know what he was looking at on that glorious Venice Beach day in the beginning of May 2004. The Los Angeles supermarkets were preparing for Cinco de Mayo, one of the city's big festivities, and people were walking the Venice boardwalk enjoying the sea breeze.

Los Angeles is a patchwork of microclimates. What is a triple-digit temperature downtown in the Garment District or at the county courts building is easily in the 70s at the beach. And with the approach of summer when Westside Angelinos take a break from the office and head out to the boardwalk for an iced cappuccino and a walk in the sun, the appearance of something strange in the sky draws a lot of attention. So it was with Pat Uskert, working on software development for an education company, when something in the sky caught his eye and he looked up.

As Pat wrote about the event in *UFO Magazine*:

Wearing flip-flops and backpacks stuffed with towels and magazines, my girlfriend and I had just left our apartment to start the
four-block journey to the beach with big plans of lying around and
doing a whole lot of nothing—a perfect Southern California beach
day. It was about 11:30 in the morning. We shuffled down the block
and took the shortcut through an alley of garage doors and garbage
dumpsters, now heading west towards the ocean.

I don't remember exactly what we were chatting about—most
likely the weather. The sun was high and strong, and the blue sky
was flawless. Well, almost flawless. We noticed a dark spot above the
rooftops to the south. At first glance, it appeared to be a high school
prank—a hubcap thrown up and left to dangle like an old pair of
shoes. But no, there was something terribly wrong with this
hubcap—it wasn't hanging.

"Check it out. UFO over Venice!" I joked. "I know! Wouldn't that
be wild?" she added, and the conversation returned to whether or
not we had brought suntan lotion.

When we got to the street, we turned south towards Rose Avenue, making our way to the corner. We walked, again seeing the
dark spot and feeling it to be a nuisance blemishing an otherwise
perfect canvas of blue. We continued south, now walking and looking
up, both observing the black ball in the sky, just above the telephone
lines. Our pace slowed, and then our flip-flops came to a stop. The
dark spot had our attention. Hanna and I ran through a checklist of
what it could be: airplane, helicopter, balloon, huge wingless bird,
all of which we crossed off the list. The black ball begged to be identified. "I can't be seeing a UFO," I kept telling myself. "This has to be
some kind of stray blimp." Then, from behind us, came a cry from a
grown man. "Jesus Christ! Do you see that?" I turned back to see a
male in his late 30s in a T-shirt, shorts, and sunglasses, pointing up.
"Do you see that?" His voice conveyed alarm and anxiety. He was
clearly agitated. "Holy shit!" he exclaimed, stepping away from his
car. "Do you guys see that?" His voice, his nervous face, the black spot
in the sky—the moment was coming into focus. My heart started

pumping. And then things got interesting. The dark spot turned. It turned and as it caught the sun, a sheen of brilliance streaked across it, revealing a smooth metallic surface and a concentric ring within the outer edge of the object. The sun glazed over the whole side of the craft, the way it might on a car turning a corner. As it continued its turn, the object's outline revealed a slight, convex dome. The object wasn't near at all, but far behind the telephone lines, perhaps a mile or so away over Marina del Rey. I had this feeling in my gut. It was the nervousness I would feel before going to bat in peewee baseball. This was like nothing I had ever seen in my life: I was looking at a flying metal disk. "This is it," I thought to myself. "I'm having a UFO sighting."

The object gleamed like tinted stainless steel, like a DeLorean seen through a dark lens. When seen from the side, it seemed to flicker as a pinwheel might. Hanna later described it as having a cockroach finish. It had the same glimmer of light you would see flashing across the back of a brown cockroach. Yes, that would about describe it—somewhere between tinted steel and a shimmering exoskeleton.

Nothing could have prepared us for this. Like anybody else who has rented sci-fi movies, we imagined what it might be like, but there's nothing quite like standing on a street corner holding a beach umbrella and looking at a steely disk floating overhead. The mind doesn't understand. The mind doesn't want to believe. The mind rejects. We could only stand there, feeling very strange.

"Video camera!" I thought. I told Hanna that I was going to run home for it. "Stay here and keep an eye on the disk. I'll be right back," I said, breaking away from the sky-gazers and dashing home as fast as my flip-flops would take me.

I fumbled my keys and pushed the apartment door open, heading straight for my camcorder over by the computer. I rummaged for a fresh tape in the camera bag, discovering that those tapes are surprisingly difficult to unwrap when you're in a real hurry. Unable to find the little pull-tab with my fingernail, I started to scrape at the whole plastic wrapping like a squirrel clawing at a nut, finally tearing it off. I popped the tape in the camera, grabbed a battery, and told myself that I was gonna get this thing. "I'm gonna do it right. No shaky footage."

In minutes, I was back out the door, clutching my camera and tripod, stumbling on the run, and thinking, "Sweet Jesus, please let that thing still be there."

The whole round trip must have taken ten minutes. I came up behind Hanna, who was still watching the object. The ranting man had left. "Do you still see it?" I asked her while attaching the camera to the tripod. She said yes and pointed it out, but my eyes couldn't bring the object into focus. I set the camera and tripod down, camera turned on. I followed her arm from elbow to wrist, and on the straight ray from her pointing finger I followed into the blue canvas. "Got it." It was further south, and much smaller now.

I knelt down and peered through the viewfinder to discover an opaque window of black—technical difficulties. With precious UFO-seconds stealing by, I was dealing with last minute camera trouble. My tripod's horizontal swivel was sticking, giving me the jerky camera motion that it was supposed to prevent, and the viewfinder must have shorted out on a prior excursion. With the grave countenance of a heart surgeon encountering complications, I flipped out the accessory screen, loosened the swivel knob and again scanned the sky in the direction Hanna was pointing.

Further south now, the object was no longer the size of a hubcap, but the size a silver dollar—a mischievous silver dollar floating among the phone lines. I managed to catch the coin descending at an angle until it came to a complete stop and hovered, halting in the air for several seconds. It was perfectly still. Then it ascended, accelerating upward in a wide arc, revealing its lustrous, silvery surface. It then assumed a perfectly horizontal flight path moving steadily from west to east, disappearing behind the top corner of the church. I lifted the tripod and stepped briskly away from the church, taking a few minutes to locate the increasingly tiny object—it was like trying to find a dust speck. It changed its course, now heading north.

The northern movement was significant. Since the coastal breeze was blowing southwest on this day, the most obvious explanation of this thing—that it was a derelict balloon—was weakened. The object had greatly increased its altitude, and it was up with the LAX and Santa Monica air traffic now, maybe a thousand feet. I later wondered: Who could see a single balloon at one thousand feet? The object began to give off its brilliant luster again, becoming a lighthouse beacon overhead. Whether it was a luminance of its own or it was simply reflecting the sun, I can't say. If it was a reflection, it was the piercing reflection of sun on glass or metal. It was a strong light, a white light.

With the relentless noon sun bleaching the viewing screen, I could only manage to catch the object for a few seconds. We watched it, now a brilliant orb high in the heavens, continuing north toward the Santa Monica Mountains until it was out of sight. As it faded from view, I was filled with a vague feeling of loss. I wondered if I would see such a thing ever again. I wondered if I had managed to catch anything at all.

Drained and bewildered, we returned to our apartment to drop off the camera and sort things out. I sat down wearily on the couch, feeling as though I had just walked away from a car wreck. Adrenaline coursed through me. My legs were shaking. My mind raced, exploring the depths of what this meant, trying to grasp what I had just seen. The object was real. It was as real as dogs and cats, as physical as pots and pans. And yet it was so unreal.

Whatever it was, I had seen it with my own eyes. This was not some show on television, but an experience as solid as mowing the lawn. My familiarity with the topic of UFOs did not mitigate the shock. Speculation had been replaced by knowledge. I no longer had to *believe*. I *knew*. And the knowledge was both a relief and a new burden.

Hanna reminded me that we still had a date with the beach. We left the camera and video behind and set out again to find a place to plant our beach umbrella. We both lay down that afternoon, pinned against our towels by the weight of pure wonder. The universe, after all, had just drawn back its curtain to give us a glimpse of its infinite possibilities. It whispered to us that there is more to the world than we will ever know. "We saw it, right?" I asked her again. "Yes," she said. "We saw it."

The weeks that followed our sighting were filled with inflamed, passionate discussion with friends, families, and neighbors about the event and the video footage. I showed the video and rattled on until I could say no more—a pause welcomed by everyone around me, I'm sure. Eventually normal routine and topics of conversation had returned to our lives. But not for long.

About four weeks after the first sighting, on May 27, around 8:30 in the evening, I saw something in the sky that was unmistakably foreign to this world. I had just jumped into my car with our German shepherd to pick up some groceries, and was halfway down the block when I saw it through the windshield. My stomach tightened. I was looking into the sky at something my mind could not comprehend. It was an animated apparition, a nightmarish cartoon—a huge cluster of about ten black spheres swirling and dancing above the intersection. These were individual black orbs, leap-frogging and interweaving like cavorting organisms under a microscope. I hit the brakes. At a complete stop, I peered through my windshield and took a moment to consider what to do. I shifted into reverse, drove back into my driveway, dashed inside for my video camera, and stepped back outside to videotape it.

To my astonishment, this object had managed to move miles away in about four minutes. I videotaped what I could, and once again found myself sitting on my couch in a daze. What the hell was going on? Is this some kind of UFO wave? How could I have never seen a UFO my whole life, and then see *two* in one month?

With the second sighting, my pledge to pursue an understanding of the phenomenon had become a blood pact. Clearly, there was something going on that needed to be looked into. I reported my sightings to several UFO organizations and soon created a website to share the footage with others. From the exposure on the Internet, I received hundreds of emails from people around the world who had seen similar objects. I have also made two contacts that are helping me to explore my sightings. One is Mark Olson, a minister in Sonora, California who has also recently videotaped multiple UFOs over his home.

I suppose I could pretend that these sightings never happened. It would be much easier that way. But in doing so, I would be turning my back on one heck of an invitation. It is an invitation to explore the mystery of reality itself, of elusive truth, of a universe only barely understood. I choose to embrace the phenomenon, acknowledging that to do so is to chase specters into a void of the unknowable. Here, I can at least take some comfort in the reality of the video footage. It assures me that these objects in the sky are very real indeed, that they are not a fabrication of the mind. Exactly what they are, however, I wish I knew. Like most people, I have no answers. Just questions.

(*UFO Magazine*, Vol. 19, issue 5 Oct./Nov. 2004)

Pat accepted the invitation to investigate the phenomenon and experience. He had stepped right to the edge of reality and peered over it. Most people, of course, when they see something that challenges the way they understand their world, quickly yank a conventional explanation off the shelf, slap it on, and put it back on the shelf to gather dust in the corner of their memories. But not Pat.

Pat Uskert contacted my wife, Nancy Hayfield, the editor in chief of *UFO Magazine*, to tell her about his sighting and point her to the footage on a Web site he assembled. Nancy printed Pat's story along with stills from the video he took. But it didn't stop there. Sighting reports began pouring in from all over California—from Burbank to San Diego to all the way up in Sonora, hard-core sky watchers as well as people who had casual chance sightings sent in descriptions of what they saw. In fact, the sighting reports became so intense that *UFO Magazine* hired Pat to write his own sighting column in every issue.

Nancy soon realized that just publishing a column of sightings in every issue wasn't enough. Someone had to get out there on the road to interview people, to capture these interviews on video, to hang out to see what people saw and get to know them. There was a whole world of real people having real sightings out there that never made it to *UFO Magazine*, to the different UFO reporting centers, or to the official Mutual UFO Network newsletter. People having Fourth of July barbecues in their backyards, trick-or-treating with their kids on Halloween, heading back from the local mall, or just walking their dogs were all seeing strange lights in the sky. Just lights. And they didn't know what they were.

Certainly, most of these strange lights had conventional explanations. Some were airplanes, to be sure, coming in to local airports from far away so they looked like they were standing still. Others could be explained by meteors that suddenly came into view and disappeared. Then there were the omnipresent Chinese lanterns, flares attached to balloons sent into the air by either party celebrants or pranksters on New Year's Eve. We've had more than our share of these sightings on *UFO Hunters*. And still others might well have been exotic military test craft such as neutral buoyancy vehicles or even experimental blimps that hovered, had strange lights on them, and might have projected images to make it seem as if they were jetting off at fantastic speeds. We do have these craft. The CIA even wrote a report about them.

At least 95 percent of all UFO sightings, according to the Mutual UFO Network, can be explained away as conventional events. But there are those 5 percent, those tantalizing other sightings that continue to defy conventional explanation. These sightings, such as the one Pat Uskert had, involve flying objects that seem to be self-illuminated, fly in a direction opposite to the direction of the prevailing wind, hover or stop in midair before changing direction, seem to have lights that are clearly not aircraft navigation lights, are clearly shaped unlike any conventional aircraft, or fly very close to the ground so that their shapes can be determined but make no sound whatsoever. And this is just the short list.

Nancy wondered, could Pat have seen a balloon flying so high that the winds aloft were blowing in an opposite direction than the winds closer to the ground? If so, that might explain the phenomenon of a silvery disk-shaped object flying into the wind. Maybe a test was in order. What if Pat tried to re-create the same conditions with a balloon and film that experiment? If the two videos, displayed side by side on a monitor, looked exactly alike, then one couldn't eliminate the balloon possibility. Go after every traditional explanation, re-create the sighting, and examine the results. If you can eliminate the conventional by conventional testing, then maybe you could consider the unconventional. It was worth a shot, she said, and asked Pat what he would need to do the experiment.

It would be a pretty straightforward deal, Pat agreed, and contacted one of his friends to help him out. He picked a day much like the day when he had his sighting—not a big challenge in California, where every day is much like the rest—bought a disk-shaped balloon, and met a friend at Venice Beach.

The experiment, often repeated throughout the ensuing three seasons of *UFO Hunters*, worked. Pat's friend launched the balloon while Pat tracked it through the viewfinder until it reached the approximate height of his first sighting. Then, as the balloon caught the winds aloft, it was carried in the direction of the wind, constantly ascending until it was out of sight. He brought the video back to the magazine, where we watched with him.

Comparing the two videos on a split-screen display on the monitor, we could plainly see that whatever Pat had seen that first day on the beach did not behave in the same way that the balloon did. Were they different objects? Nothing definitive to prove that. But were their flight patterns different? Most definitely. The experiment had worked in that the dissimilar flight patterns showed that Pat's balloon flew differently in the air than the object Pat had caught on film at Venice Beach. Was it dispositive evidence that Pat did not see a balloon? No. But the weight of evidence leaned against a balloon, and that was, at least, a start.

Pat's experiment posed another question for Nancy. What if all the people writing to the magazine and posting on Pat's Web site could also be convinced to try their own experiments? Better, what if Pat himself could visit some of the nearby witnesses and run experiments there? It only took a few balloons, a video camera, and the witnesses' permission. And, in fact, the witnesses were so thrilled to get callbacks about this that many invited Pat to stay overnight to see if he could capture the phenomenon on his own camera and review the video that the witnesses shot. When Pat reported the extent of his Web site traffic to Nancy, she had another idea. Why not set up mini road trips to visit these witnesses? Some were as close as Burbank, and Pat was living in Venice, only forty-five minutes away. Other witnesses were as far away as Phoenix, a long drive, but they wanted to meet Pat and show him their videos. Then there was Mark Olson's sighting up in Sonora, big triangles flying over the mountains in California's gold country. This was getting promising. We fueled up Pat's car, and he set out on the road to share experiences, get stories, and shoot some video. Pat was a good filmmaker and Nancy had a talent for video editing. The plan was simple. Put together a compelling video about Pat's journey on the road to find out more about UFOs.

Meanwhile, my own odyssey, starting, as it did, with a simple magazine interview, was bringing me closer to these UFO experiments. The year was 1997, and Nancy and I had just gotten back from Roswell, where we launched *The Day After Roswell* with Phil Corso at the Roswell crash's fiftieth anniversary.

Back in 1995, when I first met Lieutenant Colonel Philip Corso, I was fascinated with Roswell literature and the breaking news about Representative Steve Schiff of New Mexico and his proposed investigations into Roswell, and I was still more perplexed by my own sighting of a huge bright circular light in the skies over New York City in 1953. But I was not actively pursuing UFO stories until the motion picture company I was working for as a literary publishing agent introduced me to the man we called the colonel.

I never expected, when I first walked into a restaurant in Colorado to meet Phil Corso, that I would wind up pitching a television show about UFOs to television production companies for cable networks. Never in a million years. I had been introduced to Colonel Corso to interview him about POW/MIAs left behind in Southeast Asia at the end of the Korean War. Corso had worked on the prisoner exchange called Little Switch / Big Switch when the armistice was signed ending hostilities in 1953. Corso was testifying before the Dornan subcommittee on POWs left behind in Vietnam when he dropped the bomb that President Eisenhower signed a finding in 1953 acknowledging that the United States accepted the fact that the North Koreans and their Chinese and Soviet allies had held American POWs. Most of these men would never return to the United States, would never see their families, and would never be the people they once were. There might still be POWs from that war in North Korea or in a psychiatric facility somewhere in Russia, their identities lost to time and to the government that sent them there.

When Bob Dornan's staff members found the actual finding signed by President Eisenhower in the Eisenhower Presidential Library, thus proving that Corso was testifying truthfully about that finding's existence and that his memory was still sharp, Corso became the cover story in all the major news magazines. And this was the man I was going to meet to talk about POWs and his years as a military liaison in the Eisenhower White House during the mid-1950s. That was the story I was expecting to hear going in, but it was not the story I heard or the story I carried with me going out.

By the end of that week, I had sent a proposal for a book about Phil Corso and the Roswell debris to my New York publisher, and by the end of the month I had signed an agreement with the motion picture company and the publisher to write *The Day After Roswell* with Corso.

It was the book that would send my wife and me to Roswell for its publication-release date in July 1997, where we met the owners of *UFO Magazine*.

Truth be told, I wrote *Day After Roswell* because I found Philip Corso to be an interesting and engaging person who had been personally involved in three serious events in American history: the case of the missing POWs from three wars; an agreement with the American organized crime figures Lucky Luciano and Meyer Lansky to smuggle displaced Jewish concentration camp survivors into what was then Transjordan, the former British protectorate of Palestine; and the investigation into the assassination of President Kennedy. I was not at all interested in the Roswell crash at our first meeting because any truth to the Roswell story had been lost to history. Moreover, I had no intention at the outset of ever getting involved in the UFO field because, although interesting, the government, by its own admission, had so exploited UFO popular culture that whatever truth there was had been inextricably mixed with myth, science fiction, and bizarre stories fed to the tabloid media. Or so I believed.

Corso, however, told a convincing story about an aspect of American history that few people had ever explored. Ten years earlier, in the mid-1980s, I had explored this aspect of the same story in a book called *The Squad*, a personal memoir told to me by an individual who, like Corso, had played a background role in a much bigger story involving the CIA. Corso had also been at odds with the CIA, and he showed me some fascinating documents regarding CIA activity in Southeast Asia during the 1950s, when Vietnam was still a French colony.

Corso's story, at its core, involved a cold war between U.S. intelligence agencies during the 1950s, which boiled over in 1957 with Lieutenant General Arthur Trudeau's discovery of a cache of debris, allegedly from the crash of an alien craft at Roswell, in a Pentagon file that was the object of a search by the CIA. It was in the army's possession, and Trudeau, who had already had a serious run-in with CIA Director Allen Dulles, was determined not to disclose the nature of his find and to keep the entire discovery a secret until he could install a person he could trust inside his army R&D command. That person turned out to be Philip Corso, who, in 1960, was completing his final year in the Maryland National Guard after returning from the Seventh Army in Germany.

In 1961, Corso moved in to his office at the Foreign Technology desk in the Pentagon, where Arthur Trudeau disclosed the contents of the Roswell file to him and told him his problem. Essentially, as Trudeau later wrote in his memoirs, the army had possession of certain items of foreign technology that it wanted to develop as military weapons and sought a budget from friendly U.S. senators for that purpose. One of those senators, Strom Thurmond, told Trudeau explicitly that he wouldn't get one dime of development money unless those foreign pieces of technology had U.S. patents awarded to U.S. defense contractors. Corso said that those pieces of foreign technology were indeed foreign. They originated from another planet. They came into the army's possession when Major Jesse Marcel collected them from a ranch outside Roswell, New Mexico, in July 1947 and escorted them back to Fort Worth, Texas, days later.

Parts of that debris found their way into the Pentagon and were locked in an old file cabinet. No one, especially in the CIA, knew that the file was there, and Arthur Trudeau, having already fought a bureaucratic battle with CIA Director Allen Dulles, was more concerned about keeping this secret from the CIA than he was about keeping it from the KGB. And that was why he turned to one of the toughest intelligence officers he could fine: Philip J. Corso.

Corso had outsmarted the Soviets, the Nazis, and the OSS in Rome during the occupation. He had identified targets for nuclear destruction during the Korean War and was a psychological-warfare officer before he worked on President Eisenhower's White House national security staff. He was one of the few army field officers in the late 1950s to have personal control of nuclear weapons in Germany. Besides, Corso had led a band of army officers who protested to friendly senators when Trudeau was in danger of being forced to retire from the army after he broke the news that Dulles's prized West German

spy ring had been penetrated by the Stasi. They saved Trudeau's career, and it was time to reward Corso for loyalty.

The story of Phil Corso's two years in army R&D, initially as the
head of the Foreign Technology Division and then as the deputy
director of R&D became *The Day After Roswell*, which was officially
launched at the Roswell fiftieth-anniversary commemoration of the
crash. Corso became an instant celebrity inside the UFO community,
the subject of a quick, but ultimately unsuccessful, attempt at an A-list
studio-release feature even though it was a *New York Times* bestseller
for most of the summer of 1997.

It was at the Roswell fiftieth anniversary that I met the then owners of *UFO Magazine*, and, at their urging, I introduced them to the
motion-picture-company executives who had optioned the life-story
rights—the right to use his name and story for an intellectual
property—to Philip Corso and owned the literary and theatrical rights
to *The Day After Roswell*. Being Hollywood executives, who saw in *UFO
Magazine* a rights magnet to make lots of television features, they purchased the magazine from the owners and, eight years and over a million dollars later, finally sold the publishing rights to what had become
the UFO licensing company. They sold it to me and the original owners, and that was why Pat Uskert contacted my wife, the editor of the
magazine.

Even as we began publishing the magazine in 2003, another event
was happening that was directly responsible for our setting up *UFO
Hunters* on History. That event was the start-up of our electronic book
company called Filament Books. We got into an arrangement with
the group of developers who had licensed the technology from the
old Gemstar corporation, which had been purchased by Newscorp
after Gemstar closed down. The group who had licensed the technology sought to develop enterprise platforms for corporations. Along
with the developers' acquisition of the rights in and to the e-book
technology from Gemstar came thousands of handheld electronic-
reader devices that had since been updated with new firmware and an
online component.

It was Nancy's idea to create a subscription-book-club service with this device, and, in order to do this, we got into a number of publishing agreements with *UFO Magazine* writers and contributors. Our first list of electronic books on Filament included writers such as Philip Mantle, Paul Stonehill, and Bruce Goldberg, just to name a few. And it was because a Santa Monica–based production company wanted to include one of our authors in their *UFO Files* segment on History Channel called "Russian Roswell" that I became involved.

Initially, I was very hesitant to give the OK for Paul Stonehill, the proposed guest, to go on camera because I was wary of any rights that would be conveyed for the book to the History Channel. However, because our distributor for *UFO Magazine* was good friends with the director of the production company and asked me as a personal favor to OK the deal, I agreed. Then the director, Jon Walz of Walz-O'Malley, contacted me to ask if I could give a couple of on-camera quotes about *Kapustin Yar* and the stories circulating around UFO crashes in the old USSR. California Mutual UFO Network (MUFON) investigator Harold Burt and I had written about them in a chapter in our book *Unsolved UFO Mysteries*.

I agreed to sit for an on-camera interview to support Paul and the magazine, since it needed all the television exposure it could get, and the company agreed to film where I docked my boat rather than have me come to a studio location. And thus it was because we were doing a dockside interview in the afternoon sun on the day after I had undergone laser eye surgery, which required me to wear sunglasses in direct sunlight, that I was videotaped on camera with sunglasses and my *UFO Magazine* hat. The executive producer of the *UFO Files* episode for History saw some of the stills from the interview while we were setting up the camera, liked the way the shots looked, and gave her blessing for my wearing sunglasses and the baseball hat. And that was the first time I appeared on camera for History and the beginning of what would become the way I had to appear on camera for *UFO Hunters*.

In late 2004, six years after Corso's death, I proposed to Hearst Actuality Television, a reality-TV production company, creating a one-hour documentary on the day after Roswell, which would address Corso's claims in the book and balance them against what was public record about Corso's career in the army and his subsequent years as a security investigator for the United States Senate. The History Channel liked the idea, and I became what amounted to a consulting producer on the project as one of the television experts on Corso. That program, *The Day After Roswell*, became one of the higher-rated specials on History and was the germ of an idea.

Looking at the success of the Corso special and my ongoing appearances on different episodes of *UFO Files* over the course of 2005 as well as the impact those appearances were having on *UFO Magazine*, my wife, Nancy, suggested that we take the video that Pat Uskert was shooting about his journeys through California's Sonora Gold Rush country, the San Fernando Valley, and even Phoenix and the Arizona desert and edit it into a reel I could take to the History Channel.

We first approached Hearst, who suggested that Pat should not be a lone investigator. Rather, they said, he should bring along with him a fully credentialed scientist and an out-and-out skeptic. They should be friends, but they should be able to banter among themselves on a personal level about what they were seeing. They should be able to argue about what the witnesses were saying and to debate over the nature of the videos they were being shown. Were these videos, for example, distortions from a camera, too indistinguishable to make any judgments about, conventional objects that the camera operator could not otherwise identify, or straight-out hoaxes? We followed Hearst's instructions, and the team—Pat Uskert, Kevin Brun, and Julius Willis—set out on a journey to be entitled "UFO Road Trip."

As Nancy, Pat, and I assembled the show from the edits Pat and Nancy made, our intent was to create a special or a series that explored what witnesses had to say about their experiences and sightings. It was a quest, Pat's quest, to find out what he might have seen that day on Venice Beach. We did not intend to establish an official truth about UFOs, because, quite honestly, there exists no official truth about UFOs.

Oh, sure, anyone can tell you what the truth is about UFOs. It's almost a Sartre-like exercise in existentialism in that you know in advance what someone will say about UFOs by the nature of that person's background. Ask a high-ranking someone in the Pentagon and he or she will say that UFOs simply don't exist and that after years of military investigation, we have not been able to define the phenomenon or prove anything about it or any potential threat to the security of the Unites States. And that would be a lie. The military has been tracking UFOs since World War II, has gotten into aerial dogfights with UFOs, has discovered UFO crashes, and has kept, according to some, humanoid aliens in isolation.

Ask a skeptic and he or she will say that unless a UFO lands right on the White House lawn in front of the media and announces or presents itself, then UFOs don't exist. Guess what? They did just that in July, 1952: President Truman acknowledged their presence, and then General Samford of the Air Force said the whole thing was a mistake. A skeptic may also argue that unless a piece of UFO technology falls into his or her hands, then UFOs are at best hypothetical. Common statement: "Show me a piece of a UFO. Let me take it to a lab to see if it's 'Unkownium' and then I'll believe." Problem with that is, what if a piece of a UFO came down and it was made of the same stuff you can find in your car, only better refined? So it's magnesium or titanium. So what?

The other skeptic argument is based on what we take to be conventional science. "Why would an advanced culture travel eight million light years to visit us? It would take eight million years traveling at the speed of light." Again, my answer usually is, "How do you know they weren't here already, here before us, are us, live inside the planet, live on the moon, can travel eight million times faster than the speed of light, got here through a wormhole, made their wormhole, use warp drive just like the Star Trek *Enterprise*, make hyperspace jumps, or just materialize through another dimension?" In other words, a skeptic likes to pose an argument that only a skeptic can answer because, most often, his or her mind is already made up. Worse, a skeptic or debunker has already made the decision, in Stanton Fried-man's words, "Anything but Alien," discounting any anomalous phe-nomenon right from the outset of the argument.

Ask a true believer and you get a spectrum of answers ranging from personal contact and friendship to a multitude of sightings to spiritual insight to alien abduction and a close encounter of the fourth kind to the person who is actually a hybrid and maybe even an ET. I've heard all of it.

I trust the cautious scholars myself, the document researchers, the history specialists, and the government specialists who can point to evidence in the archives. I also trust different types of witnesses such as pilots, police officers, military personnel, and some scientists who have been exposed to the truth but run from it as if the devil were chasing them down the street. They know what they've seen or learned but want no part of it.

All of this means that the answer you'll get depends on whom you ask. It's almost predetermined. So if you want to know the truth about UFOs, don't ask a skeptic unless you want to learn that there are no UFOs. If you want the truth about UFOs, don't ask a true believer be-cause you'll get an answer that will take about a month to explain and you still won't understand it at the end. I know because those are most of the phone calls I get.

But Nancy and Pat's approach was far more elegant and straight-forward. Their approach seeks to find the truth not about UFOs but about what people think the truth is. "UFO Road Trip" was to be a quest show, like the quest for the Holy Grail. You'll never find the Holy Grail, nor did most of King Arthur's knights, but the quest hero grows along the way until he realizes the success is in the quest itself because that's where the truth lies. And that was our original demo reel that we passed around.

There is an old adage about Hollywood, often told to young film-makers who get the call to head west from their cramped studio apart-ments on Manhattan's Lower East Side. You never make what you come out to make, but opportunity will spring from that endeavor. So it was with Nancy and me when we came out to Los Angeles in 1990 to make our first television show, *The Squad*. And so it was with "UFO Road Trip," which every network eventually passed on.

At the time, however, I was appearing in one episode after another of History Channel's *UFO Files*, and I was more than anxious to get my own show. I brought our demo reel to Jon Alon Walz, by then the head of his own production company, Motion Picture Production, in the hopes that I could get some feedback on what we needed to do in order to capture some interest. Jon, like most successful motion picture executives, has a knack for seeing the entire picture in a Malcolm Gladwell blink. And when he saw the demo, it gave him an idea. What if the three UFO quest heroes—Pat Uskert, Kevin Brun, and Julius Willis—appeared together in an episode of *UFO Files* as a team? And could I appear with them?

Yes, yes, yes, and yes. And within a couple of weeks we were shoving off from King Harbor in Redondo Beach on Captain Dave's *Pacific Star* to hunt for unidentified submersible objects, or USOs, in the murky waters of the Redondo Trench in Santa Monica Bay. That segment, in which we found no USOs but left a lot of our lunch in the water, became part of the episode "Red Alert USOs" on *UFO Files* and was the first official appearance of what would become *UFO Hunters*.

That episode did very well for History, so well, in fact, that the network asked Jon to build parts of the Redondo Beach segment into a new demo combing Pat's footage, Nancy's editing, and a frame around the characters. It also featured me as one of the UFO road-tripping characters. The network showed it to various focus groups, ruminated about getting into the UFO series business, and finally, almost a year later, ordered a two-hour pilot episode. *UFO Hunters*, the new name given to us by the network, was born.

THE EPISODE THAT WASN'T:
THE LAS VEGAS UFO

In the official schedule of *UFO Hunters*, season 1, the first episode was titled "The UFO Before Roswell" and concerned the Maury Island case and the Kelso crash. But that was not how the season actually started. It started on a hilltop in a dense national forest just outside Las Vegas and with special guest James Sanders, author of *The Downing of TWA Flight 800* (Kensington, 1997), a book that actually prompted an FBI raid on New York publisher Kensington Books. Sanders and I have a penchant for getting into trouble, and this first episode of *UFO Hunters* set the pace for the series that wound out over three seasons. It captured on camera a UFO over Area 51; a bovine-human hybrid fetus C-sectioned from a mutilated cow lying along the side of a country road in Dulce, New Mexico; and an encounter with a federal police officer from the army base at Dugway, Utah, trying to confiscate our cameras and videotape by claiming—falsely—that we were filming on a military reservation without permits. Yes, we got into a lot of trouble during our three seasons, and it was this first excursion to Las Vegas that set the tone.

The story began in late summer 2007, even before we began planning the episodes for our first season, with an e-mail to *UFO Magazine* by someone calling himself Ben, or, alternatively, Colonel X, a United States Air Force officer stationed near Area 51. Colonel X sent us photos of what he called a "reverse-engineered UFO" simply hanging in space over the Nevada mountain ranges. He offered to meet us at a good location from where we could film the object and then reveal its existence to the world.

His report, which he submitted to *UFO Magazine*, located the object as viewable from the southeastern slope of Mount Charleston overlooking the Las Vegas strip. In his article for *UFO Magazine*, September 2007, he wrote:

Without revealing too much detail my about job which could lead the government to discover who I am, I am going to let you in on the scoop of the month. I am currently in Nevada, home to Area 51 and the best UFO hunting ground in the world. There are enough sightings here to keep most of the big organizations busy, but I just happen to know how and where to find a Roswell disc.

Of course its location is a secret. For those of you with a compass it can be found near the southeastern side of Mt. Charleston that overlooks Las Vegas. Since June I have been corresponding secretly with the Disclosure Project concerning its location. I have a high-level rank in the Air Force. It allows me to work in the Nellis Air Force range, which is really supposed to be clear of aliens. So, in late May when a disc showed up I wrote the big disc hunters to let them in on what was going on here.

The government wasn't keeping it in a hangar, like all the books say. There were too many officers looking for it in the buildings where it might be seen and photographed. They were keeping it over near the city limits where it could only be seen using a military surveillance radar. I thought about calling the police, but the only way to see it or prove it was there would be to use the military radar, which the base commanders were not going to allow. So who was going to believe me without evidence?

I took the problem to an engineering contracting firm off Tropicana. I asked if they knew of any way to target an "aircraft" without radar. I did not have any radar so how could I find a target if it was directly overhead? Their engineer pointed out a CCD imager called an ICX429AL EXView, Sony's top-of-the-line infrared sensor. The engineer said if it gave off infrared light and was within 100 miles, this chip could see it. It would not be a very big spot on the screen, but it should appear as a white-hot group of pixels. With a good lens you would be able to zoom right up to it once the CCD picked it up.

I never told him I was going to use the imager to target a Roswell disc. Not that it made any difference. The ICX429 was not a restricted technology and could even be purchased online. It took only 48 hours to have it sent to my office, and within a few days I was able to spot the saucer without too much difficulty.

Seeing it for the first time was breathtaking. It just sat there motionless. It did not move to the left or to the right. It did not even look like it was flying. It was a few minutes before I realized it was hovering. The darn thing was hovering! I could not believe it. I was imaging a hovering disc. You really had to see it to believe how it looked. It could hold its position better than any helicopter I had ever seen. I took some images and sent them to Richard Hall, Dennis Balthaser, and the Disclosure Project.

The first to respond was the Disclosure Project. After a little debate among the staff who monitor the organization's email, they sent everything over to Dr. Steven M. Greer. The images did not go to him right away. I guess they reviewed everything before it went to Greer. The first staff member sent the images to another staff member who then sent them to their big office. When Greer saw the shape of the saucer he wanted a meeting right away and anything I could get him.

Richard Hall had seen the photos and got Don Berliner to use a separate email at konsulting.com to begin correspondence. However, Berliner learned that Greer was involved and did not want to intrude on the find. I had thought that Berliner would have wanted his photo analyst ready to help the Disclosure Project with any technical expertise they might need, but he said, "Now that we know Dr. Greer is involved in your project, there will be no need to send us any further information and pictures." It was a finder's-keepers situation for them. If the Disclosure Project was first on the scene then that is who they wanted to handle it.

The Disclosure team arriving to view the saucer was from Phoenix. This had to be a dream-come-true assignment for them since Phoenix is where the first photographs of the suspected Roswell craft were taken. Those photos are referred to as the shoe-heel saucer photos or the William Rhodes photographs from July 7, 1947. Their appointment was for 2:30 P.M. and at 2:00 P.M. the photographer began setting up the imager while I waited nearby hoping the disc was still there. All I needed was for Greer's investigators to come all the way from Phoenix to what they would have to call a hoax if they did not get to see the disc.

When they first saw it at 2:40 P.M. they did not even ask if it was anything but the disc. They wanted a CD burnt of the event right there. They had just become the first investigators to see live hover flight under planned or predetermined conditions. The official term which was used to describe the saucer to Greer was "floating."

At *UFO Magazine* that August, when Colonel X's report and accompanying photos arrived, we were thrilled. Imagine the possibilities of featuring an issue with real Greer-approved photos of an actual unidentified floating object right over Area 51. But our publishing the Colonel X report did not go without a reaction from the Disclosure Project folks themselves, admonishing us for publishing his article without the Disclosure Project's official OK. In other words, the Disclosure Project made it clear that we were not allowed to disclose anything at the risk of blowing open their entire investigation.

UFO Magazine is just that, a magazine, and we don't take kindly to being told we can't publish a story simply because someone wants to jump on it first. Besides, Colonel X himself wrote the story that we published in the magazine, so we ran with it. At the same time, however, we were meeting at the *UFO Hunters* production offices in Santa Monica to set up the first episodes for the coming season, and we were looking for an interview that would start the season off with a brand new case. Because we were already in communication with Colonel X, I suggested we talk to him about going to his location to film the object and bring along some equipment to figure out what it was.

At the same time we were meeting, I also received a call from my old friend Jim Sanders. Sanders, who had written a number of books about the misdeeds of the U.S. government concerning POWs from previous wars and about the shooting down of TWA Flight 800 in 1996, had called to say that there was a strange, very bright star hanging just over the downtown Las Vegas horizon every night. It wasn't Venus, he said, because the object didn't move. Also, he could see Venus at the same time. It wasn't the moon. He didn't know what it was and invited the newly formed UFO hunters to come out for a look.

With the possibility of meeting Colonel X and of seeing something that fit the bill of a UFO from Sanders's house, we loaded the cars and Pat, Ronnie Millione, and I drove off to Las Vegas from Los Angeles in our first convoy with crew and producers. Believe it or not, the trip to Vegas back in 2007 was the first time I had ever seen a GPS plot a route, talking to us as we drove through East Los Angeles and into the intense triple-digit heat of California desert. Although you might think that taking this trip was a no-brainer—we were following up on a great photo spread in *UFO Magazine* to see a floating object that we might capture on television—our ability to organize it was actually in question. What I didn't know as we set up the episodes for that first season was that budgets didn't allow us the freedom to change schedules and insert trips into the pre-planning shooting scheme. Therefore, it took a lot of negotiating with time and schedules to fit this trip in. Also, we wanted Colonel X to meet us on-site so we could get an interview with him as well. We needed to go right from Las Vegas to Vashon Island in Washington State for our next episode about the Maury Island and Kelso incidents, and we needed to do this as expeditiously as possible. But it didn't work out that way.

The initial problem we had was setting the meeting and location with Colonel X. As a network crew, we couldn't just pull up in a van, unload, and set up the equipment and begin shooting. We had to have location permits and be able to show them to the network before anything was allowed to be broadcast. Networks and motion picture studios are very strict about this because of the high liability they can incur by capturing something on camera and broadcasting it without permission. Shooting permits are just that, permission from the property owner or municipality governing the land that allows images of that property to appear on television or in a movie. Therefore, we had to have someone give us permission to shoot at the location Colonel X was talking about. Also, because the story was coming from Colonel X, we really couldn't use his name and cite him as an authority without his permission. But Colonel X was telling us that he was afraid his identity would be revealed and that he would wind up in a pack of trouble. Moreover, he said he was doing this without the permission of his superior officers. In the end, he said he wasn't going to show up for the interview, but that if we had the right equipment, we could go to the location he suggested and capture the object on camera for ourselves. We had committed to going to Las Vegas at a cost of $10,000 a day, which meant we had to get something or a head would roll. Mine, actually.

Our backup was the Jim Sanders interview. He said we could see the object from his driveway in the front of his house, hanging low over the horizon and brighter than any star. Sanders is not given to fantasy. If anything, he is more a skeptic than anything else, especially when it comes to being given stories from official sources. Here's an example, the example that launched the two of us from the comfort of our living room couches to subpoenas coming over our fax machines at daybreak from the FBI and a date in federal court on Long Island.

It began on a hot summer night in July 1996, when Sanders was watching a breaking news feed from CNN about the crash of a TWA 747 heading from JFK to Paris. The plane, according to the news report, exploded over Jamaica Bay and fell into the ocean. All on board were presumed dead. Liz Sanders, Jim's wife, was at the point of tears. She was a senior flight attendant for TWA and had personally trained much of the flight crew on that jet. Sanders was also in shock until he heard a strange comment from the news reader. The navy, Sanders heard, was denying reports that a missile, a U.S. Navy missile, had brought down the jet. Wait a minute, Sanders said to himself, why would the navy deny that one of its missiles had brought down the jet when nobody reported that a missile had brought down the jet. The story for him had just taken another turn.

Sanders had been down this road before, dealing with government denials before there was anything to deny. First, you deny a story so as to turn any news agency away from reporting the story you already denied. Then, evidence pops up showing that you are culpable. Next, you deny it again, pointing out, with due annoyance, that you already denied this, so why raise it? Should a reporter pursue the story in the face of your denials, you simply ban that reporter from your circle of access. Access journalism at its best.

In his previous books, Sanders had stood in the face of withering denials from the government: he presented evidence showing that the military had left POWs behind in Southeast Asia after the Paris peace talks ended the Vietnam War. He also showed that the military had left POWs behind in Soviet hands at the end of World War II. Sanders also faced a tirade by Senator John McCain when Sanders asked him questions about his involvement in the savings and loan scandal that marked the U.S. recession of the early 1990s. Yes, Sanders had been there and knew when a cover-up was in the making. Therefore, when he heard the navy denials, he knew that there was something the government didn't want Americans to know. And it was that something Sanders had to learn.

A year after that night, Sanders had discovered not only that it was most likely a missile that had brought down TWA Flight 800 but that tests he had conducted on one of the seat backs from that plane—tests indicating the seat had residue on it from a solid-fuel rocket engine—had been falsified by the government in an attempt to debunk him. In fact, more than thirteen years after the crash, the FAA still hadn't been able to prove that the explosion of the center wing tank was the cause of that crash. I actually saw the FAA's test plane at a lab in New Mexico, where we filmed a segment for *UFO Hunters*. And I asked the technician directly whether they developed any proof that it was the center wing tank. The technician just rolled his eyes and said that it was no accidental explosion that brought the plane down. Thus not only was Sanders the guy who could smell a rat from the other side of town, he was usually right when it came to stories over the edge. Sanders's reputation and past experience meant to me that if Sanders saw a bright object hovering over the horizon that wasn't a planet, a star, or a satellite, then something was indeed there, and we were on our way to Las Vegas to see it with our own eyes.

This was our first trip together as a brand new crew as we caravanned across the desert through the small towns along the interstates on our way to Las Vegas, chattering from car to car by walkie-talkie. It was a trip many in our crew had made before, and we talked about other famous travelers who took this route, including Sam Kinison, who was killed in a car crash as he returned to Los Angeles from a performance gig in a Las Vegas club. Sam had called me from the road, hours before his fateful encounter, because we were planning a meeting to talk about a book we wanted to write together about his life and his comedy.

Interstate 10, the Lincoln Highway, which runs from the Pacific coast, across the United States, and right to the Atlantic, is the first freeway you take on the way to Las Vegas. From our office in Santa Monica, the 10 takes you past downtown LA, past East LA, and into the desert, the landscape changing from the yuppie corporate towers of downtown to the glass and steel urban landscape of East LA to what Southern California and the inland valleys really are: cactus, scrub brush, and chaparral.

As the caravan wound east, SUVs holding the cast, minivans holding the crew and production staff, and the huge van holding the cameras and equipment, it was just setting up on rush hour, when downtown empties in all four directions. Downtown LA is a commuter's town, fed by a metro subway and light rail, bus lines, and endless freeways. Along the way, driving is like an obstacle course as frenzied drivers battle for every inch of a lane, the bigger the SUV, the more aggressive the driving.

As members of a traveling show, we were just getting to know one another, playing hometown and high school geography and girlfriend bingo, sharing songs from our iPods and demonstrating whose device had more features than the others. On a new crew, when you know you're going to be thrown together in some of the most uncomfortable circumstances imaginable—such as a chartered bus driving across Mexico for forty-eight hours without a usable bathroom—you start out being as polite as possible before you start getting down and dirty, playing the dozens, and laughing at each other.

Riding shotgun, the seat I wound up occupying for three seasons, I could see what looked like a mirage in front of me in the middle lane of the 10 freeway. It was a minivan, no taillights, and it looked like it was dead stopped. On an LA freeway, that was a prescription for disaster, especially in the days before holding a cell phone while driving was illegal.

Our production assistant, driving our van, noticed the stalled car up ahead in our lane and, as the converging freeway traffic began to swerve and the lanes turned into a string of red brake lights, he turned onto the shoulder and gunned the car into passing gear. We sped through the sound of screeching brakes and passed the stalled car with no one in the driver's seat and into the clear. While I called out a warning to other cars in our convoy over the walkie-talkie, we could hear the crashes behind us as the freeway turned into a scene from a disaster movie.

When I think about it, had it not been for our freewheeling production assistant, the entire *UFO Hunters* series could have ended right then and there on the 10 freeway heading out of LA. But it didn't. In fact, we made the trip to Las Vegas, stopping only once at the legendary

Greek Oasis along the 15 freeway for gas, Greek coffee, and lots of spanakopita and baklava, and reached Vegas by early evening. By nine, we had checked in to our hotel—not on the strip or even remotely close to it—and I was on the phone to Sanders.

Yes, he said, the object was still there, still burning bright and hovering low over the horizon, and still stationary, unlike any star or planet. Sanders said he could see Venus rising, see the North Star late at night, and see that the object seemed to hover in place and not travel across the sky. As far as he was concerned it was a UFO because he couldn't figure out how to identify it. But was it Colonel X's reverse-engineered flying saucer? That was the subject of the investigation.

Our first stop was Sanders's house, where the cast arrived first and waited for the rest of the crew to arrive and set up a camera. We would film in the house, letting Jim explain how he discovered the object in the sky and why he thought it was so strange. Then, we would film outside to see how well we could capture the object on camera. Sanders explained that you could see lots of strange things over Las Vegas, but this bright light in the east was stranger than most. It was there every night without fail. It didn't move across the sky the way a star did. And it was just too bright to be anything but an artificially illuminated object.

Could it have been the space station, we asked?

No, because it didn't move. In fact, we would be able to see satellites make their way across the sky, Jim told us, if we went up to the Humboldt-Toiyabe National Forest high above Las Vegas and found a place to shoot where no light pollution would get in our way. So we set up our gear to see if we could spot the object, and when Jim pointed it out, it was there.

To the naked eye, it was almost like a very bright planet, bigger than Venus but not bigger than the moon. But it was the brightness that fascinated us. It seemed too bright to be a star and too big to be Venus. And, as Jim said, it wasn't moving across the sky and wasn't twinkling. But the light pollution from the nearby Las Vegas strip was overpowering. We watched it, talked with Sanders some more about his books, and then packed up for the night and the trip to the national forest the following day.

The next day, following Jim Sanders's advice, we made reservations at a restaurant and way station up in the national forest to find a place to assemble our camera-mounted telescope and capture a wireless signal to use the automated star chart on our computer. If Colonel X was right, we should be able to see something hanging off in the night sky, stationary and brightly illuminated, just as we saw from Jim Sanders's driveway. It would appear, Colonel X said, as the sky turned black over the eastern horizon.

We knew it was there because we'd seen it before from the city at Jim's house. But what would it look like without the light pollution distorting the sky, and what could we capture on video? It got tense as we assembled the camera and loaded the star-mapping software into the Alienware laptop computer that the company had given us to use for the show. Mounting the huge telescopic lens was a chore that the crew had to undertake very carefully. The lens assembly was delicate as well as expensive and was the heart and soul of the entire shoot. If we could capture a close-up of what the colonel told us was there, it would certainly be a coup.

We started filming the segment. With the telescopic lens on the camera locked in place, we each took turns looking through the eyepiece as the camera itself recorded the object. At first neither Pat nor I could believe our eyes. The object had a definite shape. It was almost like a flat platform very brightly lit. We checked the star maps on the computer wired into the camera and could find nothing in the sky. According to the computer chart, what we were looking at through the eyepiece was simply empty sky. But what we could see through the eyepiece was a large platform just hanging in the air as if it were suspended on invisible wire. What was it?

I was thrilled. We had confirmed Colonel X's observation. Next question: was this our UFO, our flying disk, which is how Colonel X described it and the object in the photos we had published in *UFO Magazine*? I went back inside the restaurant to text message the editor in chief of *UFO Magazine,* my wife, Nancy. I wrote that we had found it, that we had Colonel X's flying saucer in view. I hit send. And then I heard shrieks from outside on the patio deck. "Where is it?" someone said.

I ran back outside only to see the object was no longer there. "It just went out," one of the crew said.

"I saw the lights flicker," Pat said. "And then it just started to drop."

I checked the camera telescope myself, and the object had disappeared. We mumbled; checked the memory cards to make sure that he had actually captured the images, which he had; struck the telescopic equipment while we shot our on-the-fly interviews with the cast; and then wrapped the scene. We piled into the SUVs and headed back down the mountain to the city and our hotel.

Along the way I called Sanders, who confirmed that he could not see the object from his location. But just to make sure, we took a detour over to Jim's house while he waited up for us. In fact, he was in the driveway with his telescope set up as we pulled around the corner. "It just went out," he said as we all stared at the empty sky. "Lights just went out and the thing seemed to disappear."

We stood there for a little while, staring at the sky, and then got back into the cars. Nothing we could do there except stare and wait for the sun to come up. And we had a full day of driving the next day back to Los Angeles. But as we drove across the strip to the hotel, I got a call from Sanders.

"It's back up," he said. "As soon as you guys drove down the street, the lights came on and the object seemed to rise to its original position. Damndest thing."

We'd already captured the object on tape when we were up in the national forest, which obviated the need for any more filming. We were wrapped and ready for the drive back to Los Angeles the next morning. Whatever happened to that object, whatever it was, was a mystery that only a few people could solve. But as far as we were concerned, at least this first segment was over.

On the way back to Los Angeles the next day, I called Bill Scott, my coauthor on *Space Wars* and, subsequently, *Counterspace*, both at Forge Books, to ask him what he thought we had seen. For all the years Bill had been the Rocky Mountain bureau chief at *Aviation Week*, he knew about some of the secret craft the air force had in development. Bill would become one of our frequent guests on *UFO Hunters*, commenting about conventional and exotic aircraft and the way the black-operations world kept secret weapons out of public view. I told Bill about what we had seen, and he suggested we had come across one of the top intelligence-gathering platforms.

"These platforms can scrub just about any e-mail, phone call, and text message," he said. "And they're surveillance platforms, too. They probably picked up your license plates when you texted the office, and when you left Jim's house, they brought the platform back up." I didn't even know we had that capability. "They were funnin' with you," Bill said. "Just a little reminder that they knew you were there."

BILL'S BLOG

The Colonel X story of the mysterious object between Area 51 and the Las Vegas strip and the photos Colonel X sent came to us before we got the call from the network to start setting up the production structure for the series. In the moments that we first got the story for the magazine, I had this thrill—more like a chill—that this could be the big IT. This could be the crack in the wall of silence, and, by just putting our shoulders against it, the wall would crumble. We published the story and the photos, but no wall came down. And when the time came to hook up with Colonel X at the site and unlimber our huge telescopic camera, the colonel told us that he couldn't be there. Someone was onto him. The story had been leaked. Well, of course the story had been leaked because it was the cover story in *UFO Magazine*. In fact, everybody who read the magazine knew about it. But to do the story for *UFO Hunters* would be the coup of all coups. Imagine breaking a story on national television not that UFOs were real, but that the government had one and was flying it over an American city.

I consoled myself with the thought that even if this wasn't

the reverse-engineered UFO that Area 51 commentators Bob Lazar, John Lear, and George Knapp talked about, at least it was something. And if we managed to photograph one of our top-secret intelligence-gathering platforms and stayed out of trouble, then it was worth it. The trip taught me that as a crew and a team, we had the ability to accomplish something, to undertake some serious research.

The trip to Las Vegas, one of many more that would follow, also set the stage for how the team on *UFO Hunters* would comport itself over the next thirty or so months. We would focus on the conventional, evaluate the possible, and eliminate the obvious with science. Check and double-check and make sure that as many skeptical arguments were considered: even if they couldn't be completely answered, they could at least be held up to the light and scrutinized. Like any good trial litigator, you always, always take the opposing side and argue against yourself so that you know what your evidence and argument must do before a finder of fact. And in our case, the television audience was the finder of fact, weighing our evidence and argument, and even if it disagreed with us, at least it should be able to do it on the basis of the facts and not for our lack of trying.

I felt that in that first episode, the episode that never saw the light of day on television, we set the pace and set the stage for the ensuing episode on Maury Island in one of the strangest cases of America's UFO history.

BEFORE ROSWELL:
THE MAURY ISLAND INCIDENT

In the weeks before the reports of a UFO crash at Roswell and three days before the Kenneth Arnold UFO sighting over Mount Rainier in Washington State, a little-known incident set the stage for what would become the modern UFO craze. This was a report by a log-salvage boatman on Puget Sound that his boat had been hit by debris from a struggling flying saucer. The subsequent investigation into this report and the twists and turns that the case later took, resulting in the deaths of two intelligence officers from the Army Air Force, has become UFO lore.

As we were setting up the early episodes in *UFO Hunters*, season 1, this case, the Maury Island UFO, was on the agenda as one of the first cases to tackle. There was a lot of debate about this sighting as we discussed the strongest cases for the early first season. First, was it really an investigation worth pursuing? Was there actually a UFO sighting or simply a wild report, or, worse, a hoax? The only eyewitness that we knew about was the boatman himself, Harold Dahl, long since deceased. Dahl had first reported the experience to his employer and boat owner Fred Crisman, a fellow with a highly checkered past, and then recanted the case to FBI agents who later investigated it. He later recanted the recantation.

Second, Dahl's story was actually investigated by one of the first UFO witnesses in 1947, Kenneth Arnold. But Arnold later said that he could find no real physical evidence to support Dahl's contention that his boat had been hit by UFO debris other than the boat's having been repainted and that, if molten metal had hit that boat, there should have been more damage to it.

Third, it was clear that Fred Crisman, looking for an opportunity to collaborate on books and magazine articles in the wake of Kenneth Arnold's UFO sighting a few days after Dahl's sighting, was out to promote this case. Crisman, later linked in the Jim Garrison investigation into the assassination of President John F. Kennedy, had been an intelligence-agent wannabe and was reportedly always looking for an angle.

Fourth, the real tragedy in this case was the crash of a B-25 Mitchell bomber that was reportedly carrying the molten metal material—Dahl had called it "slag"—that Dahl said he collected after the UFO passed over his boat. What caused that plane crash and how might it have been related to Dahl's claimed UFO sighting?

Fifth, was this really a UFO case or was it a series of strange stories where the conspiracy angle was more important than the reported UFO sighting?

These were the questions the cast and crew talked about in our production office in Santa Monica as we planned the first flight into the Seattle-Tacoma International Airport and the drive to Vashon Island, where we would catch a research boat out onto Puget Sound for an in-the-water investigation along the route ostensibly traveled by Harold Dahl sixty years earlier.

THE INCIDENT

The case began at just about 2:00 P.M. on June 21, 1947, with Harold Dahl, a boatman on Puget Sound, motoring off Maury Island,

Washington, looking for logs that had fallen off barges floating timber along the coast. Dahl was a salvager for logs, collecting a bounty on each log he loaded and brought back to his partner, Fred Crisman. Dahl was on his boat with his son, another mate, and Dahl's dog.

In 1947, the war having ended two years earlier, America was building homes for all the soldiers that had returned from overseas, married, and were raising families. The builders needed lumber for homes in subdivisions popping up across the country in the postwar baby boom. The demand for timber was intense, and loggers in the Northwest needed to sell every tree they had cut. Therefore, Dahl's job, snagging cut logs floating in Puget Sound, brought in a nice bounty to him and Crisman, a self-described former secret agent during World War II who was the owner of the boat that Dahl worked on.

Dahl said that his attention was caught by lights in the sky, which he described as a loose formation of six circular "doughnut-shaped" objects flying over the sound between Tacoma and Maury Island, an extension of Vashon Island. Dahl called the objects doughnuts because, he said, he could see the sky through them and as they got closer, he said he remembered seeing windows or portholes along the rings of the objects.

Five of the objects seemed to be flying, but a sixth one, surrounded by the other five, seemed to be in trouble. Dahl said that it looked like it was wobbling in the air, struggling, as if it were having trouble staying aloft. It also looked like the other objects were helping stabilize it or protect it from falling out of the sky as they closed in around it in a formation. One of the circular craft seemed to get even closer to the wobbling craft.

Suddenly, Dahl reported, the object that was wobbling and was having trouble staying above the water ejected a metallic substance from inside its ring, a substance that Dahl said reminded him of "slag," molten metal that he'd seen as the residue from the smelting works on the Tacoma side of the small bay in Puget Sound. The ejection of this substance seemed to stabilize the craft. But the burning or molten metallic substance actually hit his boat, he said, breaking his son's arm and killing the dog. The burning metal charred Dahl's boat along the deck railing. There were also leafy shards of a white metal that fell out of the wobbling craft, and Dahl said that he collected both the slag and the metal.

At first, Dahl told no one about the incident. But a strange incident occurred that was reported only by Dahl: the next morning, Dahl said, a person who Dahl assumed was from the military or from some type of law-enforcement agency showed up at his residence. He had a very official attitude and convinced Dahl to join him for breakfast at a local establishment. Dahl accepted the invitation, and the two met the next morning.

The man was wearing a dark suit, had an authoritative bearing, but showed no identification, and he repeated to Dahl the details of his sighting the day before. This was surprising because Dahl had made no public statement about it and had not even told Crisman. The man advised Dahl that he tell no one about what he saw. He should simply forget about it, because if he disregarded this advice and started talking about the event publicly, things would not go well for him and his family. While he made no direct threats, the implication that Dahl took away from this conversation was that he and his family would be harmed. How this person knew that Dahl was actually thinking of telling Crisman, Dahl did not know. Nor did he know how the man was able to repeat the details of his sighting the day before. But the stranger's advice was very clear. Just forget about what he saw and it would all go away. Ultimately, this was advice that Dahl did not take, but that would have benefitted him had he heeded it.

Had Harold Dahl kept his own counsel about the sighting he'd had and not gone to the boat owner Fred Crisman, perhaps the strange events that followed would not have taken place. But perhaps the impression left by what he allegedly saw was so great that, despite the warnings of the strange man at breakfast, Dahl had to let the secret out. Of course, the damage to the boat Dahl was piloting the day before, damage, Dahl said, that was very apparent, would ultimately have to be repaired. And it was damage that couldn't be completely explained except by something's having fallen from the sky. What was that something? It was a molten metallic substance, maybe a type of fuel for an exotic propulsion system. Whatever it was, perhaps Dahl felt that he had to account for it, and the only way was to tell Crisman the story of what he saw.

Fred Crisman, the boat owner, had pursued a prior career during World War II as an intelligence operative in the Far East. Subsequent to the events on Maury Island, Crisman would be linked to the Kennedy assassination in Jim Garrison's investigation sixteen years later. He was named by Jim Garrison in connection with Clay Shaw and activities in Dallas. Some have suggested that Crisman was one of the three tramps on the grassy knoll, who were stopped and released. In the 1960s, Crisman was the host of his own radio talk show in Tacoma, broadcasting under the name of Jon Gold. Crisman was a mysterious figure.

In 1946, Crisman had written to the *Amazing Stories* magazine publisher Ray Palmer, who started *Fate Magazine*, that he believed there were demonic entities living under the earth who had attacked him with a beam weapon while he was fighting against the Japanese. Crisman was a self-styled writer who wanted Palmer to publish his stories of robotic demons who lived beneath the planet's surface. He was looking to get into business with Palmer, and when he eventually learned about Harold Dahl's story, he realized he had an angle.

Dahl waited yet another day before approaching Crisman, but after he did, Crisman had to investigate the area for himself, so he took a boat out onto Puget Sound, where he later claimed to have seen his own doughnut-shaped UFO. But the spectacle that Dahl allegedly witnessed was not seen by Palmer, because the craft disappeared behind a cloud before he got the chance to get a good look. However, he said that he found some of the material that Dahl referred to as "slag" along the Maury Island beach, which he retrieved and sent to a researcher in Chicago for analysis.

In a comprehensive FBI report on this incident after Dahl had retracted his story, there was some confusion over whether Crisman sent the slag samples to the University of Chicago or to his acquaintance Ray Palmer. Either way, ultimately Ray Palmer learned of the story through Fred Crisman's activities, a factor that would be critical in the next few days.

On June 24, 1947, an event took place that hit the national news and, at least in Ray Palmer's mind, turned the Harold Dahl sighting into just the kind of event that would open the door to a publishing career because Palmer saw the opportunity of working with Kenneth Arnold on a story about UFOs. On the afternoon of June 24, the pilot Kenneth Arnold, flying over Mount Rainier in Washington in search of a lost plane, saw a formation of bright lights in the distance. At first, he thought he was seeing reflections, flashes off the fuselage of another plane. Then, he believed he was looking at a flock of birds. But the flashes were too high in the sky and flying too fast to be birds. Eventually, Arnold got a better look at the source of the flashes and realized they were solid objects.

He believed them to be test aircraft, possibly a new type of air force jet, but when he looked closer he saw that they had no tail assembly of any kind. To him, they did not look conventional at all. As the formation passed in front of him, some of the craft turned over on their side, and Arnold marveled at their thinness. He said later that, although the craft were generally circular, he could make out a clear crescent shape in one or two of them. He said they moved in a fluttering fashion as if someone were skipping a saucer across the surface of the water. And that was how the name "flying saucer" came into existence. Arnold never used the term, but a newspaper carrying the story of Arnold's sighting did.

After Arnold reported what he saw to friends and to other pilots at the airport in Yakima, news of his sighting spread. It was covered in newspapers, and Arnold immediately became something of a celebrity, which he did not want. People who initially thought the whole thing was a delusion on his part or a made-up story were stunned into silence when another witness, Fred Johnson, said he saw the same objects through his telescope while he was on Mount Adams. He reported that the objects had a similar shape and configuration as those reported by Arnold and that he saw them at the same time Arnold had his sighting. Now, suddenly, flying saucers were in newspaper headlines all over the country. And in Fred Crisman's mind, the Harold Dahl sighting took on a whole new significance and presented to him a whole new opportunity.

By the time the Arnold story hit the newspapers, the magazine publisher Ray Palmer was in possession of the slag material, and he, too, suddenly saw an opportunity with the media interest. Kenneth Arnold and flying saucers were at a celebrity status, and Ray Palmer was not only in possession of something he hoped would test out to be a piece of a flying saucer, but he had a witness in his pocket. Palmer wrote to Arnold and invited him to investigate the Harold Dahl sighting and the slag material Dahl and Crisman had recovered. This would be the beginning of a relationship that would result in a Kenneth Arnold article in Ray Palmer's *Fate Magazine* in early 1948.

Palmer contacted Arnold to ask him to investigate the Dahl sighting just as the media interest in flying saucers was reaching a fever pitch. Meanwhile, the military was also investigating the Kenneth Arnold sighting, and a young intelligence officer named Frank Brown from the Army Air Force had made contact with Arnold to interview him and to determine, as best he could, Arnold's character and the veracity of his story. At the same time, Arnold agreed to investigate Dahl's story.

Kenneth Arnold's investigation focused on Dahl's boat at first. His inspection revealed that the boat had been recently painted in areas that had some evidence of charring, but he couldn't find any evidence of extensive damage to the wood or any structural damage to the areas along the deck where Dahl said the slag hit. Harold Dahl's son had run away at this point and was unable to confirm any of the story, and Dahl was unable to locate the photographs he said he had taken. The slag itself was a ferrous material, and test results returned no unknown elements or especially exotic alloys of known elements. In short, all Arnold had to go on was Dahl's story.

At this point, however, Kenneth Arnold had contacted Army Air Force intelligence officer Lieutenant Frank Brown because Brown had investigated Kenneth Arnold's character and found him to be highly credible. Therefore, when Arnold asked Frank Brown to investigate the Dahl mystery, he flew up along with Captain William Davidson in a B-25 Mitchell bomber from Hamilton Army Air Force Base in California. The two officers interviewed Crisman, at Arnold's suggestion, but, as Kenneth Arnold found, without Dahl's photos, there was no evidence to corroborate Dahl's story except for the slag. And Dahl was not present at the Davidson and Brown interview with Crisman, which detracted from the credibility of the story. There was nothing but a cereal box full of the ferrous material gathered by Crisman and Dahl and tested for Ray Palmer at the lab in Chicago. The lab had found no unusual elements and no unusual alloys. Crisman pushed the box on Lieutenant Frank Brown, asking him to fly it back to Hamilton so that it could be analyzed. Brown took it. Then, the two pilots, along with sergeants Elmer Taft and Woodrow Matthews, headed back to Hamilton Army Air Force Base.

Tragically, the B-25 never made it back to California. Instead, the plane developed engine trouble, lost its left wing, and crashed in a desolate area of Kelso, Washington, thus adding another element to the Harold Dahl mystery. What caused the plane to crash? Was it, like a scene from the movie *Repo Man*, something from Dahl's cache of alien slag that brought the plane down, or was it something else? This was a mystery that *UFO Hunters* wanted most to solve.

At first, there were thoughts that the plane had been sabotaged. The army and air force were mum about the cause of the crash and about the reason for the officers' mysterious visit to Tacoma. Was there something in the box of slag that Crisman had given to Lieutenant Brown and Captain Davidson that caused the crash? The mystery lingered for sixty years, and, some would say, is still unsolved.

All the investigators could go on at first were the reports by the two sergeants aboard the plane, who had safely parachuted out on orders of Captain Davidson. Davidson and Brown believed up to the very last moments that they could bring the plane in for a safe land-ing. They refused to jump because they felt that if they left the plane, its crash would kill innocent civilians. Therefore, they wanted to bring the plane to a safe place, where they could set it down. But it was not to be.

According to one of the briefings from the flight-crew sergeant, he noticed smoke coming out of the bomb bay and believed it was a fire in the junction box. The other sergeant who had parachuted to safety said that he saw smoke coming out of the left wing engine. The cap-tain ordered both of his sergeants to jump as the smoke continued to pour out of the left engine. Then, the wing caught fire. The sergeants jumped, and in their briefings they said that they saw the wing fall off the plane. The B-25 then crashed into a logging area in Kelso, broke apart, and both Captain Davidson and Lieutenant Brown were killed. The army moved in the next day and cleared as much of the wreckage as they could. But parts of the plane remained buried in the dirt in Kelso for the next sixty years.

The crash of an air force plane allegedly carrying material that had been discharged by a UFO, the deaths of two pilots, Kenneth Arnold's involvement in the Dahl UFO story, and all of it taking place amid the UFO craze that was sweeping the country quickly brought the FBI in to investigate. The crash took place on August 1, 1947, and was the first crash of an official air force plane, the air force preparing to sepa-rate from the army and on that day Davidson and Brown had been ordered back to headquarters. The crash, occurring just a little under a month after the headline-making UFO retrieval from Roswell and over a month after the Kenneth Arnold sighting, was part of a matrix of events that had captured FBI Director J. Edgar Hoover's interest. The bureau dispatched agents to look into the crash and especially to find out whether there really existed a flying saucer connection and, if there was such a connection, whether it was the cause of the crash.

Of paramount interest, of course, was the credibility of the only witness, Harold Dahl. Dahl's wife had been complaining that her hus-band had been drinking a lot and that ever since he told Crisman about his alleged sighting, their lives had been disrupted. In the FBI report, Mrs. Dahl is alleged to have said to her husband that he should just tell the truth and admit that the whole scheme was a fraud, cooked up for some publicity. Dahl then admitted to the FBI, especially in the light of two deaths having been attributed to the entire incident, that it was a fraud and he wanted out of it.

What did his retraction mean? Did it mean that Dahl cooked up the whole story himself and foisted it upon Crisman? Did it mean that he really saw something and Crisman concocted the rest of it? Or did it mean that Crisman, who subsequently disappeared and then re-appeared as a teacher at a Tacoma high school and then as a radio talk show host, had come up with the idea to get himself published in Ray Palmer's magazine? To this date, the intertwining stories are such that one can only speculate. However, after the FBI dismissed the story as a fraud, Dahl recanted his fraud admission and said he was forced into it.

And what of the two pilots, William Davidson and Frank Brown, who heroically tried to steer the plane into a safe place to bring it down where they would avoid causing injuries to innocent people on the ground? The big question that always surfaced as we looked into the details of the Maury Island and Kelso incidents was, why? Why did these intelligence officers show up to investigate the event? Partly, that was a mystery that UFO Hunters sought to solve even if we couldn't definitively find an answer to whether Harold Dahl saw flying sau-cers. Happily, we did find some evidence to explain why Frank Brown and William Davidson showed up in Washington, and through test-ing we think we figured out what brought their B-25 down.

Our lab work on Maury Island beach slag was perfunctory at best. However, we brought back to our test facility in Los Angeles material that Pat recovered from the bottom of Puget Sound in the area where we believe Dahl had his sighting and slag from the beach. A quick analysis of that material revealed that the highly ferrous nature of the slag material inside the bomb bay might have caused critical junction and relay boxes to overload. The resulting short circuit could have sent an electrical discharge to the junction and relay box at the left wing engine, causing a fire, which burned the wing and caused the plane to crash. The army itself never determined the conclusive reason for the crash, saying it was due to a mechanical failure. However, when we placed the material next to a junction box that our special-effects producer constructed, the magnetic field generated by the slag overrode the breakers on the junction box and allowed what might have been an electrical overload. Had that happened next to the junction box inside the B-25's bomb bay, both Ted Acworth and producer John Tindall suggested, it could have resulted in a fire in the circuitry. The fire, spotted by the crew chief sergeant, could have spread to the wing, started a fire in the left wing engine, and brought the plane down. Only a theory, but not impossible.

THE EPISODE

Almost every one of our episodes on *UFO Hunters* included some witnesses—living witnesses or descendents of witnesses—and an attempt to analyze evidence such as photos of the events. In this episode, "The UFO Before Roswell," however, we had none of that. We had to go on sixty-year-old rumor and physical evidence with no provenance. We had to ask, at the end of the day, what were we really trying to prove? The answer was as surprising to us as it might have been to viewers. But to get to that answer, we had to travel a very winding road.

Most roads in UFO investigations wind. They wind for lots of reasons, but mostly because the people who study these cases sit within their bailiwicks and either share information with a close-knit group or simply sit there waiting for the moment when a publisher or motion picture comes up to them with an offer to tell the story. We partly realized the issue this presented because of all our years working on the *UFO Files*, but when it came to the very treacherous road of the Maury Island and Kelso cases, we had no idea of the residue of frustration and downright contentiousness that existed from those folks claiming to be sitting on the truth.

Setting up an episode for *UFO Hunters* involved talking to sources in our contact list, laying out the story beat-points that would present the case, and then locating and talking to witnesses and experts. If there is any video of the incident, we had to find it. If there might be even a hint of trace evidence, we had to find that, too. Our mandate for each episode over the three seasons was that we needed live people who witnessed the event, video or still images of the event, and some trace evidence we could test. We tried to pound evidence and science in every episode to investigate the conventional explanation, eliminate it if we could, and see what remained. And this is what we tried to do with the Maury Island and Kelso cases.

Even though we had different opinions concerning the value of the Maury Island case and even debated whether it was actually something much more than a concocted story by a wannabe writer, because it resulted in the deaths of two Army Air Force intelligence officers and involved Kenneth Arnold as well as the FBI, we regarded it as a part of America's UFO history and, therefore, worth an episode starting off the series in season 1.

The episode was set up as a two-parter broken up, as all our episodes were, over five acts. Acts are partitions in the episodes set apart by commercial breaks. They are also progress points in the story. Because we know that the story has to move along across five acts, we set up each shoot according to what story beats, the logical dramatic steps toward the conclusion of each act, or points, the intellectual issues we have to make, have to fit into each specific act. For example, we introduce the story of the episode in act 1 and determine what role each of the UFO hunters will play in the investigation. Cameras follow each hunter along a specific story path to move the investigation along.

When it comes to scuba diving or climbing, the camera will follow Pat because of his experience in the Army Corps of Engineers. When it comes to scientific analysis and the measurement of data, as well as flying planes, the camera follows Ted Acworth. I'm usually the investigator/historian and the guy who tracks down some of the witnesses, especially police or military. We try to fit part of the story line for each separate investigative path into each act so that in act 5, the story comes together and we can each voice our opinions. This was how we set up the series from the very first Maury Island episode.

Our production organization was essentially divided into two parts. The field team included the cast, the camera and sound crew, the segment producer and field coordinator, the local production assistant, and the show runner/director. The office team consisted of the senior producer/show runner, segment producers setting up their respective episodes, the line producer and accounting department, assistant producers and production assistants, video editors, and the executive production team. At any given moment, we had one or more episodes in editing and the remaining episodes in various stages waiting to go to the network for approval. Behind the entire production team, both in the field and in the office, we had our network executive and whatever group she or he relied on at History.

When structuring the schedule for the season, the production team, including the executive producer, show runner/director, senior producer, and story editor figured out the number of production days allotted for in the budget. Production days consist of actual shooting days, travel days, editing days, and contingency days to work out story problems and wrap up any loose ends. Each day is usually allotted a specific amount of money to cover salaries and costs. For example, unless we were running tight on time, we never shot on travel days because it would convert a travel-day budget into a shooting-day budget. Very expensive. The producers tried to build in vacation days at home during the schedule so that there would be no expense for cast and crew. Every day we were on the road more than fifty miles away from the home production offices in Santa Monica, each member of the cast and crew received a per diem to cover costs. Lunch on shooting days was always covered as was dinner if we shot for more than seven hours after lunch. And this type of budgeting is minuscule compared to a network television drama or a feature film.

Critical to the setup of an episode was generating the list of witnesses and experts who appeared. We also tried to find as many background experts as possible, people we interviewed who probably wouldn't appear on camera but whose expertise would help us frame out the episode. Many times, as it happened in the Maury Island episode, that was where the trouble began.

What anyone who tries to conduct research in the pseudo-field of ufology finds is that the entire community is broken up into bailiwicks. Inside the bailiwicks, as if this were a kind of academic community, are all sorts of cliques. Just like a high school cafeteria, where you sit and who you eat with determines everything about how you spend your days. If we spoke to the wrong witness, the one who was on the outs with the rest of the community, we would find doors shut right in our face. Step into someone else's territory, and those aligned with that person would refuse to speak to you. Worse, in the age of Internet blogging, your newly found adversaries would trumpet the news of your entry into their respective bailiwicks as a trespass, as if they were the sirens of a tribal territorial early warning system.

On the other hand, if you paid homage to those who researched the field before you, were duly subservient, and promised those researchers camera time and promotion for their self-published book or self-produced video, perhaps you might obtain their cooperation until the episode aired. After an episode aired, it was anyone's guess who would be happy, who would be outraged, and who would be trumpeting disdain and a warning to other experts on his or her blog. We learned this fast and we learned it early when we began our trek into the morass of the Maury Island incident and the Kelso crash.

People in the UFO field guard the borders of their territories carefully, laying out their expertise on intricate Web sites whose extensive lists of its owners' accomplishments and contacts are meant to ward off any trespassers or predators. Encroach upon someone else's territory at your own peril, because the vituperation spread among members of the same clique is like the chemicals spread from tree to tree to warn of an impending infection from some plant disease. If this sounds bitter, it's because it is. In the field of UFO research, most of it amateur, the only truth to be disclosed is the truth as the particular researcher sees it. And there's no room for debate.

This is exactly what we found as we began our background setup of the Maury Island/Kelso episode. First, the phone call from our senior producer set off the hope, the promise, and the alarm. News that a Los Angeles–based production company was coming to town to interview experts in a location was exciting news, of course. It meant camera time, exposure of information, jobs, and money. It also posed a threat to researchers who feared encroachment. Imagine that you have been working quietly for years on a specific UFO story in the hopes that someday your book will be published or your movie will be made. Then along comes Acme Productions, Ltd., asking for your help and all your information. Is it the chance of a lifetime? Is it the dashing of your dream? Will the production company make you famous, or are they just a bunch of interlopers who'll take your valuable research and then move on? It can be any of the above depending upon how you play it.

So it was that our foray into the Maury Island/Kelso incidents was met with bristling hostility from those who had anointed themselves the keepers of the flame. In the first instance, our senior producer found that unless he followed the path of investigation laid out for him meticulously by one of the experts, not only would he get no help but the trumpeting blog would ward off any person foolish enough to help. Fortunately, we relied on the expertise of *UFO Magazine* columnist and contributor George Earley, whose research into both the Maury Island and Kenneth Arnold cases was probably the best in the field. And when it came to Kelso, even though we had established a good working relationship with one of the experts, his partner felt that we were destroying their chances for a great book deal by exposing the Kelso case to the world in advance of their writing. As a result, not only did we have to deal with a mountain of bureaucratic paperwork to gain access to the Kelso crash site, but we actually were confronted by the local sheriff and then faced hostile gunfire from the ZZ Top look-alike next-door neighbor.

We broke the episode up into three basic parts: search the beach on Maury Island and the bottom of the narrow strait of water to retrieve anything that might be construed as slag so as to analyze it in our lab; perform background research on the case, the players, and the victims; visit the Kelso crash site to retrieve whatever we could for analysis and lay out what might have happened. The final segment would be the lab segment, where we tried to come up with explanations for the incident from an analysis of what we retrieved. And this became the basic five-act structure for all the ensuing episodes over three seasons.

Our trip to Washington took us directly to a Vashon Island bed and breakfast in a very charming and unique Victorian-style building. It was warm, given the early October chill on Puget Sound, and the bedrooms were very well furnished. It was a great way to start a series. Our show runner and director for season 1, Al LaGarde, who had spent two seasons on *Paranormal State,* assembled the cast and crew in the downstairs sitting room the night before we began shooting to go over what the next day's schedule would entail.

We were to begin with a beach walk, a survey of the beach where Harold Dahl said he saw the slag fall. On the beach, we were scheduled to meet George Earley, whom I would interview about his research into the case and the influence the Kenneth Arnold sighting had on the Harold Dahl report, at least as far as Fred Crisman was concerned. George Earley, whose *UFO Magazine* column, "The Opinionated Oregonian," usually focused on in-depth research and commentary concerning historic cases, studied the Dahl and Kelso cases for years, and his role in our first episode was to start our investigation off by providing background on the case and pointing out the directions we had to take in order to find any answers.

After the beach search and our meeting with George Earley, we would retrace the route Harold Dahl's salvage boat took on the day he said he saw the flying saucers. With our own dive boat, Pat, a certified dive master, would search the bottom of the narrow strait for any piece of rock or debris that might look like what Harold Dahl allegedly saw being ejected from the flying saucer.

In actuality, we shot the beach scene first, but when the episode was edited, the dive-boat scene came first and the beach search second. I remember that on the days we spent on Vashon and Maury Islands, the wind was blowing so furiously that we were all wearing multiple layers of clothing when we weren't actually shooting. It was a very raw couple of days on that beach and on that boat.

The search on the beach told us very little about what Dahl might have actually retrieved. It was hard to tell basic ferrous rock that might have washed ashore from anything else. The pebbles that were rounded and smooth showed the results of being rolled around on the bottom of the strait of water and then being rolled along the shoreline as they washed ashore. Our guest researcher, Ron Millione, collected samples, along with the ones that Pat brought up from the sea bottom and some strange striated rocks that Pat believed might have been solidified molten material. These we tagged and bagged for later analysis at a lab we had set up and for use in our special-effects producer's lab. John Tindall, who was setting up the experiments at his facility, indicated that he had an idea about what effect the ferrous rocks might have on a junction box, based on the official air force report on the crash of Davidson and Brown's B-25.

On the beach, we met up with George Earley, who explained that the events that took place after the Dahl sighting might say more about the mystery surrounding those events than the actual sighting itself. For example, he asked, what was the relationship between Fred Crisman and Ray Palmer? What was the relationship between Palmer and Kenneth Arnold, which resulted not only in the 1948 *Fate Magazine* article on Dahl sighting but also in Kenneth Arnold's article on flying saucers in Ray Palmer's January 1952, self-described "book-length novel" entitled *Other Worlds Science Stories*. The story, George Earley has said, kept changing, a critique of the case echoed by other researchers as well.

This pointed us to the Kelso crash as the possible big reveal. Is it the hype or spin that Ray Palmer put on the case, which brought Kenneth Arnold into it and resulted in the crash of the B-25, that really makes this case stand out? Was this case a true-life version of the movie *Repo Man*?

The next stop was Kelso, but on the way we stopped to visit a local library to look up some of the history on the Kelso case and on Davidson and Brown to see if news from sixty years before could help us shed some light on the mystery we were trying to solve.

In the newspaper microfilms, we certainly found lots of information about flying-saucer sightings in the summer of 1947. In fact, there were sightings in thirty-nine states, not just in Washington and New Mexico. But the real clue Pat picked up from the papers was that the copilot and army intelligence officer Lieutenant Frank Brown has a great-nephew, Barry Fisher, who was researching the case and trying to find out what happened to his great-uncle by looking at pieces of the downed bomber. We had to get Barry Fisher to the crash site.

At the Kelso site, a truly remote and still relatively desolate area, we met up with Garth Baldwin, our archaeologist, who specializes in historic-site archaeology and whose presence was required by the state of Washington to oversee the exploration and analysis of the crash site. Even though the crash site was currently located on private land, the state still required that any investigation of an historic site involved the presence of and a filed investigation by an archaeologist registered and certified by the state. We worked from an approved list of archaeologists and found Garth Baldwin, a fascinating and intelligent individual, an ex-marine, and a graduate student. He was intrigued by the mystery we were hoping to unravel—why did the plane crash, and what can be found at the crash site that would help us answer that question?—and believed that looking at the spread of debris and aligning that with the crash reports from the air force would be useful. Washington State was very strict about the requirements for exploring the site and forbade any use of digging equipment or even shovels and spades. We were allowed the use of garden trowels for the purpose of scraping dirt off debris or looking under debris, but going beneath the ground surface was not allowed. Garth was also in charge of making sure that we obeyed the rules for surveying the site.

We were also joined by a ground-penetrating-radar operator and his rig for the purposes of conducting a noninvasive search under the surface. Might there be parts of the plane that the air force, which, with three hundred volunteers, scoured the site and removed debris in the days after the crash, missed? What might still be lurking underground that was never recovered? A ground-penetrating-radar survey might show us something that had been missed for sixty years.

The air force refused to allow any photographs of the crash site and guarded it heavily, leading to the suspicion in local newspapers that the plane was carrying secret cargo. One had to wonder whether, in the wake of the Kenneth Arnold sighting and the Roswell incident, the air force was being especially careful just in case there was any UFO slag spread all over the crash site. This was yet another reason for our bringing a ground-penetrating-radar unit to the site. The unit was operated by Rob Shaw from Geo Radar Imaging, who explained the process of the 3-D imaging the radar unit returned and how that imaging would show if anything significant was lurking below the ground up to a depth of twenty-five feet.

Working from the original air force crash reports, Garth first laid out the scenario of the crash against what he saw from exploring the physical site. He suggested that because the fires in the cargo junction box and then on the left wing engine certainly eroded the integrity of the wing, the plane didn't come down in one piece. The wing fell off first, and then, even as the pilots tried to exert some control, the weight of the right wing and the engine flipped the plane over on its right side and arced it into trees, where it broke up and was consumed in flames. Garth walked us to the center point of the impact area, where we found pieces of an engine cowling, possibly a rubber bladder from a fuel tank, and other pieces of the bomber's frame.

We were using the radar on the off chance that if the pilots were actually carrying some unknown material that might have impeded the plane's ability to remain aloft, the density of that material could have sunk it so deep during the crash that not only would the air force volunteers have missed it, but our metal detectors would have missed it as well. Although the radar generated an image for us, the amount of moisture in the ground—it was actually soaked through—combined with the dense foliage and leaf cover and the very uneven terrain, diminished the radar imaging ability of the unit so that the results were inconclusive at best.

However, during our radar scanning our next guest appeared: Barry Fisher, the great nephew of Lieutenant Frank Brown. In his initial conversation with Pat, Barry revealed that one of the things he discovered about his great-uncle still puzzled him. Why would Lieutenant Frank Brown, an intelligence officer, also be a counterespionage agent dispatched to Washington to meet with Kenneth Arnold and investigate the Dahl sighting? What was the connection? Also, why would Frank Brown have bequeathed his military identification to Kenneth Arnold? What was their relationship, and why would he not bequeath his identification documents to his family?

The answer, it seems, came from Frank Brown himself, who was the army's principal investigator of the Kenneth Arnold sighting. Brown wrote in his report on Kenneth Arnold that he found Arnold to be of a very high moral character. In fact, he wrote that, because of Arnold's strong family values and commitment to telling the truth, he had a very high confidence that Arnold actually saw something anomalous over Mount Rainier. That's why, when Kenneth Arnold contacted Brown to investigate the Harold Dahl sighting, Brown asked the Army Air Force for permission to fly to Washington to look into the case. It was Arnold who was the key. And the key to Kenneth Arnold was Ray Palmer. In turn, the key to Ray Palmer was Fred Crisman. And thus we established the links in the chain from Dahl all the way to Frank Brown and his death in a plane crash while carrying the material that Dahl allegedly collected. What was that material, and could it have brought down the B-25?

Our first step was to visit with Dr. Sam Iyengar at his laboratory in

Orange County, California, where he was analyzing both the rocks that Pat collected and material we recovered from the Kelso crash site. Dr. Ted Acworth, who holds a PhD in physics from Stanford and an MBA from MIT, already suggested that one of the rocks that Ronnie Millione said looked particularly suspicious because it bore the results of having been molten and then hardening was, more than likely, simple igneous rock that had been molten at one point under the Earth's mantle, was forced to the surface, and subsequently hardened. But the rocks and the airplane debris would become the subject of Sam's and Ted's analyses.

We brought soil samples, the rubber strip from what we believed to be the downed B-25, as well as some struts and an aluminum piece of skin from the plane for Dr. Iyengar and Ted to examine with Dr. Iyengar's sophisticated instruments. As Sam explained, the purpose of the tests was to see whether the material we brought was anomalous or conventional. If conventional, were there any outstanding anomalies about the evidence that we should think about? And, if the material the plane was carrying was anomalous itself, did the material that came into contact with the plane, either during the flight or as a result of the crash, change the nature of the conventional aircraft material?

The first scan of the aluminum piece that we recovered indicated that the piece displayed the results of having come into contact with a high heat source because its edges were converted into aluminum oxide. This compound could have also resulted from the aluminum's having been exposed to moisture and groundwater from sixty years in the dirt at Kelso. Other pieces that Dr. Iyengar tested, however, also returned results consistent with having been exposed to a very high heat source such as a fire. The soil samples we recovered from the areas closest to the crash site were subjected to X-ray diffraction, which revealed a crystalline structure consistent with exposure to a very high heat source. This, in conjunction with the aluminum test results, suggests that an intense fire broke out on board the plane, which continued burning even after the crash.

But, Pat and Ted both asked, what could have caused the fire on board? Did a fuel tank simply explode on its own? Unlikely, because the ignition would have needed a source. What about the official report that said that a fire broke out in a junction box inside the bomb bay? What could have caused that fire? Radiation from UFO material? Or, as our science researcher and special-effects producer John Tindall suggested, perhaps it was a heavy magnetic field that caused the junction boxes and relays to fail, thereby overloading the plane's electronic circuitry. He suggested and then proceeded to demonstrate that a magnetic field close to a relay could have caused it to fail. It could have overloaded, and then the surge in current could have caused other relay boxes to fail. If the circuit relays were short-circuited, then 120 amps of current would be shooting through wires that could only handle 20 amps. The result, which Tindall demonstrated on camera, was that the wire itself would vaporize in a burst of flame in a matter of seconds. Imagine, he suggested, that this wire vaporization happened all along the left wing, causing the left engine to burst into flame. It is a very plausible disaster scenario.

What, we asked, could have caused that intense magnetic field that tripped the relays in the junction box? It could have been, Tindall said, the very ferrous nature of the slag material itself. We passed magnetic compasses over the rocks collected from the sea bottom and beach, and, sure enough, the compass dials spun around, locking on the magnetic source. Then, Tindall held a magnet close to the junction box he built, mimicking the large amount of ferrous material the plane might have been carrying, and the junction-box switches immediately failed. They locked up, and the junction box simply passed along intense current into the wiring. The demonstration of overloading the wiring showed just how quickly it could vaporize. Now we had a plausible source of the magnetic field and a plausible cause of the fire.

Taking it one step further, we considered whether the slag itself, sitting in the bomb bay, could have been ignited by an electrical fire. A quick experiment in which Tindall exposed the slag material to an arc welder demonstrated that the slag caught fire, burning at 4,000 degrees Fahrenheit, and it would have burned right through the aluminum, which would have melted at 1,200 degrees Fahrenheit. And to demonstrate the chain reaction that caused the combustion, Tindall exposed the aluminum compound in the plane's structure to a 4,000-degree source. The result? The aluminum caught fire and became completely oxidized, becoming aluminum oxide, the same compound that Dr. Iyengar identified in the sample he analyzed. As Pat Uskert put it, this type of white-hot fire was very different from a gasoline fire or a simple electrical fire.

Now we had a plausible scenario for the cascading effect that essentially burned up the plane in midair and caused the left wing to fall off. The highly magnetic slag, stored next to a junction box in the bomb bay, caused the circuits in the junction box to fail, sending a 120-amp current through 20-amp wire, which started a fire. The fire in the junction box ignited the slag, which in turn ignited the aluminum as the electrical fire continued along the wing, caused other junction boxes to fail, and set the left engine on fire. The burning wing fell off, and the plane flopped over on its right wing as it lost altitude and burned in midair while it crashed into the dense forest canopy at Kelso.

In our team wrap-up we were able to conclude that, regardless of the UFO provenance of the slag material that both Crisman and Palmer forced on Davidson and Brown, the rocks' ferrous nature alone certainly could have generated a magnetic field powerful enough to trip the switches in a junction box. This, in turn, could have created a short circuit and resulted in an electrical fire igniting the slag, which would have burned at a temperature hot enough to destroy the aluminum and cause a structural failure in the plane. Science corroborated the official descriptions of the final moments of the plane and the air force crash report. We were able to attach witness testimony to the cargo the B-25 was carrying, which the air force subsequently admitted it was carrying. And it was very gratifying for us that we were able to bring some closure to Lieutenant Frank Brown's family. We were able to provide a plausible explanation for Lieutenant Brown's bequeathing his military identification to Kenneth Arnold and to explain why Arnold's honesty and the strength of his moral character so influenced Brown that when Arnold asked him to fly to Washington State to investigate Dahl's story, he didn't hesitate. Thus the Dahl-Crisman connection, the Crisman-Palmer connection, the Palmer-Arnold connection, and the Arnold-Brown connection became the chain of causality that brought Lieutenant Brown and Captain Davidson to their deaths when their plane, carrying Dahl's slag, caught fire and crashed. You can imagine why, under scrutiny from the FBI after the crash, Harold Dahl recanted the entire story and Fred Crisman simply disappeared for a while.

This was our first real venture into an actual historic case, and the entire team of producers, investigators, crew, and on-screen cast members turned in an episode that was entertaining and that brought science and good background research to a mysterious set of events. We never concluded whether Dahl actually saw flying saucers and retrieved UFO debris or not, but we did explain how the plane might have crashed as a result of its cargo and why Frank Brown was drawn into the case. It was a good first episode.

BILL'S BLOG

I had always believed the Maury Island UFO sighting by local boatman Harold Dahl and the events that followed to be more a tale of conspiracy and fraud than a real UFO sighting. It was a case mired in controversy with shadowy wannabe intelligence agents, magazine publishers, and even the FBI. It was a case that the witness, Harold Dahl, eventually admitted was a fraud and then recanted on his admission. But it was a case that led to the very tragic deaths of two B-25 pilots over Kelso, Washington, as they were carrying a box full of slag that was said to have dropped from a flying saucer in trouble over Maury Island, Washington. In short, it was a case more about the controversy than about the actual UFO.

At first, I have to admit, I thought this was the worst possible case to begin with on *UFO Hunters*, season 1, during the fall of 2007. The case took place sixty years earlier, all the witnesses were dead, and the debris from the crash of the B-25 over Kelso was now part of an historic site. But the more we investigated the history of this case and the various players in the twists and turns that took place during early summer 1947, the summer that saw the crash at Roswell only a week or so after Maury Island, the more we realized that this case was inextricably linked to the very beginning of the flying-saucer craze in America. So we decided to see if we could really figure out what might have actually happened. And the episode turned out better than anyone thought.

This episode also showed me the dangers of working with the prickly UFO community. Yes, ten years earlier I had brought retired Lieutenant Colonel Philip Corso to the fiftieth anniversary of the Roswell crash and watched as his then-rock-star status both inspired and infuriated the UFO community. Who was this retired old guy who popped up from under the radar with a big-time publisher and a blockbuster whistle-blower story about having handled UFO debris? Here was a field in which people had been working in quiet frustration for most of their adult lives only to be overshadowed by a storyteller who provided not one iota of hard evidence to support his claims. Of course they were angry, even while they wanted to latch onto every piece of the Corso story they could. This conflict is still going on today.

Much the same thing happened when *UFO Hunters* came to town in Kelso. The researchers were furious that we were coming in, possibly to ruin their plans for the big book, the big movie, and the big appearance on *Larry King Live*. That wasn't our intention, but that's how we were perceived. And this would happen over and over again, no matter how much we tried to explain to researchers what we were about.

Producing a television show is just that: producing a television show. Of course we would have loved to have found pieces of a UFO on the beach at Maury Island or, better still, on the sea bottom, where Pat would have retrieved it. But what does a piece of a UFO look like? Is it made of "unknownium," the magical element all UFOs are made of? Does it have a strange alloy of compounds that are common to us but can't be fabricated on planet Earth? Does it display properties like the memory metal rumored to have been retrieved from the Roswell debris field? We don't know, and we didn't find anything that would have led us to any conclusive knowledge.

We were there to produce an entertaining and informative television series. Changing the world is great, but producing a television series is what the contract said and what we had to do. Most important, and what people began to grasp over the course of the first season, is that we were there to support the existence of the UFO community.

When you look at most network shows, there is always the requisite smirking skeptic through whose bluster and il-logic one can hear the basic debunker argument: all UFO re-searchers are simply delusional kooks grasping at any straws they can find. Our plan was just the opposite in season 1. We wanted to show that UFO researchers were applying as much science and logical thinking as they could to solving mysteries. We wanted to display that logic and science and to show that by employing a scientific method we could eliminate conven-tional explanations to bring us to the core mystery. We wanted to debunk the debunkers.

The Maury Island episode, taking us down a winding road of illusion, tragic deception, self-serving career moves, and the too-naive belief in some witness testimony, was an introduc-tion into the hostile world of ufology. We found that even as we began to contact the key researchers in the case, they were align-ing against any outsiders they felt were poaching from their territory. Like book reviewers who write their reviews before they even receive the review copy of the book, commentators formed their opinions before they even met us. Maybe the Corso curse hung over us too closely.

When faced with hostility from local researchers, however, our only course was to try to make as many friends as possible. We never promised instant fame. We never said the show is "all about you." And we never said we were there to promote Joan's or Joe's newest book or DVD. But we weren't there to steal anyone's thunder. Sure, the Kelso Museum folks complained about our presence at the Kelso crash site to the local sheriff. But when the deputy saw our paperwork and that we had complied with every existing regulation, he shook our hands and went on his way. The Kelso crash site neighbor paid us a visit with a handgun tucked into his pocket. Then, after going back to his own property, we believed, he fired shots over our heads. This episode was an introduction to what we would face for the next three seasons. But it was a great episode that brought real laboratory science and solid background-historical research to a case that was simply hiding under a cloud of unknowing for sixty years. We focused a light on history and on scientific experimentation, and we came up with answers. We established a pattern and a methodology that carried us to the Roswell debris field, to Area 51, and to horrific photographs of a strange human-bovine-hybrid fetus delivered postmortem from a mutilated cow. We had ventured into the unknown.

USOS:
UNIDENTIFIED SUBMERGED OBJECTS

The second episode of season 1 was actually developed from two earlier *UFO Files* episodes on deep-sea UFO phenomena called USOs: "unidentified submerged (or submersible) objects." In the air they're UFOs, but once they dive into the water they're USOs. Therefore, USOs are the underwater equivalent of UFOs and, reportedly, lurk in the darkness of the deepwater Redondo Trench just off Catalina Island in Southern California as well as in the deepwater trenches of the Gulf of Mexico and the Atlantic Trench in the Bermuda Triangle.

If we are to believe a log entry made by Christopher Columbus on October 11, 1492, a day before he made landfall in the New World, while on his quarterdeck he saw a brightly illuminated object under the water moving ahead of his flagship, the *Santa Maria*. He saw the object exit the water and fly into the sky. If his sighting was accurate, Christopher Columbus probably recorded the first sighting of a USO.

Our two earlier USO *UFO Files* episodes were very successful for the production company and for the History Channel. Therefore, given the amount of information available to us and the fact that the Redondo Trench in Santa Monica Bay was in our neighborhood, a

USO episode was an obvious choice. Besides, we had a number of very informative witnesses, an expert and author we had relied on in previous episodes named Preston Dennett, a very formidable abductee (also referred to as experiencer) and private pilot named Noah Felice, and 911 tapes from the Lost Hills sheriff's station documenting at least one very important USO sighting. We also had some great video showing a UFO over the Redondo Trench and Catalina Island.

THE CASES: USOS IN THE REDONDO TRENCH OFF CATALINA ISLAND

The area of Santa Monica Bay between the mainland and Catalina Island first caught the attention of the media all the way back on April 15, 1966, at 9:45 A.M., when a professional photographer captured a saucer-shaped craft, one with no tail assembly or wings and no visible means of propulsion, traveling at about two hundred miles an hour over Catalina. It startled the photographer, who shot some compelling footage of the craft. This was real film, and it was unnerving to see the object that was captured on it.

Just about two years later, in the late afternoon on December 29, 1968, a Palos Verdes attorney saw a string of lights hovering over the Catalina Channel. Palos Verdes, a beautiful isthmus of land near Long Beach, California, is almost directly across the bay from the Catalina Channel. The attorney said that he watched the string of lights move slowly over the water until they almost stopped in midair and then tilted in unison diagonally over the water just above the surface. Then, the lights simply stopped moving and hovered over the water.

The witness said that it was the strangest thing he had ever seen because the lights operated as if they were attached to a rigid object, but he couldn't see the object, only the lights. Thinking that he might be able to contact the lights, whatever they were, on a walkie-talkie, the witness ran into his garage, pulled out his walkie-talkie unit, and turned it on. But what he heard was a brief ship-to-shore transmission from boats on the water that night, one telling the other that the lights he was observing from the deck were nothing like anything he had ever seen before. "I don't know what the hell it is," the speaker said. Then, the speaker described the position of the lights exactly the way that the attorney was seeing it, completely confirming the sighting from another position. The attorney told Pat Uskert that the transmission "really freaked me out."

The next day, the local Los Angeles news carried the story of the Catalina lights, telling viewers that they had received lots of phone calls from other witnesses. However, they explained that the lights were really a set of balloons with candles or flares affixed to them launched by "two crazy college kids." Not so for the Palos Verdes witness, who said that the lights he saw bore no resemblance to lights on a balloon. What he saw were lights that moved in unison, not lights hanging from separate objects. The balloon explanation, used before to explain away the Roswell crash, simply didn't work for him.

In January 1968, a Los Angeles County Sheriff's Office deputy named Richard Callen saw a large vessel sailing in the channel with "lights in its portholes." The object seemed to explode. A bright light illuminated from the object, and then flares shot into the air from the bright light. He could give no explanation for what he saw, and, presumably, there was no report of a conventional vessel exploding in the Catalina Channel that night.

On March 23, 1977, Sheriff Sergeant Vincent Rupp received dozens of phone calls reporting UFO sightings between Sacramento in the north, to Salinas farther south, and all the way down to Los Angeles, Orange County, and March Air Force Base in the Moreno Valley between 3:45 and 4:00 A.M. In a *Los Angeles Times* report on the incident, the witnesses who had called in were March Air Force Base personnel, local police, and officers from the California Highway Patrol based in Los Angeles. One witness, Mark Hogan, a runway worker at Los Angeles International Airport, referred to the formation of lights as "tin-can" or "teardrop" shaped and said that they flew in from the direction of Santa Catalina at 3:30 A.M. and swept across the runway. He said, from his experience of seeing conventional aircraft of all types every day on the job, that the lights "weren't natural." A military spokesperson from March Air Force Base confirmed that the objects had been seen from the base even though there were no aircraft or missile tests taking place at the base at that time.

Another witness that Pat Uskert interviewed was David Russo, who, upon seeing the strange object over Santa Monica Bay, took the time to make a sketch of what he saw. Russo, a retired attorney living in Long Beach just a couple of blocks from the water, saw bright lights in formation over the bay at approximately 11:30 P.M. on August 4, 2006, while he was walking along the shore. He saw the lights heading toward Long Beach from nearby San Pedro, and when the object got to about a mile in front of him, he said, "it just stopped" about ten to fifteen feet above the surface of the water. He could make out different colored lights on different sides of what he depicted on paper as a triangular-shaped object. The object rotated above the water and then, from a dead stop, shot off toward Catalina Island in, Russo said, "less than a second."

These incidents set the background for our main case, the crash of a small private plane on January 26, 1980, which, the pilot said, was the direct result of a USO off the city of Avalon on Catalina Island, shooting it down with a beam of "liquid light." The pilot's name is Noah Felice, and his story became the major incident of the episode because we hoped that by diving in the area where his plane went down—and this was a documented crash—we would find a piece of wreckage that might have shown some evidence of contact with an anomalous weapon.

NOAH'S STORY

On January 26, 1980, Noah, a private detective and a pilot with four-teen years' experience, and his cousin Mark took off from Catalina in Noah's Piper Cherokee when Mark told him that he was dying of cancer and had only five or six months to live. The two men had grown up together and were each other's closest friends. They were, in

Noah's words, closer than biological brothers. Noah said that the news was so shocking to him, losing his cousin to cancer, that instead of heading back to work, he decided to fly them to Las Vegas for a blow-out vacation.

As they circled around the island, Noah spotted a strange object just below the surface of the water. It was very unusual, and he had never seen anything like that before. Noah looped around to get a better look at the object, descending just a bit to get a good angle on it. What he saw startled him at first. The object was a craft, not a submarine but something different. It was metallic, large, the size of two houses, and he said that it had something like a door or an observation porthole on top, through which he could see a humanoid figure. "It looked human, but it wasn't human," he said.

But as soon as he looped around the island to descend to get a better look at the object, the object shot a bright white beam of light at him, completely engulfing the cockpit and making it impossible to see anything. More chilling, Noah said, the light seemed to take control of the plane, rendering the plane inoperable. The light seemed alive, as if it were a presence in the plane. The sound of the engine became silent, his instruments went dead, and he couldn't even feel the vibration of the propeller-driven Cherokee anymore. It was as if the light separated the plane and its occupants from the reality of the world they knew and placed them in a kind of isolation booth.

As Noah became disoriented and lost his bearings in the brightness, he believed that the object shot another beam at him. The second beam took even greater control of the plane; instead of making it inoperable, it was sucking the plane toward the strange craft in the water even as the beam engulfed Noah and his cousin in a feeling of being in thick liquid. He was floating in it, unable to move, unable to manipulate the controls of his plane even as the light grew brighter.

"I knew the plane was moving," Noah said. "I knew we were being drawn into the light, drawn down toward the source of the light, and there was nothing I could do about it."

The liquid that surrounded them, not the ocean, but the light, was so thick that Noah could barely feel anything, even though he knew he was being sucked toward the source of the light.

"I knew we were being pulled into the framework of the light, like being drawn into a portal. But it was the source of whatever was shooting that light at us. And then it was, Bang!"

The plane fell into the ocean.

Noah told us that he had a feeling of complete helplessness, bordering on panic, because in all his years as a pilot and as a private detective investigating homicides and cold cases, he never felt afraid. He was always able to work his way through tight situations. But this was unlike anything he had felt before. Even though Noah was pulled from the water by the bay watch twenty minutes after impact, what really happened to Noah and his cousin Mark Anthony Felice is another story.

Being in a plane crashing into the water at over a hundred miles an hour would be like hitting a cement wall. Noah's body should have sustained broken bones as his seat belt slammed him back before it tore. His skin should have been shredded off him by broken, sharp-edged glass as his body hurtled through the windshield. His spinal column should have been injured by the sudden shock of hitting the water at a high speed. Noah should have drowned because he was underwater for twenty minutes unconscious. Yet none of that happened. When Noah was pulled from the water by bay watch, he had a concussion and that was it. What had happened, and how was it that he was alive?

"It was horrible," he said. "There was blood everywhere in the cockpit. I was dead for at least fifteen minutes before they found me, actually dead."

As bad as that was, Noah explained, with all the blood floating in the water, "I can't understand why the sharks didn't get me."

Noah's cousin did not survive the crash. He was killed. And today, over thirty years later, Noah still doesn't understand what happened to him and his cousin after they hit the water.

If Noah didn't go crashing through the windshield, didn't get torn from his seat from the impact, who rescued him? Bay watch said they retrieved him from the water. And the bay-watch diver actually discovered the plane wreckage. But, unless the diver managed to open the cockpit door, release the seat belt, and bring Noah to the surface, how did he get out? And, even more puzzling, unless Noah's body went into a hibernation-preservation mode and shut down his systems so that he didn't require the level of oxygen of a waking person, sometimes called "drownproofing," how did he survive without permanent brain damage?

The Los Angeles County Sheriff's Office report on Noah's plane crash speculated that there were two possible locations for the plane wreckage, both on the Los Angeles mainland side of the island, Empire Landing and Ripper's Cove. If the wreckage had not been drawn out to sea by the underwater currents, then, quite possibly, the wreckage could have still been in one of those two spots even after twenty-eight years, when we were investigating the crash. And if the wreckage could be located on the sea bottom, a diver could tell if the windshield had been broken or if the seat belt had been torn. Even better, if we could salvage some of the instruments, we might be able to determine if there remained any residual magnetic field or even radiation. Finding those types of anomalies would be evidence that something strange happened to the plane and it wasn't just pilot error that sent the plane into the ocean.

Noah's recovery from the water was truly incredible. Where had his conscious mind been during this time? He was told that he drifted in and out of consciousness while underwater for fifteen to twenty minutes, and he literally came back from the dead. What did he remember? Where had his conscious mind been during this time? And upon his recovery, was he a changed person?

Noah told us that, to this day, he is not 100 percent sure whether he had a near-death experience or was actually under the care of extraterrestrials or some sort of spiritual entities. He truly cannot say. However, he remembers images, clear images, of what he was able to see while he was bathed by the light and he has his own theories about what might have happened to him.

Noah remembers that from the moment he felt the liquid surrounding him and his awareness that the plane was underwater, he felt that he was not only not inside the plane but also not within this reality. He said that he was six years old again and that he and his cousin Mark were both playing on the lawn of the house where they grew up. They were tumbling and running and in what developmental psychologists call childhood bliss. This is a form of theta state prior to adult-onset brain development in which children are actually open to far more sensory input than adults. In order to compensate for this flood of sensory activity, the normal child brain filters itself away from any negative or hostile input and generates a pleasure feedback loop. This is entirely normal and accounts for the happiness that most children seem to be able to experience despite the difficulties their families may have. In Noah's vision, Noah and Mark were in this state of bliss. They were children. Mark was not dying. The plane did not crash. And whatever would befall each of them in later life was not even on the horizon. They were young again.

Noah told me that he remembered that a presence came into his mind, even though he was a child, and that presence told him it was time to say good-bye to Mark. Was this Noah's own mind speaking to him as he went into a hibernation state to preserve what little oxygen he had left in his bloodstream? Was he in the midst of a true spiritual experience? Or were extraterrestrials, having inadvertently shot down his plane, now aware of the pain and suffering that would befall Mark and saving him from that while implanting in Noah's mind his fondest memories before sending him back to experience the pain of loss and the pain of physical recovery? Noah has his own ideas, but all he knows is that he had one day. One day free of everything. One day in complete innocence. One day. Who wouldn't want just one day?

Noah remembers waking up in a hospital and then lapsing back into twilight sleep. He was injured, suffering a bad concussion. But he was alive and awash in the memories of his childhood vision with his cousin. He remembers being told that he was the only survivor of the plane crash and feeling grief at the loss of his cousin. But he also remembers seeing figures around him in his vision, figures telling him that he would go back but that his cousin would stay.

Since the crash, Noah told us, his life has changed completely. Maybe it was a standard near-death experience that put him in touch with another realm, an otherworldly realm; maybe it was an actual extraterrestrial contact; or maybe it was an oxygen-deprivation-generated hallucination. Whatever it was, Noah has said that since that day, he has been in touch with the entities from the world he visited and they maintain contact with him.

Our mission, in this episode, was not only to get as many witnesses' stories as possible and to interview experts such as Preston Dennett but also to find the wreckage of Noah Felice's plane, even if only to retrieve a piece of it that might reveal an anomalous event to give him some peace of mind.

THE EPISODE

We had the incident and the event interviews recorded on video. Pat had interviewed two witnesses who had seen configurations of lights over the Bay toward Catalina and had those sightings corroborated by multiple witness reports and television news reports. But the heart and soul of the episode would be to see if we could find any real measurable evidence of a UFO contact. In order to do that, we headed off to Catalina, where, while Pat was interviewing his witnesses, I flew the route of Noah Felice's plane while Noah himself sitting in the copilot's seat narrated the events preceding his crash.

Our next step was meeting up with Captain Dave on the *Pacific Star* to sail from the mainland to both Empire Landing and Ripper's Cove to see if we could find the spot where Noah's plane went down and estimate where the wreckage might have ended up twenty-eight years later. But to do that, we needed sonar-imaging equipment to map the sea bottom before sending Pat to dive to the bottom to see what he could bring up. Sailing along with us on this trip were Noah Felice and Ronnie Millione.

For Noah, this was a return to a tragedy and to a place where, he said, he went to the outer edge of reality, crossed over, and came back. Maybe by finding the wreckage of his plane we could put puzzle pieces together to find out what really happened to Noah Felice.

As Pat and Ronnie helped the side-scan radar crew pay out the cable over the stern diving step, Noah helped our captain navigate the boat to the coordinates in Empire Landing, where he believed the plane wreckage might still be. This was not as easy as one might think because the small cove was still large enough to require a grid search, and, of course, we didn't know how far out to sea the wreckage might have drifted. The coastal shelf around Catalina Island drops off very steeply so that if the wreckage originally came to rest near the ledge of the slope, the heavy undertow would have drawn the pieces of the plane over the edge and from there carried out into much deeper water. As it was, we were searching a bottom at a depth of sixty feet.

Side-scan radar is effective for searching and imaging shallow brown-water areas. Like standard radar and ground-penetrating radar, the sending unit bounces radio waves off the bottom and sends back the signal to a computer that converts the sounds to a three-dimensional image of anything it pings along the bottom. Our sonar operators were a team from Aqua Survey, a professional sea-bottom-surveying organization. And as we stared at the computer screen and the radar began transmitting and receiving, they advised us to look for anything bright, shiny, and metallic and also straight-edged. Straight-lined metallic objects would likely be parts of the aircraft assemblage, especially parts of the wing or tailpiece.

Our boat motored back and forth across straight lines called "transits" as if it were etching lines across a blank sheet of loose-leaf paper. But after transiting Empire Landing for over two hours and picking up readings on clumps of kelp and stray debris along the bottom, we finally confirmed that the wreckage of Noah's plane was not resting in this location. We headed to Ripper's Cove.

On a Coast Guard map of the Catalina sector, Noah traced out the route of his flight, indicating where he turned to loop around after he spotted the glint off the object for the first time. He was convinced, even though we had to scour Empire Landing because of the sheriff's report, that he hit the water in Ripper's Cove. But, a question for all of us, would the driving seaward current over twenty-eight years pump the wreckage along the bottom until it rolled off the shelf and was dragged out to sea or broken up?

Once in Ripper's Cove, we had a hit. The side-scan radar picked up a large straight-edged metallic object that Noah identified as a possible tail rudder. He couldn't tell if it was the tail from his Piper because we couldn't read the tail numbers, but, Noah said, it looked like a tail piece. The *Pacific Star* was in seventy feet of choppy water, and it was time for Captain Dave's diver, Jake, to go over the side to scour the bottom for the wreckage.

"Look for the registration number eight-one Mike," Noah instructed Jake. The number 81-M had been on the tail rudder of Noah's Piper.

It was exciting to think that after almost three decades, we might have hit just the right spot and found the wreckage. And as Jake looked over what we thought, through the video camera, was a very suspicious piece of debris, our hopes rose. But when Jake bobbed back up to the surface, all he could report was that the metallic, shiny straight-edged object was in reality the transom of a boat that had sunk many years before. It was rusted and decaying, but Jake said that, as he approached it, he could tell that it was no plane.

The mystery continued. If both the Avalon sheriff's station and the Santa Monica Bay watch positioned Ripper's Cove as the most likely of the two crash sites, what happened to the plane? One thought, which we were embarrassed to consider, was that if ETs had shot down Noah's plane, they disposed of the wreckage to avoid giving themselves away. The other, far more logical, explanation was that the underwater currents off the shelf had drawn the wreckage out to sea. But how could we test out this theory rather than simply move on? Ted Acworth and John Tindall came up with a simulation/demonstration that made sense.

Tindall suggested that the wreckage could have shifted because of the Bernoulli effect, a law that says that fluid in motion has less pressure than static fluid. How might this work on the sea bottom? To demonstrate, Tindall suspended two cards from a pole and blew air between them. The fluid in that case was air, and the air in motion, because it had less pressure than static air, drew the two cards together. This effect is also called lift, the principle that allows a winged craft heavier than air to fly. Air, drawn over the wing as the plane moves forward, moves faster than the air beneath the wing. As a result, the pressure is lighter on the top surface of the wing and the plane rises. Changing the shape of the wing, which you can see a pilot doing if you look out the window of a jetliner that's landing, gives the plane more lift and the pilot more control as the plane loses speed before it touches down on the runway. This is also the same effect that allows a sailboat, with a deep-enough keel, to sail into the wind as well as off the wind.

The Bernoulli effect on the wreckage on the sea shelf might have worked in the same way as lift. Faster current moving over the top of the wreckage would have lifted the wreckage off the bottom just enough to move it over the shelf, where gravity itself would have forced it to tumble to a greater depth. Once it was no longer embedded in the soft bottom, the undertow would have dragged it out to sea. The demonstration of the Bernoulli effect, therefore, would have to show that a faster current passing over the top of the wreckage would actually lift it.

In a fish tank full of water, Tindall set a simulated piece of wreckage on a sandy-gravel-sloped bottom. As he blew a current of water over it, the wreckage actually lifted off the bottom. Once it did, the natural force of gravity on the sloped bottom sent it slipping forward into the trench. The speed with which the simulated wreckage moved and the angle of the incline suggested to Ted Acworth that another effect might be working as well. This was known as mass waste. And if this worked on the wreckage, then we had been looking in the wrong spot. We should have been looking farther out to sea and deeper in the Redondo Trench.

Mass waste, according to Tindall, explains mudslides and the collapse of the walls along an underwater shelf. It is the mass of material sliding down, taking everything with it and increasing its mass because of the lack of cohesion of the mass as it falls. If this happened, then it might be possible, Ted suggested, to plot the course the wreckage might have taken in order to set up a new search grid. Tindall demonstrated this possible trajectory of the wreckage by increasing the angle of the incline of the soil in the fish tank and pouring loose gravel and sand into the tank. As the sand built up, it moved very quickly, carrying even the top level of the newly poured sand along with it. Thus, Ted argued, it was clear that the wreckage could have slid much farther down the slope, possibly into a spot where it might not be retrievable. But it was worth looking for it. And to demonstrate the Bernoulli effect even further, Ted set a simulated fuselage on top of a much steeper incline as the bottom began to shift and then blew water current against the force of gravity over the fuselage, and immediately the fuselage slid right down the incline all the way to the bottom. In other words, mass waste combined with the Bernoulli effect moved the wreckage far away from where it might have initially come to rest after the crash. The experiment was, as Ted Acworth said, "our smoking gun."

With the results of Tindall's and Ted's experiments, we moved back out into the channel off Catalina to see if we could find an underwater debris field deeper into the trench. This time, we set up the search grid two miles east—toward the mainland—of our original location off Ripper's Cove. Unfortunately, this new search area was in the San Pedro Basin at a depth of one mile. This is one of the most impenetrable sections of the bay and well beyond the diving reach of Pat and Ted. A mile-deep basin, some theorists believed, would make a perfect hiding place for USOs, were they to navigate in that area. But our hope, as our dive boat moved farther out into the bay, was that the wreckage had not slid all the way to the bottom but had come to rest along the slope.

Our expert Preston Dennett, whom we interviewed as part of this search, also had a theory. He theorized that the USO activity in the San Pedro Basin and the Redondo Trench had been so extensive over the previous forty or fifty years that he wouldn't be surprised if Noah's plane had been taken away by the USO. Dennett theorized that if an extraterrestrial presence wanted to remove hard evidence from investigators, evidence that would have shown that a conventional apparatus had come into contact with an anomalous force, the simple solution would be to destroy the evidence or take it someplace where it would not be found.

With all the sightings of craft going back to 1947, we asked why a USO would go to such lengths to hide evidence. Dennett said that since the water was so deep and the military and naval presence in Southern California waters so extensive, he believed that there may be an actual alien base underwater. Why Los Angeles? Dennett believed that not only would a military presence attract them but also that the base would be a "hunter's blind." They could hide their craft, observe human beings while staying largely unobserved themselves, and have direct access to a huge ocean.

"The entire Southern California shoreline," Dennett also pointed out, "is riddled with caves and tunnels that go inland." He said that the underwater tunnels extend all the way from the ocean to Edwards Air Force Base and that an underground tunnel connects Edwards to Vandenberg Air Force Base. In fact, navy submarines can go from Edwards all the way to Catalina Island without being seen. This would be a perfect location for USOs.

Back on the water, Pat and Ted worked with another side-scan unit to get an image off the bottom. In the new search area, they picked up a cylindrical object. It could have been a fuselage or something else, but we continued our search of the outer edge of Ripper's Cove until we got a solid image of what Ted said had to be a plane. We saw the tail, probably part of an engine, and the outline of wings. Definitely a plane, even though we couldn't tell whether it was Noah's plane. This time, Ted Acworth and Pat Uskert went into the water, both of them experienced divers and both of them going to a limit of one hundred feet to see if they could make a positive identification.

At the bottom of the cove, Ted and Pat made contact with the plane, largely intact. Although they couldn't make out a tail number, which would conclusively confirm the identity of the plane, Ted said that because he noticed a cargo door on the fuselage it could not have been a Piper Cherokee. Ted identified the plane as a Piper Warrior, a larger aircraft with a cargo door. The Cherokee was smaller and did not have a cargo door.

It was unfortunate on this return trip to Catalina that it was a last-minute assembly of crew so that Noah Felice, who was in upstate New York, couldn't join us on the trip. Noah said that he would have wanted to have been there for the discovery of the underwater wreckage.

Ted's theory was that after twenty-eight years, the wreckage could easily have drifted much farther down the slope, possibly even into the mile-deep trench. If that were the case, it is likely the wreckage, which we know was in the water because the rescuers took a photo of it, will be irretrievable. It simply has tumbled too deep for a dive team to recover and might even have broken up and spread all over the floor of the trench or basin.

With no plane wreckage to analyze, we returned to Tindall's lab to examine the possibilities of whether a beam of some form of energy could disable a plane to the point where it would fall out of the sky. What type of beam could do that? Tindall and Ted suggested that if the beam of white light that Noah saw was really a beam carrying an electromagnetic pulse, an EMP, then perhaps a heavy EMP beam could knock out the controls of a plane, especially if one of the beams was a targeting mechanism to lock onto the craft and another, more powerful beam did the damage. Tindall set up a demonstration to illustrate this possibility.

The first thing that Tindall and Ted demonstrated was the power of an alternating-current magnet. Instead of a magnet with north and south poles that remained fixed, the AC magnet that Tindall built actually directed a magnetic current in a narrow direction when Tindall pointed it in close proximity to an electric motor wired to a light. The magnet, once powered, generated a current into the motor, actually turned it on, and illuminated the bulb. Next step: could this magnetic wave shut down an engine?

Tindall constructed a basic model of an airplane engine with a magneto permanently generating a current to the spark plug that fired the cylinder turning the propeller. Tindall started the engine with a power drill to turn the prop over until the engine caught—just like cranking a car before the advent of electric starters—and then took the powerful AC magnet, placed it near the cylinder, and had our lab assistant Jeff Tomlinson turn on the current. The result was exactly what Ted had predicted. The electromagnetic beam from the magnet interrupted the electron flow to the spark plug, causing it to stop firing. Once it stopped firing, the engine stopped and the prop stopped turning. Had that been Noah Felice's plane, the engine would have been shut down and the plane would have fallen into the water. Our experiment showed that a powerful EMP would definitely have had the juice to cause Noah's plane to crash.

Knowing this, we could only speculate about the nature of whatever took down Noah's plane. However, by taking Noah's story at face value and modeling out the physical forces that could have stopped the engine on his plane with a powerful electromagnetic current and then swept the wreckage out to sea, we demonstrated that it was possible to use scientific experimentation to test the effects of a UFO on a piece of modern machinery.

The Catalina Channel, the Redondo Trench, and the San Pedro Basin, we found, were indeed sources of speculation, incredible eyewitness testimony, and lore. All the way from the Battle of Los Angeles in January 1942, when coastal antiaircraft artillery opened fire on a tubular object hovering over Redondo and Hermosa Beaches, to sightings as recent as the 1980s, the Southern California coast from

Point Dume all the way to Long Beach has been a hot spot for eyewitness accounts of UFOs and USOs. Even as far south as San Diego's Coronado Island, witnesses have told vivid stories of UFO encounters and abductions by alien creatures. While our episode, in Ted's words, did not come up with any dispositive evidence that proved scientifically that USOs were real, we did use science to model out how they might have worked on a conventional engine.

BILL'S BLOG

Because this episode had its roots in two previous *UFO Files* episodes on deep-sea USOs, including the segment where Pat Uskert, Kevin Brun, Julius Willis—the original UFO hunters—and I went deep-sea diving off Redondo Beach for a USO, I was far more enthusiastic about this episode as we started out. This was familiar territory for us and actually was the first episode we planned out. The Noah Felice story had caught my attention over the summer when Nancy and I had returned from our boat in California to our place on the Delaware River in New Jersey to spend the summer after we had finished shooting the pilot for *UFO Hunters*. I brought Noah's story up to our co-executive producer, Alan LaGarde, as soon as Nancy had gotten back to our boat in September.

We had begun setting up the episodes for season 1 while the production company was still in very small quarters on the edge of Santa Monica. But in a week, we moved to a larger space more centrally along the Colorado Avenue corridor in Santa Monica. We finally had the room to spread out while the editing bays were set up, and we hired staff to begin the administrative process of organizing a five-month production. It was on the second day in our new offices that I brought the story of Noah Felice to LaGarde as the main through-story for the episode. The story would rest on Noah's camera presence, his ability to relate his story to a television audience, and, of course, his credibility.

Noah's telling of the story brought a lot to the episode because we built each episode on witness testimony, action sequences, and as much time as we could spend in Tindall's lab testing and modeling to demonstrate to a television audience just how science worked in UFO studies. In fact, if a major story for a proposed episode didn't have science behind it, science that could be demonstrated in a lab, the network stepped in to tell us to find another story. And as a result, we became uncompromising in seasons 1 and 2 about finding only stories that we could bring back to a lab for testing. The episode featuring Noah's story, with its underwater currents, the possibility of underwater sequences with Pat and Ted, flyovers of the island, and finally demonstrations of electromagnetic beams, worked.

I have to admit that when we first set out on our expedition to Catalina Island I was excited about finding Noah's wreckage. Ultimately, I was very disappointed that the wreckage eluded us. I had seen the photo of the rescue diver and, therefore, had seen the actual photo of the plane underwater. It was an incredible photo. I knew, as a result of having seen it, that the aircraft wreckage existed at one point and that it was possible to locate it. But the shooting scheduling for this episode was very tight because we were squeezed between the Maury Island trip and an upcoming long trip to New Hampshire and then to New York State for the "Abductions" and "Vortex" episodes. By this time, we were already planning the trip to Mexico for the "Mexico's Roswell" episode as well, so there was a very narrow shooting schedule for Catalina, even though we were at our home base in Los Angeles.

Our underwater excursion also had to rely on the reports, but not the actual personnel, from bay watch. We couldn't find the original diver who rescued Noah Felice, and this made our search for the crash site very difficult. I was, however, glad that we could bring Noah Felice back to the area where he went down and where he lost his cousin.

Noah and I have remained friends over the years. He does say that his life changed after the crash not only because of the loss of his cousin but also because, he says, part of him seems to remain in contact with the other side. He has no answers, but the effects of the near-death experience or the contact with alien or spiritual entities, whatever it was, continues to this day.

The Catalina episode also taught me a lot about working with the producers. In reality television, the general rule of thumb, at least five years ago, was to let the episode develop out of the organic relationships among the cast, in this case, Pat, Ted, Ronnie, Jeff Tomlinson, John Tindall, and me. However, on a series that is more of a story- and action-driven documentary instead of a show about personalities, organic-relationship television tends to slow the episode down. Therefore, shooting this episode, which was more like History's old *UFO Files* than anything else, required that each member of the cast had to play a position and stay with his own investigative path instead of interact with the other members of the team on minor issues. That's why, especially in the first season, we began each episode with a scene at *UFO Hunters/UFO Magazine* headquarters and ended each episode with a headquarters wrap-up. That would change in season 2. But in season 1, it was a very safe way to set the course of the investigation up, lay out the roles for each member of the team, and keep track of where the investigation was going so that we could end with a "what have we learned?" at the end of each episode. And it worked.

As interesting as the dive and lab scenes were in the USO episode, as fascinating as the witness stories were, even the ones that didn't make it into the final cut because the episode was running too long, our first real excursion into a famous case of the unknown would be the "Abductions" episode and the case of Barney and Betty Hill.

ABDUCTIONS

Episode 103, the third official episode in our first season, dealt with the historic case of the Betty and Barney Hill abduction and two relatively modern cases of abductees who believe that their ET abductors left them with subcutaneous devices to monitor their every move. In particular, the devices could locate them for future abductions. In some respects, this was a very dark episode about a threat to humankind, the kind of threat documented by Whitley Strieber in *Communion,* his personal and very frightening memoir of his abduction experiences. In other respects, the stories of Betty and Barney Hill, Tim Cullen, and other abductees, stories that we returned to in our third season, were a wake-up call that, despite what skeptics and debunkers say, we are not alone in the universe.

THE BACKGROUND OF ALIEN ABDUCTIONS

The Basic Story of Alien Abductions

What is an alien abduction? Is it merely a contact experience, seeing something otherworldly, or is it something more? Simply put, an alien abduction is the taking of a human being by an entity not of this world to a different place, either physically or psychically, where some sort of exchange takes place between the taken and the entities who take them. In the J. Allen Hynek official classification of encounters with otherworldly things and entities, a close encounter in which a human being observes actual visible life-forms is called a "close encounter of the third kind." Subsequent to Hynek's system, UFO researchers added two more classifications, a "close encounter of the fourth kind," which is an alien abduction, and a "close encounter of the fifth kind," which takes place when there is actual communication between an alien entity and a human being. In the abduction cases we covered in this episode, we realized that we were well into close encounters of the fourth and fifth kinds.

Core Elements of an Alien Abduction Case

In abduction case reports that we've heard from a number of experiencers, there is a core story:

Feeling a Presence. The abductee is aware, perhaps even psychically if not physiologically, that something is about to happen. There may be a sound, like a buzzing or a humming, a strange direct or diffused light, a tingling and then a paralysis, and then a sense of floating or being moved against one's will.

A Transportation. Many abductees report being taken aboard some type of craft. They are either floated aboard, as actual witnesses on the Brooklyn Bridge said they saw in the Linda Cortile abduction, or physically grabbed and dragged aboard, as Betty and Barney Hill reported they were. In the Gulf Breeze abductions, near-abductee Ed Walters said that he was trapped in a blue beam from a craft overhead, a beam that paralyzed him and started to levitate him toward the source of the light. Such transportation is usually preceded either by the subject's being put to sleep or put into a twilight sleep or simply being paralyzed so that, even though awake, the person is powerless to resist.

An Alien Presence. The abductee may find himself strapped to or immobilized on an examination table. Or the person may have voluntarily submitted to the abduction and being hosted by his captors aboard a craft. Children usually have reported going aboard willingly because they are far more suggestible than adults and follow instructions without question. Once abducted, the person realizes he or she is in the presence of otherworldly beings. These beings may look like large-headed, squiggly armed, four-foot gray beings or they may look like tall, blond-haired Nordic beings, but they always seem nonhuman even if they look human. In the case of voluntary abductions, the abductee has had a long history of contact with these otherworldly beings and knows, sometimes from the time he or she was a child, that these are extraterrestrials.

The Encounter. What do the aliens want? Are they experimenting on their human subject, extracting male sperm or a female ovum for the purposes of a human-ET hybrid, simply examining a repeat abductee to see if an implanted communications device requires any maintenance, or actually imparting a message to the abductee? The nature of contact reported by various abductees shows that alien abduction encounters can be far more complex than aliens' simply picking up a human being and returning the abductee to the same location.

What happens during the alien encounter may trigger any number of memories about prior abductions and previous meetings that may go back to a subject's childhood. Sometimes, and we heard this from more than one person who's encountered ETs, the encounter may go back to the actual root of the person's existence. In at least one case, the subject, Michael Lee Hill, found out more about his lineage, his biological history, from his alien encounters than he learned from his adopted parents.

The Nature of the Testing. Some alien species seem fascinated with the human body and conduct sometimes very callous types of experiments that inflict pain on the subject. There are alien species that have no concept of emotion and therefore are almost careless about the level of fear they instill. Others are sympathetic toward their human subjects and actually try to communicate to them that what's happening is beneficial for both life-forms: the human and the extra-terrestrial. Most encounters, researchers have said, involve the sampling of human fluids, human sperm and ova, primarily for the purposes of hybridizing a species. Whether this species is created for the purpose of taking over on Earth, a "childhood's end" scenario, or for infusing human DNA into an alien race to evolve them for living on their own changing planet, is still a mystery. But the tests conducted on subjects seem to point to a larger purpose.

Messages. In many cases of alien abduction, there is hardly any communication between the aliens and their human subjects. Many people have said that the extraterrestrials simply conduct their tests, try to impart a telepathic message that the human subjects are not in any danger and should not be afraid, complete the tests, and return their subjects to the place from where they were originally taken. In many long-term abduction scenarios, however, the abductees report that the aliens explain to them the purpose of their mission. In cases where a woman has been impregnated by aliens, the abductors show her the child that they have taken from her, allow her maternal bonding with the child, and then send her back. In other cases, human beings discover that they are really hybrids and are abducted to bond with other hybrids.

In many cases the humans that are taken report that their abductors are actually very benevolent creatures who impart messages of pending disasters. The most prevalent message is that human beings are either destroying the planet or that our natural inclination for warfare will ultimately destroy our species. Contactees back in the 1950s consistently reported that aliens were warning them about the disasters that would befall humanity if we relied on our animal instincts for conflict. Aliens also were reported to have told their human contactees that if human beings couldn't control themselves, then the aliens would.

The Return. After the abduction and testing have been completed, the human subjects are returned to their homes, places from where they were abducted, and awaken with either a hazy memory of the events or no memory at all. Hours may have passed, but the abductees can't account for this passage, and it has become known as "missing time." For many abductees, missing time is the only clue that they were abducted in the first place, and they have a sense that something traumatic might have happened to them, but they can't remember any of it.

In many, many instances subjects have missing-time issues without any abduction's having taken place. This happens when a witness is so awed by the presence of an otherworldly craft that the person loses all sense of time, realizing that significant time has passed only when the abductee believes he or she has been transfixed for a matter of minutes. Missing time can also be a function of physiological disorientation in the presence of a very heavy static electricity field. This is sometimes called the Oz effect.

In some cases, missing time is the subject's mind's self-defense mechanism deployed to keep the truth from the conscious mind. After all, contact with an otherworldly species can be a trauma in and of itself. Missing time just by itself doesn't automatically mean that the person has been abducted by an alien life-form. But for those who do believe they have been abducted, missing time can be a clue.

THE STORY OF BETTY AND BARNEY HILL

The main story line in this episode of season 1 dealt with the abductions of Betty and Barney Hill from a lonely country road in Portsmouth, New Hampshire, in 1961. At a time when only a very small community of UFO devotees were following the alien-contact exploits of writers like Howard Menger, George Adamski, George Van Tassel, and Frank Stranges, all of whom were self-described alien contactees in the 1950s and led their own flocks of true believers, the story of Betty and Barney and their interrupted journey home from Canada shocked and frightened the nation and put them right on the cover of *Look Magazine*. In a community where stories of a UFO presence are short on evidence but long on fantastic testimony, the physical evidence and strange anomalies in the Hill case still make a lot of skeptics cringe and even caused one physics professor at MIT to fall back on the argument of "statistically accounted for." Our conversation was all caught on video in this episode.

Barney and Betty were a very private couple. Spouses in a mixed-race marriage, uncommon enough in New Hampshire or anywhere else in 1961, they both worked for social causes in addition to their regular jobs. Barney worked for the United States Post Office and sat on the local Civil Rights Commission. Betty was a social worker, and both of them were members of the NAACP. At the dawn of the 1960s, a time before the civil rights movement began in earnest legislatively under President Lyndon Johnson with the civil rights and voting rights acts, Betty and Barney were advocates of social change. In the tiny towns of America's conservative New England, the last thing the Hills wanted was national publicity. But that was exactly what they got—the cover of *Look Magazine*—when they had the misfortune to spot a huge bright light up in the air following their car along a lonely country road outside of Groveton, New Hampshire, on September, 19, 1961.

Barney suffered from hypertension at the time and also suffered from the symptoms of a stomach ulcer. Maybe it was the pressure from his job at the post office. Whatever it was, the Hills needed a break and took a vacation in Quebec. On the night of September 19, their vacation over, they were driving home to Portsmouth along Route 3 in the darkness when, right around midnight, a very bright light way off in the distance caught their attention. It could have been a star, but it was unlike any star they had seen before. Betty believed that it was one of the satellites that the United States had just put up. Barney, however, thought that it was a plane that seemed unusually bright against the very dark sky. He was worried and said during a hypnotic regression session with Dr. Benjamin Simon, "I first saw it in front of the car, but then it swung around to the rear."

The light was brighter than a conventional aircraft and seemed to be tracking them. Just the thought that there was a plane following the route they were taking made Barney nervous. He said, "Look, it's following us, Betty." He later told Dr. Simon that he was "hurrying to get away."

As they drove, Barney constantly looking out his window to keep track of the light, the light seemed to get closer. The two of them kept talking about what the light might be, Barney now believing he was looking at a disk-shaped object. He made a turn, later telling Dr. Simon that he didn't know why he had to make that turn. Then, he realized that he was no longer on the right road home.

The light kept following them and seemed to be positioning itself right above the car. Finally, at Betty's urging, because she wanted to determine what the object was, Barney stopped the car at the Mount Cleveland picnic area and the couple got out. Once outside the car, Betty pulled out a pair of binoculars and got a better look at the object against the light of the moon. It wasn't a satellite at all, she realized, but something else, a circular object that was illuminated with multi-colored lights. The object crossed the face of the moon and then swooped down. It was rotating and flashing a blue-white light. It passed them heading north toward Vermont, and Betty could see it fly above the tramway over the Franconia Notch.

The Hills got back in the car and started driving again, heading for the safety of the nearest town. Whatever the thing was, Betty told her niece Kathy Marden over the phone the following morning, she and Barney had the feeling that the object had noticed them. They were nervous, all alone on that New England country road at night, with nothing between them and that strange object. They soon found that what initially had been a nervous reaction to something anomalous in the sky became downright frightful as the object suddenly shifted its direction and now seemed to be tracking their car, staying low to the horizon and matching their speed.

The object seemed to track them for a few more miles, and then it suddenly began a descent toward their car. When the object stopped, hovering about a hundred feet above the car, directly in front of the windshield, Barney stopped the car in the middle of the road and stared up at the object. Through what looked to him to be a row of windows, Barney could see eight to ten figures, not people, but humanoid shapes, and they were looking down at him. Barney wanted out of there, and fast. As he told Dr. Simon, "I was driving and driving, and I made a turn." He made a left-hand turn onto a dirt road.

Ahead of him he saw what he believed to be six to eight men in the road. Barney was confused. What were these men doing in the middle of the road after midnight? What Barney and Betty thought as they saw the men break into two groups and approach them was that these figures weren't men at all. They weren't human.

Barney reached for the pistol he had been carrying, but it was too late. The figures approached the doors and forced them open. While Barney struggled to run away, Betty also tried to escape. As she told her niece the next day, she remembered trying to flee the car through her door but, before she could get any distance, was immediately grabbed by the small humanoids and dragged, against her will, to a small clearing in the woods about a hundred and fifty feet away. In the meantime, the humanoids had already grabbed Barney, preventing his escape, and dragged him to the clearing, too. Betty told her niece that she remembered this part of the incident consciously, that she even recalled seeing Barney next to her in the clearing. She remembered struggling with the humanoids, who tore her dress, and then she saw a ramp descend. And that was all she remembered until she and Barney found themselves driving along a very familiar road coming up to their driveway. It was almost dawn, and they had no idea where they had been for the previous few hours.

Later that day, Betty phoned her sister and talked to her niece, Kathy, about the incident. She described the craft, talked about the small humanoids who grabbed her, and said being dragged into the clearing with Barney was the last thing she remembered before returning to awareness just as they pulled up the road near their home. She remembered nothing in between, except for the disconcerting feeling that in the two hours that were missing from her life something had happened to her after she struggled with those creatures.

All she knew at that point was that there was a strange pink powder residue on the dress she had been wearing, and the dress was torn. That pink residue resonated with a missing part of her memory, telling her that something very traumatic had happened.

This would be the beginning of a very revealing inner journey for Betty, as well as for Barney, because, try as they might, the Hills simply could not return to a normal life. Betty said in interviews years later that Barney, who had suffered from hypertension—a disease that finally killed him—continued to be uneasy and complained of all sorts of physical problems. In particular, Betty said, Barney was unusually worried about his genitals and complained of pains in that region. He said his stomach was bothering him, and he was having trouble sleeping at night. Moreover, try as they might to calm down, Barney seemed to be unusually irritable, as if something was eating at him that he couldn't resolve. Thinking that this was some kind of underlying physical condition, Betty took him to their family doctor. But after a series of exams, the doctor could find nothing wrong with Barney except that his blood pressure was elevated.

While Barney was manifesting physical symptoms, Betty was having serious nightmares, repressed memories of what had happened to her after the humanoid creatures had taken her. She kept the dress she was wearing that night, a dress that had pink stains where she remembered the humanoids had touched her. She never had that dress cleaned because she believed she had an actual piece of physical evidence from what had happened to her that night. But beyond that she had only her conscious memories and her dreams.

Betty Hill also reported the incident to Pease Air Force Base, the local base in that area of New Hampshire. An investigator from Pease called her back, interviewed her, and then reported that Betty had probably seen the planet Jupiter. Betty had left out many important details of her encounter, she said years later, because she was afraid of being thought insane. The Hill incident became part of the air force's Project Blue Book, the most significant—almost entirely false—official report of the air force's investigation of UFOs. Air force officials knew that there had been an unidentified object in the area, but in keeping with their protocols, they denied its having anything to do with a UFO.

Barney Hill's condition continued to deteriorate. His doctor, after hearing repeated complaints of physical ailments from his patient and after finding nothing physically wrong with him that he could correlate to Barney's symptoms, finally suggested that the problem may be emotional. Emotional problems, he advised, do, many times, create the impression of physical symptoms even though there might be no underlying physical causes. What Barney's doctor told him was also reinforced by Air Force Captain Ben Swett, who talked about hypnosis at the Hills' church in November 1962. Although the Hills asked Swett to hypnotize them to help them remember, Swett declined, saying he was not qualified. But he advised them to speak to their doctor to find a qualified therapist. Barney brought this up to his doctor.

Upon his doctor's advice, Barney visited a psychiatrist, who, after a session with him in which he learned of Barney's loss of memory, referred him to Dr. Benjamin Simon. Dr. Simon had played an important role in World War II, helping pilots suffering from hysterical symptoms recover lost memories and confront and integrate the underlying trauma.

During the two years between their encounter and their visits to Dr. Benjamin Simon, Betty was also suffering from nightmares, dreams that played back a version of the events that had taken place aboard the ship, but not a dream because it seemed all too real. She dreamed about communicating with her abductors, now referring to them as otherworldly; and dreamed about what she called the medical experiments in which the alien humanoids probed her body. And she dreamed about being taken aboard the craft. These nightmares were persistent and would ultimately play a role in Dr. Simon's opinions about what might have been the origin of the stories the Hills told under hypnosis.

Dr. Simon regressed both Barney and Betty during separate treatment sessions, recording their responses on tape and asking his assistant to transcribe the recordings. Upon the conclusion of each session, he instructed both Betty and Barney not to remember what they told him, believing they were not ready to integrate what they told him under hypnosis into their conscious memories until they saw him in follow-up sessions. Kathleen Marden and Stanton Friedman, authors of the book *Captured!* (New Page, 2007), write that Barney's emotional reactions during his regression sessions were so intense that Dr. Simon had to stop them at points because he was afraid of Barney's high blood pressure problems.

As the sessions progressed, the stories Barney and Betty told were nevertheless astounding. Separately, each told the same story of being placed into a trancelike state by the humanoid creatures, taken from the clearing by force onto what Barney and Betty described as a craft of some sort, restrained on examination tables, and then probed and examined by creatures they described as "aliens" from another world. The details of the incident they both reported were so precise that Dr. Simon was shocked by these revelations, accounts he believed that his patients believed to be true even if he couldn't lend his professional credibility to the actuality of extraterrestrials abducting human beings.

Among the elements of the Hills' story that rang credible for Dr. Simon—including his patients' belief that the incident had actually taken place—were the correlations of the descriptions of the events from two different perspectives that supported each other. He believed from his initial examinations of the Hills that they had experienced true memory loss, a form of amnesia that seemed to have resulted from some sort of trauma. He heard from Betty's sessions that the amnesia was induced by their abductors, by a command they placed in her mind. They had been instructed, ordered, to forget everything and restart their memories only when they realized they were driving home at dawn. Yet when the Hills told their separate stories under hypnosis, they both described being placed into a twilight state, taken aboard what seemed like the same craft, and made the subject of painful and invasive medical-type examinations.

Barney, in particular, described an examination of his genitals, embarrassing as well as painful, that resulted in his being overly concerned about his genitals in his post-traumatic waking state. Physical examinations of Barney's genitals also showed that a pattern of warts had developed around them, a pattern that was consistent with his description of the place where his examiners placed their examination instrument. Many people overlooked this extrinsic evidence corroborating that something had happened to Barney.

For her part, Betty related that her exchanges with entities she described as extraterrestrials were more cordial than Barney's. In one instance, an examiner tried to pull out her teeth but could not. It turned out that it had pulled out Barney's dentures and couldn't understand why Betty's wouldn't come out. When Betty explained that some people lose their teeth as they age, the creature asked her to explain aging because it couldn't understand the concept. But perhaps the most important part of the story that Betty related to Dr. Simon was the star map, a drawing that she was able to make under hypnosis of a map shown to her by one of the creatures to explain where they had come from. This star map, a depiction of an unknown part of the heavens, would, years later, become an important piece of evidence that Betty would be able to provide to substantiate her story.

At first, when the star map became public in John G. Fuller's 1966 *Interrupted Journey* (which features an introduction by Dr. Simon) (Dial, 1966), about Betty's and Barney's two lost hours aboard a spaceship, astronomers had not yet discovered the existence of the twin-star Zeta Reticuli system. But Ohio elementary schoolteacher and amateur astronomer Marjorie Fish was intrigued by the map that Betty drew. Betty said under hypnosis that she had seen the map on the spaceship and that the aliens had told her that it depicted their home star system and indicated different "trade routes" to different sectors of that section of the galaxy. These were stunning revelations, if true, and Fish set out to find the unknown star system.

Fish used Betty's descriptions and the map in Fuller's book to examine many different stars and systems, comparing them to the 1969

Gliese star catalog, a catalog not available to Betty Hill in 1961 or in 1963 when she drew the map for Dr. Simon. Fish hypothesized that the system Betty saw on the map in the spaceship was the Zeta Reticuli system, a twin-star system, and the home system of the aliens. This conjecture was debated back and forth for almost a decade and, interestingly enough, became the basis of a 1974 article in *Astronomy* magazine and that generated much discussion. Supporters argue that Betty Hill could not have known about the existence of Zeta Reticuli on her own because the existence of the twin star was not published until 1969 and the discovery of planets in that star system also did not take place until years later.

Another interesting element that Betty related to Dr. Simon was a medical procedure in which the creatures examining her inserted a thin rod into her abdomen. It was a procedure to sample fluid in her womb, extracting DNA for fertilization purposes. The entities had also extracted sperm from Barney, an examination that Barney did not remember but that still caused him some physical reactions and emotional anxiety. These examinations, the stories about which were related under hypnosis, indicated that perhaps the Hills were being used as test cases for some sort of alien-human cross-fertilization program.

Dr. Simon was very skeptical about the nature of the Hills' encounter with an alien nonterrestrial species, hypothesizing that Betty's nightmares of having been abducted by aliens and taken to their spacecraft suggested the same story to Barney, who repeated it under hypnosis. However, in an early 1970s interview with radio talk show host George Noory, Dr. Simon stated that he believed that Betty and Barney believed the story and that they were not fabricating anything. In that interview, George Noory remembers, Dr. Simon didn't say whether he believed or not, only that he believed that they believed, and that was as far as he would go. In an article in the journal *Psychiatric Opinion* (October, 1967) essentially endorsing the value of hypnosis for lost-memory recall, Dr. Simon said he saw the Hills' experience as a psychological aberration. Because there is no alien abduction category in the DSM, the basic manual for psychological symptoms, Simon found himself in a tough place. He believed from what he heard in the sessions that Betty and Barney actually lived out these stories, but investing his medical reputation in an alien presence was professional suicide. So he took the "psychological-aberration route" and relied on Betty's nightmares for Barney's story without ever having to deal with the physical evidence of the dress or the skin warts around Barney's genitals corresponding to where Barney said he was examined.

According to Marden,

At first ... Simon was dumbfounded by the fact that the Hills' hypnotic recall matched in so much detail. He even muttered during one hypnosis session, "It can't be." He was always searching for a viable alternative explanation. The best one that he could find was the "dream transference hypothesis." But Barney stated under hypnosis that he knew very little of the details about Betty's dreams and that they were only dreams and couldn't possibly reflect reality. Dr. Simon simply didn't believe what he had heard. (private e-mail)

Moreover, Marden suggested in a private e-mail to me, "had Dr. Simon stated publicly that he believed that the Hills had experienced an abduction by non-human beings aboard a flying saucer, it would most assuredly have been professional suicide." However, Marden said that in his personal letters to Betty Hill, Dr. Simon was positive and fully supportive of Betty.

Over the years Betty and Barney, now having fully integrated their experiences into their conscious lives, felt much better and continued to speak openly about the event at local UFO meetings. They also continued their interviews with UFO researchers and investigators and were forthcoming about their stories.

The news of the event gradually leaked out, and a reporter for the *Boston Traveler*, John Lutrell, who had heard of the interviews, got hold of one of the transcripts of the Hills' regression sessions. He published the story in the *Traveler*, a story that was picked up by the wire services,

and Betty and Barney suddenly became the center of a publicity firestorm. They did not seek publicity, trying only to figure out what
might have happened to them and why, when their private medical
sessions became public knowledge. They ultimately told their story to
John Fuller, who wrote the book *Interrupted Journey* about their adven-
ture. The book was optioned for a television movie of the week by
James Earl Jones, who played Barney. Actress Estelle Parsons por-
trayed Betty. Also interestingly, it was the publication of Fuller's book
that prompted the first public coverage of the story on radio by none
other than Long John Nebel at WOR. Long John hosted Fuller after
having read the book and told him, "This is a good tale here; it's got a
little of everything, and you will do well with it."

Over the years evidence in addition to the Gliese star catalog and
the technique known as amniocentesis has arisen to support Betty's
story. Betty's dress, for example, which she preserved in a closet after
her encounter, was analyzed by Dr. Phyllis Budinger, an organic
chemist, and found to have protein remains in the pink powder residue on the spots where Betty said the creatures grabbed her dress. Dr.
Budinger said that although she couldn't identify anything otherworldly about the organic chemical compounds in the powder residue,
the simple fact that the pink residue showed up within twenty-four
hours after Betty's claim of abduction, the correspondence of the
powder residue with the torn dress zipper indicating that someone or
something was tugging at the dress, and traces of organic compounds
in those places were suggestive of the presence of a life-form. In fact,
because there was no pink residue on other parts of the dress, Dr.
Budinger theorized that the pink residue came from something external to Betty and not from Betty herself.

Moreover, by looking at the dress, both the control sample and
the stained sample, through a high-magnification microscope, Dr.
Budinger said she was able to see that the fibers of the stained sample
had been pulled apart. There was greater spacing between them, an
indicator that the dress had been under strain, probably from being
pulled. That would account for the distresses and spaced fibers,

particularly in the stained sample. Even the normally skeptical Ted Acworth said that everything he saw from the samples was consistent with distortion of the fibers resulting from some sort of physical struggle.

Dr. Budinger said on *UFO Hunters* that it wouldn't actually be necessary to find some unknown protein-based compound on the dress even if the dress was touched by extraterrestrials. It was clear that the dress was contaminated by something, but the contaminants were quite common. Not at all otherworldly. Simply put, the universe is probably made up of all the same stuff anyway so the fact that there was no "unknownium" on the dress doesn't discount Betty's story in the least.

There was additional evidence left on the Hills' car, shiny spots, the size of silver dollars, Betty said, which marked where the entities touched the car as they tried to keep the Hills from escaping. And when a physicist friend of the Hills suggested that they try to get magnetic readings off their car where the spots were, they ran a compass over the car. Betty said that every time they brought a compass near the spots, "the compass would just go spinning and spinning around." Barney said that when he moved the compass away from the spots, the needle would just "flop down," but when brought to the spots, the needle would start to spin. This, researchers have said, is another indicator that something was present on that car that affected the normal response to a compass.

The story of the Hills' encounter, although fiercely debated among skeptics and UFO investigators, still stands as one of the most amazing revelations of human encounters with the unknown.

ALIEN IMPLANTS

That aliens implant devices subcutaneously into the bodies of abductees is also a hotly debated topic in UFO research that was investigated by *UFO Hunters'* guest Dr. Roger Leir, has been talked about by bestselling author and radio host Whitley Strieber, and is the subject of diverse medical opinions. Implants of different shapes and sizes and placed, UFO abductees say, in different parts of the body have proved to be very perplexing for medical professionals. Some say that these are little more than metal splinters, shards, that people either step on or pick up and that quickly become sealed off from the bloodstream by the body's own natural defenses. But Roger Leir, a podiatric surgeon, argues otherwise. He has said that these pieces of metal are truly anomalous because "the abductee or implantee has no memory of the device's having been inserted."

There is no entry wound or surface scar, which would have to be there if the person simply stepped on a piece of metal or picked one up. How can a piece of metal get into a human body without an entry wound?

These implants also appear in places other than hands or feet. They appear behind some persons' ears or inside their skulls, making them impossible to remove.

There is no resulting infection around the implant. Normally a person's natural defense systems fight any foreign body, creating swelling, puss, and a fever to kill off any associated viruses. However, in these implants, there is no evidence of any defense mechanism attacking it.

The implant is surrounded by the host's own neurological tissue. This is truly strange because how would neurological receptors naturally form around a foreign body? Usually, the body defends itself by swarming the foreign object with lymphocytes and launching attack by T and B cells to prevent what the host body perceives as antigens from infecting it. The lymphocyte activity is detectable even over the long term. The body also exhibits symptoms consistent with lymphocyte activity. However, in the case of claimed alien implants, there is no lymphocyte activity because the invading implant is bathed in the body's own neurological cells in a kind of gelatinous membrane so as to convince the body's defense system that no foreign object has invaded it. How could such an object find its way into a host body absent an entry wound, absent any lymphocyte activity, and surrounded by a neurological package made up of the host's own cells?

Moreover, pain sensors exist on the surface of the skin, not generally deep below the skin where the implants are generally located. Yet, any attempt to probe the implant, even with the area fully anesthetized topically, is a painful experience for the implantee.

Video from different alien implant extraction surgeries show that the implant itself can move inside the body as soon as it detects it is being probed. This also defies much basic medical understanding regarding inanimate objects because an implant, if it were simply a metal shard, shouldn't react to a probe as if it's trying to evade extraction.

What Roger Leir has said about behavior of the implant is that after it is removed and the host's neurological sack has been peeled away, the implant actually shrinks and dries up just as if it is dying outside the host's body. This is indeed strange because, why would a piece of metal shrink? Is there some form of symbiotic interaction between the implant and the host, which many implantees claim does exist? One implantee said that once his implant was removed, he felt as if another living presence in his body was no longer there. Other implantees have said that after extraction, for the first time since the implant, they felt as if they were truly alone. This leads abduction researchers to wonder whether the implants are tagging devices solely for identification or radio-locator tagging devices, just like the ones we attach to animals in the wild, or two-way communicators, listening posts inside abductees' bodies that send information to the abductors.

The Medical Science Behind Implant Surgery

There is an enormous amount of controversy concerning the extraction of alien implants. First, of course, is the categorization of alien implants. Are they real implants or simply shards of metal that have found their way into the bodies of hosts by accidents such as stepping on them? Some surgeons attest to the anomalousness of these objects, citing their behavior upon removal, the gelatinous sack they reside in inside the body, and the nature of the host's cells that surround them. Other surgeons reject the concept entirely. But Dr. Roger Leir has argued consistently that the scientific testing of an alien implant shows that

> the object exists inside a package of host neurons that shouldn't be surrounding the object at all.
>
> There are no entry wounds or scar tissue around the object, which should exist if the person simply stepped on something.
>
> The objects are broadcasting radio signals on frequencies designated for deep-space transmissions.
>
> The objects shrink and die upon removal.
>
> The objects contain metallic alloys, which don't exist on earth.
>
> The objects seem to have the host's tissue growing out of them, an amalgamation of human tissue and metal. This defies biology.

Because credible science and biological laboratories refused to get involved with testing objects that are purportedly removed from self-described abductees or implantees, the testing procedure is very difficult to complete. But this became our challenge on the alien abduction episode of UFO Hunters.

THE EPISODE

We began the episode in New Hampshire with the Betty and Barney Hill story, a story that had been covered previously on UFO Files. However, because we were covering the big picture of alien abductions, particularly alien-implant stories and the surgical procedures used to extract reported implants, we wanted to wrap the medical procedure segments within the most discussed and debated story in the history of alien abduction research. Because Kathleen Marden's and Stanton Friedman's book, Captured!, had just been published, we also wanted to include the latest information on the Hill case, including a visit to Dr. Phyllis Budinger's lab to review firsthand the evidence that both Stan and Kathy had described.

The episode also had to focus on an ongoing case, a case of a self-described alien abductee who discovered a strange object just under his skin on his inside thigh. Jeff Harvey could not remember how this object got into his body, but its presence nagged at him. We asked Dr. Leir to examine him and work with his surgeon to extract and then test the object. As background to Jeff's case we worked with certified clinical hypnotherapist Yvonne Smith to see whether any of Jeff's missing memories could account for his experiences and the implantation of what we believed to be a metallic device under his skin.

The subject of alien implants also has an historic perspective. We interviewed Tim Cullen, one of Roger Leir's early research subjects, about his operation and about the implant that Dr. Leir discovered. We also saw video footage of Cullen's operation and marveled at the way the fluoroscope revealed that the object the surgeon was after seemed to move in Cullen's body away from the probe.

We began by flying to Portsmouth to meet Kathleen Marden, to whom Betty had spoken about the incident on the morning after. Kathleen told us that her aunt was very cogent and was conscious of everything that happened to her and Barney up until the entities dragged her into a clearing and she saw a ramp descend from their craft. It was there, Kathy said, that Betty saw Barney in a trancelike state. The next thing she remembered was sitting alongside Barney in their car heading up to their driveway near dawn. Kathy drove with us to the spot in the road where Betty and Barney stopped the first time to see the circular craft. Then we drove to the spot on the highway where Barney stopped the car. We pulled our vans over to the side of the road and Kathy walked us into the clearing, now just a mound of brush in a housing subdivision, where Barney and Betty saw the craft with the ramp lowered and were dragged up the ramp and aboard. Finally, after telling us the story from her perspective,

Kathy directed us to head west to Chagrin Falls, Ohio, to visit Dr. Phyllis Budinger where we could see the swaths from the actual dress Betty was wearing that night and hear the story of why Betty kept the dress in the hopes that it would someday be tested.

From Portsmouth, we first drove down to Cambridge to meet with physics professor David Pritchard at MIT. Professor Pritchard had worked with Dr. John Mack and a group of people in 1992 at the Abduction Study Conference at MIT, who characterized themselves as alien abductees. I'm saying "characterized" because the evidence presented at this conference, although compelling and engrossing, was nevertheless subjective. Professor Pritchard, who was one of the moderators of this colloquium conducted by Dr. Mack, said that as a scientist he could only rely on evidence no matter how compelling the testimony.

I asked him specifically about the Barney and Betty Hill case, especially the physical trace evidence and Betty's revelations about the Zeta Reticuli system. Although we both agreed that the overwhelming majority of alien abduction reports from experiencers lack any hard evidence and are based almost purely on subjective testimony, Professor Pritchard did acknowledge that the Hill case was different. However, he characterized it as being within the realm of statistical possibility, albeit on the edge. And this was the basis for our discussion about a game-change piece of evidence versus something that falls with a statistical curve. In the Hill case, unless Betty's prediction of the Zeta Reticuli star system could be accounted for, the skeptics had a big problem. In fact, the Hill case, I suggested in our discussion, was more like a placebo affecting a cure of a disease. A placebo, because it has no curative abilities, by rights should have no effect whatsoever. However, as Dr. Bernie Siegel pointed out, when a placebo acts as a cure and a disease mysteriously disappears, researchers look at it as a statistical issue, not the game changer that it is. Dr. Siegel suggested that the real issue to be investigated was why the placebo seemed to work. Did the person taking the placebo believe in its curative powers to the extent that the person was cured? If so, the placebo has far more power than any researcher gives it credit for.

From Cambridge and MIT, we flew to Yuma, Colorado, for a meeting with alien-implant witness Tim Cullen and researcher Dr. Roger Leir to investigate the phenomenon of alien implants. Tim was one of Dr. Leir's early research subjects and a patient as well. We met with Tim and Roger to talk about Tim's implant extraction and to review the video footage of his operation.

In some respects, Tim's stories of his UFO encounters were not unlike Barney and Betty Hill's. He told us that he drove along Highway 59 at night twelve miles outside Yuma when he saw a cylinder-shaped object in front of him. He said the object settled onto a pasture across from the highway while Tim and his wife simply looked at it. He said that it seemed to him that only four or five minutes had passed and then Tim turned to his wife and suggested they drive into town. Years later, however, Tim said that he discovered what he believed to be a metallic object in his arm, just above his wrist.

Tim told us that when he discovered the object, there was no discernable entry wound on his arm and that he'd had MRI scans before discovering this object and the scans showed no anomalous object in his arm. Dr. Leir said that it would have been impossible for the object to have entered his arm naturally without having left an entry wound or a scar. "Medically," Leir said, "it simply makes no sense for an object that size to appear without any external marks." And, Cullen added, he had no memory of the object's entry, no pain, and no bleeding. He just discovered that it was there.

Roger Leir told us that Tim's body did not reject the metallic object at all and, in fact, that when removing it he noticed that the object was surrounded by a network of Tim's own nerve cells. This, too, Roger said, defies medical science. As we watched the video of the operation to extract the object from Tim's arm, even the skeptical Pat Uskert was amazed at the object's moving away from the hemostat every time the instrument, under the surgeon's control, approached it. It was astounding.

Before we left Yuma, Tim Cullen took us to the spot where he had seen the UFO land, a UFO whose presence might have been responsible for Cullen's abduction and the implanting of the metallic object in his arm. We walked over the open field across from the highway, looking for any signs of disruption of the soil, a high magnetic reading, or a high level of radiation. We took readings with our Geiger counter and with our magnetometer, but found no anomalies there. Either the object that Tim saw left no residual effects on the soil or the event happened so long ago that any residual magnetic fields or radiation would have long since dissipated. Of course, any skeptic would argue that since nothing was detectable in the field, nothing happened there in the first place. Relying on Tim's testimony about the event and with no other evidence, we had nothing tangible to prove or disprove that anything had taken place. But we saw the object that Dr. Leir had removed from Tim's arm and we saw the video of the surgery. So we knew that something was there that behaved very strangely. We just didn't know what it was.

Our next and final leg of this trip was back to California, where we met Jeff Harvey, another one of Dr. Leir's research subjects who was coming to Los Angeles for an implant-extraction surgery. Jeff presented us with an ongoing case of some sort of memory of a bizarre contact, missing time, and X-rays of a strange object located just under the skin of his inner thigh. The object, Jeff told us, was responsive to a magnet because when he placed a magnet over the spot, the object drew Jeff's skin to the magnet, indicating there was something metallic there. The X-rays displayed the object. Our plan with Jeff to end this episode was to introduce Jeff to certified clinical hypnotherapist Yvonne Smith and then to proceed with the extraction operation.

In 2006, Jeff became very ill with what was diagnosed as heavy metal poisoning. No cause of the poisoning was ever determined, but, we wondered, whether the cause might have been the metallic object in his thigh. This was also a question that Jeff had asked himself. He had contacted Roger Leir to find out whether, if this object were removed, it could be tested for any anomalous aspects. Jeff also had a sense that he had been contacted by an extraterrestrial presence, perhaps because his father had been in the intelligence services. Therefore, he agreed to work with Yvonne Smith to determine whether he could recover any memories from his past.

We met Jeff Harvey at the Los Angeles International Airport and started our interview with him as we drove to our production facility in Santa Monica. On the way, Jeff told us about a UFO sighting he had with his father when he was only eight years old. The father and son were fishing off the bank of the Lackawaxen River in Honesdale, Pennsylvania, when they saw a circular metallic object pass over their heads. Jeff described it as a saucer shape with a bowl shape on the bottom. He said they both got a good look at it as it passed over the river. Although he could not explain how, he said he related the object in his leg to the appearance of the flying object and told us that when he had X-rays of the object analyzed by the military, VA doctors told him that the object seemed to be consistent with the size and appearance of shrapnel. However, Jeff Harvey had never been in battle. Another VA doctor also told him that the object was most likely a fatty cyst. However, one day, to test out that theory, Jeff ran a magnet over the spot where the object was and the object flew to the magnet even through his skin. Thus, Jeff reasoned, the object inside him was metallic, and he was determined to find out what it was.

The next morning, we took Jeff Harvey to Dr. Leir's medical office for testing of the object inside Jeff's thigh for any radioactive or magnetic readings and to see if the object was emitting any radio signals. First, Roger Leir ran a magnet over the spot where the object was lodged, and the object jumped right up under the skin, an indicator that it was metallic. Then, Dr. Leir ran a gauss meter over the object to see if it was generating any electromagnetic field on its own. When the gauss meter went off, we knew that it was, in fact, generating a field, something very unusual for a simple piece of metal. What was it that could send out such a signal? The object should have not been generating a field of any measurable significance unless it was connected to a power source. What was the nature of that source?

As a next step, we tested it for the emission of a radio signal. When the radio receiver that Roger passed over the spot registered, we discovered that the metallic object was emitting a precise signal of 59 gigahertz, a reading that fell into the VHF band used by the military, which, Ted Acworth explained, could have come from any of the background radio instruments in the office. It could also have included cell phones. But the 59 gigahertz reading, Dr. Leir explained, was in the radio band used by satellites and for deep-space communication. Still, at such a low power, this device could not have been broadcasting long distance to any orbiting satellites. Until the object was out of Jeff's body, however, and under a high-power microscope, we were still in the dark as to what it was.

We next drove Jeff Harvey from Dr. Leir's office to the surgeon's operating suite, where the object would be removed and handed over to us. This would be the hour of truth.

At the surgeon's office, the operating room nurse extracted a supply of Jeff's blood so the object could be stored in it while Roger Leir set up the testing apparatus. He didn't want the object to shrink or dry out. Also, perhaps the object, if it were a robotic device, could be tricked into believing it was still inside Jeff Harvey's body and keep on transmitting its signal. After anesthetizing the location in Jeff's thigh where he would make his incision, the surgeon opened up Jeff's skin and, using the X-ray to guide him, went after the object with a hemostat and forceps. It took very little time for him to locate the object and slowly extract it. And that's when we were in for our next surprise. Jeff's tissue had attached itself to the object. As Ted explained it from the operating room, this was very strange because it looked to him as if the object was encapsulated in organic material that was actually attached to the rest of Jeff's body. That's why the object seemed to fight extraction.

The object was flat and almost rounded. Jeff said that he was surprised that an object that small was capable of generating a signal. But we discovered quickly after extracting the object that all of its radio signals had stopped and that it was no longer broadcasting on the gigahertz frequency or on the VHF band, and there was no electromagnetic signal, either. It was just as if it were a radio that had gone dead upon extraction.

JEFF'S REGRESSION SESSION

Ted and science assistant Jeff Tomlinson took the object to Seal Labs in El Segundo for an analysis of its makeup and any properties it might have possessed. Pat and I took Jeff Harvey to meet with clinical hypnotherapist and UFO abductions researcher Yvonne Smith to see what memories associated with that object might lie close to the surface of his conscious mind. Yvonne explained that in working with clients, it often takes many sessions to uncover deeply repressed and often traumatic memories of experiences that the conscious mind deems too painful to integrate. Moreover, regression researchers point out that, in cases of what they believe to be an alien abduction, the aliens may deliberately implant suggestions that the abductee forget the entire experience, thus leaving a hole in the abductee's memory, missing time.

Jeff was out to investigate what had happened to him when he was a child, particularly when he saw that object over the Lackawaxen River, and how the metallic object could have gotten into his leg. We met Yvonne at the hotel room where Jeff was staying and prepared for the session. The ensuing session, as interesting as it was, did not provide any conclusive testimonial evidence that Jeff had been abducted or that his sighting of an unidentified object when he was a child bore any relation to the object that was surgically removed from his thigh. In fact, the description Jeff gave to us while he was in a hypnotic or hypnogogic state suggested more of a childhood trauma perpetrated by an adult relative or family acquaintance than the presence of an extraterrestrial. Yvonne Smith suggested that you can't come to any conclusions after one session in these types of cases because the subject has to work through layers and layers of repressed memories to reach a point where his conscious memory can begin to put together the images. At best, Jeff would have more sessions to pull away the screen his own mind was creating, blocking him from the threatening or traumatic buried memories. And many of these sessions might not involve regression at all, but piecing together childhood memories like a patchwork quilt.

TESTING THE OBJECT EXTRACTED FROM JEFF HARVEY'S THIGH

Upon removing the object, Jeff Tomlinson and Dr. Roger Leir examined it to see if it was still broadcasting a radio signal. To Tomlinson's surprise, the object had gone dead. Not only that, despite its having been protected in serum drawn from Jeff Harvey, the object also looked as if it were no longer functioning. Dr. Leir has concluded, after a number of extractions of these types of objects, that the object actually is in a symbiotic state with the implantee/abductee and relies on the person's own body fluid and neural cells to remain active. Upon removal, the object is only a piece of metal.

The next step, however, was for Dr. Ted Acworth and Jeff Tomlinson to take it to Richard Mattson at Seal Labs, one of the leading analysis labs in the country, for further testing. And that is where Pat and I met them.

We wanted to see what the object looked like under extreme magnification. The object was very small and, in Ted's words, looked to the naked eye and even under the microscope like "a small meteorite." Under the scope, it had two distinct layers, a dark outer layer and a lighter center. The outer layer could have been oxidized, resembling rust. But under closer inspection, Tomlinson noted, there seemed to be a finlike protrusion from the object. It was odd because it didn't seem to fit the geometry of the object, and it wasn't actually protruding. Ted put it under an electron microscope, a device that scanned the object to provide us with a hypermagnified view and with a graph of what elements composed the object. We also took magnified X-rays of the object to ascertain the shape of the protrusion. Aligning the

X-rays with the electron scan of the object, Ted was able to determine that the protrusion itself was not a part of the object but was attached to the object. It was a different material altogether. In fact, unlike the object, the protrusion was actually organic. It was a piece of human tissue attached to a metallic object extracted from inside a human body.

This presented us with a riddle. As Ted explained it, there are two normal physiological reactions to a foreign object's presence in a human body. Either the body surrounds it with puss and ejects it or there is an inflammatory reaction, as with a deep splinter, which requires that the object be extracted. In this case, the body, presumably Jeff Harvey's, simply grew tissue around the object, tissue that attached itself to the metal, an unheard-of reaction. It was as if Jeff's body embraced the object.

The object, the spectrum analysis told us, was mostly iron with some phosphorus, not exactly otherworldly or anomalous. And it is also within the realm of medical possibility for an object to enter the body at one point and then move through the body to reside at another point even without causing an infection. However, the possibility that Jeff Harvey's body had embraced the object instead of rejecting it was a mystery.

This episode left us with an interesting conundrum. Although we'd shown that science can substantiate some of the claims of abductees, the criteria that skeptics establish as a requirement for veracity present a logical paradox. How can you prove something that is tangible enough for skeptics, who at the same time scoff at any evidence you set forth because it challenges them to suspend disbelief long enough to consider it? In other words, as our guest author Stan Friedman suggested, the skeptics' sine qua non is "Anything but Alien." For example, even if Jeff Harvey's metallic implant was iron, what explains the skin growing out of it? Even if the pink powder that turned up on Betty Hill's dress twenty-four hours after her statements that she was abducted by aliens is a substance composed of compounds found on our planet, what explains the presence of that organic matter in the very places where she said the aliens held on to her? And did she tear her own zipper on her dress?

These are among the many questions that are pursued by UFO researchers but dismissed by skeptics as not relevant unless a flying saucer lands on the White House lawn. Not even a UFO flying over the White House or the Washington Monument would be strong enough proof even though there are photographs from July 1952 that captured a fleet of UFOs over the Washington Monument and President Harry Truman admitted to the press that they were UFOs. If that's not public disclosure of UFOs, what is?

For that incontrovertible proof, our next episode took us to a land where we might actually find it: Mexico and the desert outside of Coyame and the mountain village of Xilitla.

BILL'S BLOG

We are driving along a lonely New England road at night outside of Portsmouth, New Hampshire. It is a chilly autumn evening with the setting sun looking like a dying star on the horizon. We've logged three episodes so far, but this is the first real substantial story that we're investigating. It has been the subject of debate and controversy since the early 1960s, spawning at least two seriously researched books, a number of magazine and journal articles, and one major television movie. This is the story of Betty and Barney Hill, and it is our point of entry into the subject of alien abductions. Are they real? Are they delusional? Choose your side and argue your case.

For me, the Hill case, breaking into the national headlines in the early 1960s just as I was entering college, was a mind blower. Seeing Betty and Barney on the cover of *Look Magazine* and reading John Fuller's book *Interrupted Journey* opened my eyes to the possibility that other realms could actually exist. It also scared the hell out of me. Imagine walking through the woods at night or along a lonely road and bumping into a small gray extraterrestrial who could force you onto a spaceship and perform painful experiments on you. But the biggest shocker was that if Betty and Barney Hill were telling the truth, it was a paradigm changer.

We're on our way to meet Kathleen Marden, Betty Hill's niece to whom Betty told her story on the morning after her encounter. Kathy Marden will explode a lot of myths about this case for us. In her book *Captured!*, written with Stanton Friedman, she reveals that Betty and Barney had conscious memories of seeing the strange ship and its strange occupants. It was only once they were actually taken, "captured," that their memories are blank.

From New Hampshire, we will go to Ohio to meet Phyllis Budinger, the chemist who actually analyzed the strange pink powder on the dress Betty wore the night she was taken. And from Ohio, we will be off to Colorado to meet with Dr. Roger Leir's patient, Tim Cullen, another person claiming to have had an encounter with a strange craft, but, this time, who took a strange metallic object away with him. It had been inserted into his arm by the aliens themselves. And from Colorado we're to go back to Los Angeles for an actual alien-implant extraction and analysis of the object we find.

This is a strange journey into the past and into the future exploring what I like best: trace evidence. Tangible evidence of something that may show that strange encounters leave their marks on the ground, on the witnesses, and on the individuals who are contacted.

The Hill, Cullen, and Jeff Harvey cases are in marked contrast to the contactee movement of the 1950s, where supposedly ordinary people crossed paths with entities from Venus or other planets and were given messages of warning and hope for the human race. Presaging the Billy Meier contact story of the 1970s and 1980s, the 1950s contactees, Van Tassel, George Adamski, Frank Stranges, and Howard Menger, talked of "space brothers" and beautiful women from Venus who foretold of disasters facing humanity. In the Betty and Barney abductions, they came for the eggs and the sperm.

It's one thing to hear or read about a story. It's another to live it, to visit the actual places where it took place, and to talk with live witnesses. Kathy Marden is a live witness. She spoke to her aunt on the morning after and probably is the closest one to the case now that Betty is dead.

I had the opportunity to interview Betty for *UFO Magazine* back in 2004, one of many interviews she gave to the magazine. She was as feisty as ever, but as lucid as could be, coughing out her story between cigarettes. She brought us all up to date on her continuing quest to get the truth to the public, making her way from talk show to talk show, sitting in the green rooms holding the cast, on her lap, of an alien head she said was the medical examiner aboard the spaceship. It was Betty Hill, a living legend of popular culture. And now *UFO Hunters* was on the story.

UFO CRASHES

UFO Hunters went to Mexico for this episode to investigate what has come to be known as Mexico's Roswell, the crash of a flying saucer into a private plane over the Coyame desert just south of the U.S. border town of El Paso. In Mexico, we also went to the small mountain village of Xilitla to investigate the crash of a UFO, a fireball that came hurtling to Earth and was retrieved by a special police unit.

THE COYAME INCIDENT

At its most simple, the crash on April 25, 1974, at 10:07 P.M. at Coyame in the state of Chihuahua, Mexico, right across the border from Texas, was the result of a collision between a small private plane and a flying saucer. This opinion was best expressed by our guests for this episode, Ruben Uriarte, MUFON state director for Northern California, and Noe Torres, authors of Mexico's Roswell: The Chihuahua UFO Crash (RoswellBooks.com, 2nd ed., 2008). But the Coyame incident was more than just a simple crash and subsequent retrieval. It involved the deaths of the Mexican army retrieval team and a cross-border search, retrieval, and disposal operation by U.S. military forces in a scene right out of a science fiction movie. Moreover, had it not been for a mysterious report filed with an entity referred to as the Deneb team, the crash might have gone completely unnoticed by the UFO community.

In 1992, the Deneb document was mailed to a number of UFO researchers, including Elaine Douglass of Operation Right to Know, currently a MUFON state director and editor of the *Journal of Abduction-Encounter Research*, who forwarded it to author Leonard Stringfield. Stringfield, in turn, included the report in his *UFO Crash/Retrievals: "Search for Proof in a Hall of Mirrors: Status Report IV"* (1994). Whether the Deneb document is real, disinformation, or an out-and-out hoax, it stirred up a lot of controversy inside the UFO community because, on the face of it, it read, in some respects, like an official report of a real incident even though, in other respects, it was less than authoritative and contained at least one very serious misspelling, as if it had been dictated. Here is the document printed here with permission of author Noe Torres, who included it in his coauthored book, *Mexico's Roswell* (VBW Publishing, 2007).

SUBJECT: THE CHIHUAHUA DISK CRASH

FILE: UFO3263

To: All Deneb Team Members

From: JS

Date: 23 Mar 92

Subject: Research Findings on the Chihuahua Disk Crash

Text:

On 25 Aug 74, at 2207 hrs, US Air Defense radar detected an unknown approaching US airspace from the Gulf of Mexico. Originally the object was tracked at 2,200 (2530 mph) knots on a bearing of 325 degrees and at an altitude of 75,000 feet, a course that would intercept US territory about forty miles southwest of Corpus Cristi [sic], Texas. After approximately sixty seconds of observation, at a position 155 miles southeast of Corpus Cristi [sic], the object simultaneously decelerated to approximately 1700 (1955 mph) knots, turned to a heading of 290 degrees, and began a slow descent. It entered Mexican airspace approximately forty miles south of Brownsville, Texas. Radar tracked it approximately 500 miles to a point near the town of Coyame, in the state of Chihuahua, not far from the US border. There the object suddenly disappeared from the radar screens.

During the flight over Mexican airspace, the object leveled off at 45,000 feet, then descended to 20,000 feet. The descent was in level steps, not a smooth curve or straight line, and each level was maintained for approximately five minutes.

The object was tracked by two different military radar installations. It would have been within range of Brownsville civilian radar, but it is assumed that no civilian radar detected the object due to a lack of any such reports.

The point of disappearance from the radar screens was over a barren and sparsely populated area of Northern Mexico. At first it was assumed that the object had descended below the radar's horizon and a watch was kept for any re-emergence of the object. None occurred.

At first it was assumed that the object might be a meteor because of the high speed and descending flight path. But meteors normally travel at higher speeds, and descend in a smooth arc, not in "steps." And meteors do not normally make a thirty-five degree change in course. Shortly after detection an air defense alert was called. However, before any form of interception could be scrambled, the object turned to a course that would not immediately take it over US territory. The alert was called off within twenty minutes after the object's disappearance from the radar screen.

Fifty-two minutes after the disappearance, civilian radio traffic indicated that a civilian aircraft had gone down in that area. But it was clear that the missing aircraft had departed El Paso International with a destination of Mexico City, and could not, therefore, have been the object tracked over the Gulf of Mexico.

It was noted, however, that they both disappeared in the same area and at the same time. With daylight the next day, Mexican authorities began a search for the missing plane. Approximately 1035 hrs there came a radio report that wreckage from the missing plane had been spotted from the air. Almost immediately came a report of a second plane on the ground a few miles from the first. A few minutes later, an additional report stated that the second "plane" was circular shaped and apparently in one piece although damaged. A few minutes after that the Mexican military clamped a radio silence on all search efforts.

The radio interceptions were reported through channels to the CIA. Possibly as many as two additional government agencies also received reports, but such has not been confirmed as of this date. The CIA immediately began forming a recovery team. The speed with which this team and its equipment was assembled suggests that this was either a well-rehearsed exercise or one that had been performed prior to this event.

In the meantime requests were initiated at the highest levels between the United States and Mexican governments that the US recovery team be allowed onto Mexican territory to "assist." These requests were met with professed ignorance and a flat refusal of any cooperation.

By 2100 hrs, 26 Aug 74, the recovery team had assembled and been staged at Fort Bliss. Several helicopters were flown in from some unknown source and assembled in a secured area. These helicopters were painted a neutral sand color and bore no markings. Eye witness indicates that there were three smaller craft, very probably UHl Hueys from the description. There was also a larger helicopter, possibly a Sea Stallion. Personnel from this team remained with their craft and had no contact with other Ft. Bliss personnel.

Satellite and recognizance [sic] aircraft overflight that day indicated that both the crashed disk and the civilian aircraft had been removed from the crash sites and loaded on flatbed trucks. Later flights confirmed that the convoy had departed the area heading south.

At that point the CIA had to make a choice, either to allow this unknown aircraft to stay in the hands of the Mexican government, or to launch the recovery team, supplemented by any required military support, to take the craft. There occurred, however, an event that took the choice out of their hands. High altitude overflights indicated that the convoy had stopped before reaching any inhabited areas or major roads. Recon showed no activity, and radio contact between the Mexican recovery team and its headquarters had ceased. A low altitude, high speed overflight was ordered.

The photos returned by that aircraft showed all trucks and jeeps stopped, some with open doors, and two human bodies laying [sic] on the ground beside two vehicles. The decision was immediately made to launch the recovery team but the actual launching was held up for the arrival of additional equipment and two additional personnel. It was not until 1438 hrs that the helicopters departed Ft. Bliss.

The four helicopters followed the boarder down towards Presido then turned and entered Mexican airspace north of Candelaria. They were over the convoy site at 1653 hrs. All convoy personnel were dead, most within the trucks. Some recovery team members, dressed [in] bioprotection suits, reconfigured the straps holding the object on the flatbed truck, then attached them to a cargo cable from the Sea Stallion. By 1714 hrs the recovered object was on its way to US territory. Before leaving the convoy site, members of the recovery team gathered together the Mexican vehicles and bodies, then destroyed all with high explosives. This included the pieces of the civilian light plane which had been involved in the mid-air collision. At 1746 hrs the Hueys departed.

The Hueys caught up with the Sea Stallion as it reentered US airspace. The recovery team then proceeded to a point in the Davis Mountains, approximately twenty-five miles north east of Valentine. There they landed and waited until 0225 hrs the next morning. At that time they resumed the flight and rendezvoused with a small convoy on a road between Van Horn and Kent. The recovered disk was transferred to a truck large enough to handle it and capable of being sealed totally. Some of the personnel from the Huey's [sic] transferred to the convoy.

All helicopters then returned to their original bases for decontamination procedures. The convoy continued non-stop, using back roads and smaller highways, and staying away from cities. The destination of the convoy reportedly was Altanta [sic], Georgia.

Here the hard evidence thins out. One unconfirmed report says the disk was eventually transferred to Wright-Patterson AF Base. Another says that the disk was either transferred after that to another unnamed base, or was taken directly to this unknown base directly from Atlanta.

The best description of the disk was that it was sixteen feet, five inches in diameter, convex on both upper and lower surfaces to the same degree, possessing no visible doors or windows. The thickness was slightly less than five feet. The color was silver, much like polished steel. There were no visible lights nor any propulsion means. There were no markings. There were two areas of the rim that showed damage, one showing an irregular hole approximately twelve inches in diameter with indented material around it. The other damage was described as a "dent" about two feet wide. The weight of the object was estimated as approximately one thousand, five hundred pounds, based on the effect of the weight on the carrying helicopter and those who transferred it to the truck.

There was no indication in the documentation available as to whether anything was visible in the "hole."

It seems likely that the damage with the hole was caused by the collision with the civilian aircraft. That collision occurred while the object was traveling approximately 1700 knots (1955 mph). Even ignoring the speed of the civilian aircraft, the impact would have been considerable at that speed. This is in agreement with the description of the civilian aircraft as being "almost totally destroyed." What was being taken from the crash site was pieces of the civilian aircraft.

The second damage may have resulted when the object impacted with the ground. The speed in that case should have been considerably less than that of the first impact.

No mention is made of the occupants of the civilian aircraft. It is not known if any body or bodies were recovered. Considering the destruction of the civilian light aircraft in mid-air, bodies may well not have come down near the larger pieces.

Unfortunately what caused the deaths of the Mexican recovery team is not known. Speculation ranges from a chemical released from the disk as a result of the damage, to a microbiological agent. There are no indications of death or illness by any of the recovery team. It would not have been illogical for the recovery team to have taken one of the bodies back with them for anaylsis [sic]. But there is no indication of that having happen [sic]. Perhaps they did not have adequate means of transporting what might have been a biologically contaminated body.

Inquires [sic] to the FAA reveal no documents conserning [sic] the civilian aircraft crash, probably because it did not involve a US aircraft[.]

It should be noted that the above facts do not tell the complete story. Nothing is known of the analysis of the craft or its contents. Nothing is known about the deaths associated with the foreign recovery team. Nor is it known if this craft was manned or not.

Other questions also remain, such as why would a recovered disk be taken to Altanta [sic]? And where did the disk come from? It was first detected approximately 200 miles from US territory, yet US air defenses extend to a much greater distance than that. If the object descended into the atmosphere, perhaps NORAD space tracking has some record of the object. Alternate possibility is that it entered the Gulf of Mexico under radar limits then "jumped" up to 75,000 feet. Considering prior behavior exhibited by disks of this size, it is probable that the entry was from orbital altitude.

The facts that are known have been gathered from two eye

witness accounts, documentation illegally copied, and a partially destroyed document. This was done in 1978 by a person who is now dead. Only in February of this year [1992] did the notes and documents come into the hands of our group.

What can one make of the Deneb report, what is the Deneb group, and is there any significance to the term Deneb? Elaine Douglass believes that the Deneb group might be an informal group of quasi-insiders commenting on what took place in the Coyame desert in 1974. Noe Torres and Ruben Uriarte comment in *Mexico's Roswell* that Deneb is the name for a very bright blue star in the constellation Cygnus and is so bright and so large—one of the brightest stars in the sky—that it is often mistaken for a UFO. Accordingly, perhaps Deneb might have been the perfect code name for a group described by Douglass as government personnel with some knowledge of the government's UFO investigations but who are not actually members of the investigative group. Deneb might be a close-knit group of watchers with insider connections but just outside of the real Special Access Projects circle.

Noe Torres, who, along with Ruben Uriarte, was a guest expert accompanying *UFO Hunters* to Mexico in this episode, also speculates that the Deneb group might actually be composed of ETs in human form who are monitoring the military's monitoring of UFOs, as if the watchers were watching the watchers. As far-fetched as that may sound, other guests on *UFO Hunters,* including author Maximillien de Lafayette, have also speculated that ETs who look just like human beings in every way have penetrated all of our country's institutions and have been pulling important strings for decades. Could the name Deneb, therefore, be either a code name for that group or, perhaps, refer to the planetary system where these ETs originated? Or maybe it's simply a code name for a group of watchers and means nothing more than the star that, because of its extreme brightness, is most often mistaken for a UFO by sky watchers.

As Torres and Uriarte point out, Deneb lies almost at the center of that portion of the Milky Way galaxy most easily observed by the ancients, called the Great Rift. It is the dark portion of the Milky Way at the center of the two spiral arms. It is from this spot that the ancient Mayans believed that life began and from where the deities would return to Earth in 2012. Thus, it also might have special significance for any UFO incident in Mexico.

In Elaine Douglass's analysis of the Deneb report, which she said she received from a post office in California, she suggests that the group that's sharing the information about UFO activities is not apprehensive about being discovered and refers to "UFO" as part of the file name for the report, indicating that the term "UFO" is used within the government. She believes that the individual who wrote the report had actually spoken to at least one eyewitness at Fort Bliss, the debarkation point of the military team that retrieved the flying saucer from the desert and disposed of the debris of the private plane.

The writer of the Deneb report seems to have been well enough connected to the goings-on at Fort Bliss to be aware of the mission the retrieval team was on, the reason the retrieval team went to Mexico, and the route of the retrieval team and its cargo after carrying out its mission. The report also describes a military mission and not a covert intelligence-gathering operation. Yet, Douglass speculates, it is probable that the person or persons who circulated the Deneb report to people outside the tight circle of the Deneb team members was not a member of the Deneb team but someone who gained access to the document.

Who are the members of the Deneb team? Whether an unofficial group of UFO watchers inside the military, a semi-official group controlled by someone with enough authority to build his own intelligence unit, ETs in influential positions, or members of a special access group monitoring all government activity involving UFO discoveries and retrievals, the report, if true, reveals that ongoing UFO monitoring activity and military involvement in UFO retrievals is taking place inside the government and the military.

With the incident fully described in the Deneb report, the proof itself would have to lie in finding the crash site and the disposal site to see if any evidence remained of the incident. Finding hard evidence would lend credence to the report and establish that, at the very least, something happened in the Coyame desert.

Anyone can see that the Coyame crash story was compelling regardless of the Deneb report's poor grammar, misspellings, and seeming lack of native English fluency. One can imagine that someone whose native language is not English wrote the report, if, indeed, this is a legitimate report. Nevertheless, the story cried out to the *UFO Hunters* team during our preparation for the series to see if any evidence still existed to substantiate any part of it.

Essentially, the report describes a flying saucer, hovering over the U.S. border near top-secret army bases that collided with a private plane. Both craft crashed in the desert on the Mexican side of the border. But when the Mexican army retrieval unit—under the watchful, but invisible, eyes of an NSA surveillance aircraft—retrieved the disk, the entire unit was stricken by some unknown virus. Radio transmissions went dead, and when the U.S. Army sent a surveillance craft over the border to find out what happened, they saw the convoy stopped on the road with soldiers spilled out of their vehicles. They were all dead.

The U.S. Army dispatched a biological-hazard retrieval team to the location within the hour, scooped up the saucer and the bodies, and rushed them off to the Centers for Disease Control outside Atlanta. They burned then buried the debris from the private plane in the desert a mile away from the crash site. The whole incident was hushed up but was documented in a classified "eyes only" report that was circulated through the Pentagon's Special Access Projects department.

An incident like this poses the question, how do you investigate it? Answer, if you believe you can find the location of the incident, go down there, find witnesses, find the location, and see if you can find any debris. And that's just what the *UFO Hunters* team did, winding up being held at gunpoint by Mexican soldiers who thought that we might actually be terrorists.

THE XILITLA INCIDENT

On August 20, 2007, at 4 A.M., only months before *UFO Hunters* arrived to investigate, a loud crash and fiery explosion in the sky sent frightened residents of the tiny community of Xilitla out into the streets to see what had happened. It was a burning craft hurtling through the sky, a fireball that streaked in from the west just above the low roofs in a sharp arc and then crashed into a nearby grove of lemon and coffee trees, starting small fires in the underbrush. But, some of the village residents said, the object didn't simply fall to Earth, it changed direction, actually gained altitude as if it were trying to navigate, and looked to them as if it were being flown.

Even before the smoke was clearing from the forest grove, residents were calling the police emergency numbers. And within the next thirty minutes police units had effectively locked down the town and told the residents to get back in their homes. The little village was a scene of chaos through the rest of the predawn darkness as police officers collected piles of dirt and ash from the area where witnesses said they saw the fireball come to rest. When the police pulled out, they took with them as much of the ash as they could collect. And then came the silence. No officer would speak to the villagers about what they found or what they discovered. It was as if the incident had never happened.

Rumors quickly began to spread among the villagers that the reports of the crash had gone all the way up to the central police intelligence bureau, an office so secret that even its agents fear for their lives about disclosing its secrets. However, one agent was willing to talk about the incident, though he refused to be seen in public. Ruben Uriarte and I, along with Mexican radio talk show host Victor Camacho, agreed to meet the officer deep in a sugarcane field, where, we hoped, Mexican military and police intelligence officers would not find us. This was serious business.

Here's what the intelligence officer said: "I took the initial report on August 19 [2007]. There were unidentified objects that had fallen. There were ongoing reports of strange objects in this area, balls of fire."

For the record, fireballs are not uncommon in this part of Mexico. Documented witness reports of fireballs hurtling across the sky go all the way back to 1969. But, if the fireballs were meteorites—probably the most conventional explanation—there would be a crater from the meteorite's impact, as there was in a neighboring village in 1969. Meteorites also leave a debris field and they usually fall straight to Earth even if at a sharp angle. But in Xilitla, none of this was the case. The object seemed to be guided down, left no crater, and whatever debris existed was taken away by the police.

The police intelligence officer told us that his report on the Xilitla incident was filed with the SDN, the top-secret central military intelligence bureau. All police and military forces report to the SDN. After his report went to the SDN, the police intelligence officer told us, it simply disappeared. There was no further word from any official at the intelligence agency about the incident and all of the ash the police recovered was filed away.

After the incident, however, the police contacted the editor of the local newspaper, indicating to him that what happened in Xilitla was a UFO incident. He told us that he had dispatched reporter Maribu Villalobos to cover the incident as well and determined that from the witness statements, it seemed as though the villagers had seen a UFO. The reporter found out that there was a considerable amount of ash residue from where the fireball crashed through a grove of trees. But the police removed the ash for analysis.

The witness reports all supported one another. Juaquin Rubio, for example, who lived directly across from the impact site, said that the object was about seven feet in diameter. He said he saw the fireball hurtle in from the west, hit the limbs causing sparks and a fire, and come to rest at the base of the tree grove. There was a small fire on the ground and fires in the trees where the fireball clipped off limbs and branches. Rubio said he was frightened at the sight of the fireball because he'd never seen anything like it before. And at seven feet across, it was very menacing.

Another witness, Satarina Gonzales, said that, on the same night as Rubio, she saw an object in the sky, which had bright flames coming out of it. She was so scared she called to her husband, who, in turn, called the local Mexican equivalent of 911 to report a crash and a fire. The police units began to arrive within a few minutes, but, Mr. Gonzales said, they were complaining to the Xilitla residents watching the commotion that their radios were not working. They said they couldn't raise their dispatch or talk to one another on their walkie-talkies. In fact, it was later reported that for twenty minutes after the police units were fully deployed—from 4:30 A.M. to 4:50 A.M.—the entire Xilitla area was under a complete radio blackout.

And still another witness said that the object seemed to skim across his roof, causing his entire house to tremble as if it were in an earthquake. He also heard a scraping sound across the top of his house and the sizzle of electricity. He couldn't explain it but was so frightened that he stayed inside his house until he saw the flashing police lights. But, he said, even the police seemed to be in a state of confusion because their radios weren't transmitting or receiving.

All the witnesses reported that they saw what they called "long ashes" in the street that were collected by the police. Reporter Maribu Villalobos actually handled the ribbonlike ashes before the police confiscated them. She said that they were about two centimeters wide, were composed of black and gray matter, and didn't just crumble because its pieces had hard surfaces. She handed the ashes over to police officer Carlos Arillano. Officer Arillano was unwilling to meet up with the team, because he still had possession of the ashes—which he should not have kept—but agreed to send them back to California to Capco, our lab in Ventura County, for analysis.

Capco uses gas chromatography to provide a quantitative analysis of what a substance contains. If, for example, the ash sample from Xilitla contained elements or substances that could not be identified as substances found on planet Earth, it might constitute a smoking gun for an otherworldly origin of the fireball. Similarly, if the substance signatures returned by Capco's analysis showed that there were elements combined in ways that no terrestrial process could accomplish, that would be another compelling piece of evidence. On the other hand, because most of the analysis that has been provided by science of planets both inside and outside our solar system has shown that the substances found there are the same chemicals that we have on Earth, it is likely that even if we were to find something fabricated by an extraterrestrial intelligence, it would likely be composed of something found right here on Earth. However, certain composites may, indeed, reveal a manufacturing process that we have not yet developed.

The best example of this, at least for me, was the composition of the transistor that John Bardeen, Walter Brattain, and William Shockley invented. According to the story, the three had been working for at least a decade at Bell Labs and Western Electric to develop an alternative to the nineteenth-century Edison tube, essentially the incandescent lightbulb. They were to invent a device that would pass electrons through it, just like the filament of a lightbulb, but only in one direction and only one at a time. They were using a silicon base but were not able to control the electron flow and the direction. After the crash at Roswell in 1947, as the story goes, the army took the most basic technologies discovered in the Roswell craft and sought the American companies whose R&D divisions could make the best use of pieces of the craft's debris. When Bardeen, Brattain, and Shockley saw the circuitry from the crashed craft and analyzed the substances therein, they found that the silicon was doped with arsenic to impede the electron flow. In just a few short months, developing a formula based on what they had analyzed from the Roswell debris, they had proof of the concept of a switch they would call the transistor. By 1948, the transistor was in development. And in 1951, the inventors had industrial patents along with the first transistor radios. It was a success story that began the march to integrated circuitry, the personal computer, and the digital matrix in which we live and work today.

One can see from that story that it wasn't the exotic materials that proved to be the clue, it was the combination of substances that had not been tried before on Earth that provided the inventors of the transistor with the solution they were looking for. Therefore, in analyzing the ribbons of ash that Carlos Arillano delivered to us from the fireball residue at Xilitla we hoped to find, at the very least, some strange combinations of substances or the residue of alloys that could not be found in the present-day industrial database of compounds.

Latin America, and Mexico in particular, is a hotbed of reported UFO activity. From the ancient Inca ruins in Peru to the Mayan ruins in southern Mexico, the indigenous peoples seemed very aware of aspects of astronomy that scientists of industrialized nations only officially discovered centuries later. Images of aircraft and humanoid figures in space suits adorn the temples of the Maya and the Incas. The Nazca lines and bottomless lakes in Peru all have legends of UFO landings intertwined with Native American lore. As in the American Southwest, stories of star people and their star ships, people from Cygnus, the Dog Star, and the cluster of stars forming the constellation of Orion, predominate the legends of creation.

Although the "Crash and Retrieval" episode only focused on the Coyame crash and the Xilitla incident, it was set against the rich background of Latin American UFO legends, the stories of witnesses and their extraterrestrial contacts, and modern-day cover-ups by the police and the military.

THE EPISODE

We were still a new crew in fall 2007 as we set out for Mexico City from Los Angeles to venture into the Coyame desert and from there to the mountain village of Xilitla. By the time the episode ended, after being held at gunpoint twice by Mexican troops and chased through the desert by a military unit that threatened to shut us down, and after evading a squad of Mexican intelligence units trying to stop us from interviewing one of their own about the Xilitla crash, we found we had to rely on ourselves and to trust the fact that we were a family on the road. We traveled across Mexico by a chartered tour bus and were robbed by a knife-wielding transient who sneaked past our bus drivers to get into our equipment. We almost didn't make it out of Mexico at the last minute, when a customs official suddenly appeared at the Mexico City Airport Jetway to tell us that our exit visas weren't properly stamped. We had to get them stamped at another terminal just as our plane began to board. And I met the friendly sheriff of Coyame, who wore a pair of six-guns, a big black Sam Elliott handlebar mustache, and a huge ten-gallon hat and introduced me to the inside of a Mexican jail. There were so many different stories in this expedition that many of them didn't make it into the final cut. It was an experience—I can tell you that.

We arrived at the Mexico City airport, where we picked up a huge Greyhound-sized pink tour bus for our drive across Mexico. This wasn't exactly the newest bus on the lot, but at least it had a semblance of air-conditioning and a bathroom in the rear with a door that actually closed. It didn't lock. It only closed. Burt for the first half of the trip, the toilet flushed. And that was a good thing.

Our first stop was a neighborhood outside Mexico City, where residents had told news commentator Victor Camacho that there had been a number of UFO incidents in the area, all of which had been investigated by the police. However, when the residents asked police investigators about their findings, the police simply said nothing had happened and it was better not to talk about it. This made the residents even more nervous. It made us nervous, too, because the police, who knew we were filming in the area, began to surveil us. Their cars were always down the street from the bus and we could see that at least one officer was wearing binoculars as he sat behind the wheel.

Our expert Ruben Uriarte, head of Northern California MUFON and author of *Mexico's Roswell*, along with Noe Torres, took careful note of the police presence around us. In the past, Ruben's and Noe's trips to the Coyame desert stirred little activity. But the presence of a huge pink tour bus with a camera crew from Los Angeles was attracting attention.

Our first interviews with local residents laid the groundwork for one of the areas we wanted to explore. Was there something that was going on that the government wasn't talking about? And we found out from our local witnesses that they had seen UFOs hovering over the area and had seen police officers watching the UFOs. One resident told us that he knew a member of a police intelligence unit that had investigated a reported fireball crash in the distant village of Xilitla. The intelligence officer said that he had written a comprehensive report of what he had learned and turned it in to the offices of the SDN. Now, however, he was willing to go on camera to reveal that he was the officer on the scene and that he made a report on the UFO incident.

Victor Camacho and a friend of the officer, whose name we never learned, set up the interview deep inside a sugarcane field. But, we learned, even as we headed to the meeting, the police were on to us. With our bus standing out like a giant pink thumb, the police had an easy time staying three or four car lengths behind so we wouldn't notice them. Besides, you're not going to pull off a *Bullitt* car chase in a tour bus.

We made it to the sugarcane field without being intercepted and conducted the interview. The intelligence officer was visibly shaking as he told us the story of how the police got the report of the Xilitla crash and put special intelligence units on alert. When the police cars that responded to the crash report lost all radio contact with their dispatch, the intelligence officers became particularly concerned. Those who analyze reports of UFO encounters, as we were to find out along our travels for the ensuing three seasons, know that in close encounters a strong field—whether an electromagnetic field or something else—can disable electrical equipment such as radios. Thus, when all the police car radios and handhelds in Xilitla went dead and the police were walking around without any instructions from dispatch, the intelligence officers knew that this was an anomalous event and that they needed to secure all the reports as quickly as possible.

As we learned from the interview, UFO reports were common in

Mexico. But it was the actual crashes and retrieval of debris that ranked very high on the intelligence priority list. And our officer, speaking out for the first time about the cloak that dropped around Xilitla, made it clear that the police and military intelligence bureau took this very seriously.

While we spoke, and as Director of Photography Kevin Graves kept the camera on everyone but the intelligence officer, except for an occasional long shot, we could hear police car sirens in the background. Our intelligence officer began getting nervous, and his brother, who brought him to our location, began to tense up. "This is getting very serious," he said to us through Ruben and Victor, both of whom were translating. "Very serious."

We tried to keep the interview going, but a sudden nearby blare of police horn made everyone jump. "¡No más!" the officer's brother said. And Camacho's face became dead serious. We had to get out of there. If we were caught together, it could mean something much worse than the drunk tank in a Tijuana jail.

The siren was almost upon us, and we split in different directions like a pool table break. Camacho headed for his car, our *Hunters* team headed for the bus. The intelligence officer headed deep into the sugarcane field. His brother headed into the nearby town. The bus doors almost closed upon us as the driver panicked, and we rolled away toward the highway, a police car lolling behind us to keep us in view. When we were safely away from the sugarcane field, the police car peeled off, and for the first time since we met with local residents outside Mexico City, we felt free. But it was a false sense of security that would not last for long.

JOURNEY TO XILITLA

From our meeting with the police intelligence officer, we drove to the village of Xilitla to investigate the facts of this case and why it was so critical for the police to send their reports directly to the SDN under a cloud of secrecy. We wanted to talk to witnesses and to see if there was any trace evidence still there that we could take back to our laboratories in California for analysis.

It was already getting dark when we arrived in Xilitla. We spoke to one or two residents, but before long the entire village came out to meet us. We were astounded at the unanimity among the witnesses, each of whom had a separate story to tell that coincided or comported with the other stories. We assembled all of them out on the main street and asked them to show us where the flaming object first came into view. As they pointed skyward for our cameras, showing us the direction of the object, a thunder and lightning storm that had been brewing all afternoon suddenly crashed overhead. The area literally shook with the booming claps of thunder as if some ancient deities were spewing their wrath upon us for daring to ask about the secrets of the unknown. Even the villagers seemed startled by the intensity of the storm.

Then, as we tried to get the first interviews in while we still had some light, there was a violent lightning strike on one house up the hill followed by a series of strikes directly across the street in the lemon grove. And, as the ground shook from the terrible thunder, all the lights in the village suddenly went dead. It was a power outage. So much for the *Close Encounters of the Third Kind* shot.

As the rain came down in torrents, we covered the cameras and reassembled the witnesses inside a large garage. Our camera and sound crew laid wires and rigged batteries to light the area so we could get our first interviews, even if that would be all we got that night. Then, amid the pounding rain and searing lightning hits, we captured the group shot, lined up our witnesses for the next day, and set up a human-umbrella assembly line to get the cameras and sound equipment back into the bus. With the streets awash with rivers of rain and mud flows, the driver eased the bus back down the steep hill to the hotel for the night. And we knew that we would only have a few hours of sleep before heading back out to the village before daybreak to catch all the light we could for a day's shooting.

It rained all night, lightning searing across the sky and thunder vibrating through the paper-thin walls of our hotel. Some of the rooms had leaky roofs, making sleep especially difficult. But by day-break, the rain had slowed to a drizzle. And by the time we reached the village, the sky was hazy, but the rain had stopped. It was very early morning, and the villagers were out to see the bus as it pulled up to the single main street. As we got off, a perfectly wonderful young woman and her little sister handed us fresh hot cornmeal cakes right off a tortilla grill, and another young woman handed us cups of coffee. It was probably the brightest moment that I remember from our trip to Mexico.

We got right to work interviewing witnesses, talking to the newspaper reporter who covered the crash and the police presence, and collecting soil samples. Reporter Maribu Villalobos gave us Officer Carlos Arillano's phone number, and we called him to get the long-ribboned ash samples that the other police had collected and sent back to SDN. He agreed to send them to us, but didn't want to appear on camera. We completed the interviews and piled back into the bus for the long trip north to Coyame to shoot the primary segment of the "Crash and Retrieval" episode, "Mexico's Roswell."

COYAME: MEXICO'S ROSWELL

It was a long bus ride to the Coyame desert as we headed north to-ward the Texas border, and it took over two long days of driving. By now the bus drivers were getting tired and the bathroom was getting full. We had to stop at a gas station to flush the toilet's holding tank and to give the drivers a rest. The heat had been relentless, but as we entered the desert area, the nights became very chilly.

We tried to get as much sleep as we could on the bus because we knew that at the windy desert of Coyame the next day, we would be trekking across the sand looking for what might be scraps of wreck-age. So we had to be sharp. But sleep came in fits that night on the uncomfortable bus seats. And there were disturbing sounds from the front of the bus and rustling amid the seats. Most of us thought it was one of the crew or cast stumbling along the aisle to the bathroom, but it wasn't. The next morning we discovered that a stranger had managed to sneak past the driver supposedly standing guard duty, rifle through all of our belongings, and help himself to our field coordinator's Macbook laptop computer with all the travel records on it. All of us felt very threatened, and the bus driver whose responsibility it was to guard the passenger section became deeply depressed because he knew it would cost him his job. Basically, it was a big downer.

We were up and on the road before sunrise, looking for any place we could get coffee and some corn cakes to sustain us until lunch. And by early morning's bright daylight, we pulled up to our first military checkpoint at the edge of the Coyame desert. Through the bus windows we could see machine gun emplacements set behind a makeshift sandbag garrison. There was a bunkhouse, a shed that seemed to function as a headquarters building with what looked like vintage World War II radio antennas set up on shaky towers alongside, and a series of guard posts with very young teenagers sporting automatic rifles and serious expressions. Except for the very real weapons, it looked like a high school play.

A small squad of soldiers surrounded the bus while a teenager wearing sergeant stripes on his very crisp camouflage uniform stepped onto the bus. He barked at us in Spanish. Ruben translated: "He wants us out of here so he can search the bus for weapons." And he whispered to us, "Take your wallets." As we waited outside the bus, Ruben looked increasingly worried. He is usually carefree in a mellow, Northern California way. This time, he appeared very concerned, even through a surface smile. He caught my eye and jerked his head toward a pile of sandbags with a huge mounted machine gun poking out between them.

"This guy's got us in his sights," Ruben said. "He could mow us down in a minute. Keep smiling at them."

Finally the sergeant asked our interpreter—a person we refer to on location as our "fixer"—what we were doing in the desert. All I could make out was "*los ovnis*," UFOs. The sergeant shook his head. That didn't look good. Then one of his men started yelling "Jaime Mausson, Jaime Mausson." Jaime Mausson is a celebrated television personality who writes about UFOs and is also well-known for releasing footage of UFOs to the world. One of the soldiers had found Noe and Ruben's book with Mausson's photo on it. We were OK.

Patting both Noe Torres and Ruben Uriarte on the back, the soldiers ushered us back on the bus and actually waved to us with their rifle barrels. We were off again, this time into one of the most desolate stretches of territory I had ever seen. Ruben and Noe had saved the day and probably kept us out of a long night's detention, especially if the police intelligence division was still looking for us after the encounter with their agent in the sugarcane field.

THE DISCOVERY IN THE DESERT

According to Ruben and Noe, who had surveyed the area using the locations given in the Deneb report, there were two important spots where we might find evidence. One was the hole where the report said a U.S. military detail buried some of the plane-crash debris. The second location would be the actual crash site itself where the private plane came down. Maybe there would still be some parts of it lying on the ground that were never retrieved. Finding evidence of a burial spot, especially with some evidence that unknown persons tried to explode or burn the material, would be supportive of the statements in the report. Also, finding a plane-crash site would be supportive, but to a lesser extent, because how could we determine what plane the material was from? And, of course, we would need soil samples to test to determine whether there was any residue from an explosion or fire.

At first there was some confusion about the location that Ruben and Noe were trying to find because we were having issues with our GPS devices. Some of them couldn't get a satellite signal, and, because we were so far out into the desert, our cell phone GPS systems weren't picking up any signal from our telephone carriers. But once out of the bus, we formed into two groups at what was supposed to be the disposal site. One group led by Noe, the other by Ruben, we searched until we both converged on what looked like a dark spot in the sand.

Amid the windswept chaparral and scrub, we formed around what looked like a closed-up mine shaft. It was a squared-off hole, big enough for a human being to lower himself into, and its opening was framed by wooden beams. We stood around the opening for a while debating what it was. And if it was a shaft, artificially dug, what was it doing in the middle of a desolately dry and empty landscape? Only one way to find out.

We pulled away the sand and wooden hatchway—a clue that this had been artificially dug—and found a six-foot hole completely framed on all sides. The hole led to a small ditch. It looked like the opening of a mine shaft. Could this be the place we were looking for?

Around the opening was dark sand that grew lighter the farther away from the hole you walked. Also, the sand just over the small shaft looked as if it had collapsed into the shaft. It looked like something had exploded underground, blew out a cavern, and the heavy sand collapsed into it. What could be inside that shaft?

Before doing any exploration of the interior of that shaft, Ronnie and Pat both lowered their Geiger counters into the hole to measure for radiation. We noticed a slight uptick in the clicks, but the dials showed that it was insignificant. No serious levels of radiation. The hole was safe from a radioactive-contamination standpoint. Safe, at least it looked that way, to explore from the inside.

Pat lowered himself into the hole while Ronnie collected soil samples, and I lowered a camera to Pat along with a small shovel while he pulled away the dirt from the opening of the shaft, making sure that there was enough support around the hole and shaft so that the dirt wouldn't collapse.

Gradually, what seemed to be only a hole at first turned out to be an entrance. What the entrance led to wasn't any bigger than a crawl space, but inside the crawl space, Pat could feel around for what might be stuffed in there. Slowly, he pulled out metal parts, struts, small beams, a rim from a wheel, and gasoline tanks that had burn marks all over them. Around the periphery of the hole and mine shaft, Ronnie Millione was filling up sample vials of soil, some of which still smelled like oil. The greater the distance from the hole, the cleaner the sand. Right on top of the hole, in the mound that had collapsed, the sand seemed saturated with oil.

Noe and Ruben were exploring the perimeter and began bringing back parts of wreckage: a landing-gear strut, an entire wheel and tire, more cans of fuel oil, shards of windshield glass, and perhaps the strut from a wing. Strange as it seemed, Pat, Noe, and Ruben were all collecting the same type of debris and similar khaki petroleum cans or gas cans that had U.S. Army labels. We didn't want to jump to any conclusions, but, we said to one another, this looked like something had been deliberately buried or exploded here inside that small mine shaft. We debated the nature of the shaft. Was it a well that turned out to be dry? Was the debris from a house or structure that someone was trying to build? But why the landing gear and the glass? Why the army gasoline cans and why the oil-soaked sand? What happened here?

Working on the scant but significant evidence that we had, we formed the theory that we had probably discovered the spot where something—debris from a plane—had been deliberately burned under the ground, disposed of to keep it secret. If this was the case, then, as UFO hunters with Ruben Uriarte and Noe Torres, we had actually discovered the spot referred to in the Deneb report where a U.S. Army retrieval team had buried the debris from a private plane that had crashed into a UFO. It was a huge find.

We bagged and tagged the evidence we collected along with the soil samples from locations A (at the shaft site) through D (farthest away from the shaft site) and packaged them for delivery to California. We also packed up our gear and headed for the next Coyame desert location, the purported site of the plane crash. We may have discovered the disposal site, but would we be as fortunate to discover anything indicating we had found the actual plane-crash site?

Using Ruben's coordinates, we drove along the road to where he believed we should form a search grid, got out of the bus, broke into separate groups, and began traversing the search pattern. It wasn't long before Noe's group called out to the rest of us across the expanse of sand. They had found something. It was a complete landing gear. We spread out across the area and found other parts as well, such as pieces of a dashboard, a portion of a window, and more struts and other pieces of metal. Ronnie Millione ran his Geiger counter over the pieces but found no radiation signature. We looked for, but did not find, any identifying numbers that we could use to check for ownership of the plane. Perhaps these had been burned at the other location. But we did find parts that looked like they had come from a plane.

We bagged and tagged these parts again, believing that if there was any trace evidence, residue of a composite that Ted Acworth called unobtainium or alternatively called unknownium, that would tell us something. If we could get these things out of Mexico, they would go to one of our laboratories in California for testing.

The sun was setting as we got back onto the bus, congratulating one another on finding some evidence, some pieces of substantiation for claims made in the Deneb report that, first, there had been a collision between two aircraft over the Coyame desert resulting in debris on the ground, and, second, that some of that debris was brought to another site, not far from the original crash site, for disposal. We had found a site where something had been exploded, burned, and buried. And we found what looked to be a crash site with parts of a plane. If that was all we would discover, at least there were parts of the Deneb report, regardless of its source, that we had shown likely to be accurate. We hadn't found any evidence of a UFO, but we had found evidence of an attempt to dispose of debris and another site where there was debris from a plane. And these sites were just over a ridge of hills from the American border and one of the largest military installations in the American Southwest.

THE TOWN OF COYAME

If it hadn't been for the Humvees with machine gun mounts and the Mexican army deuce and a half that followed us along the road from the desert, the journey would have been uneventful until we reached the village of Coyame. But the small army convoy was persistent, and, when we reached another military checkpoint, we had to exit the bus again, and again at gunpoint, while the soldiers spoke to us through our local interpreter, Ruben and Noe letting me know that what was being said was OK. This time, the soldiers wanted to know what we were doing in the desert, what we were looking for, and what we found. We were up front with them, telling them we wanted to locate the sites of a UFO crash reported decades ago. We made it clear we found no identifiable parts of a UFO, whatever those parts might look like, but did find wreckage out there, which they could look at for themselves. They shrugged, not interested in trekking through the desert, and let us go on our way after checking our passports and entry visas. They continued on their way and we headed south to the village.

We hit the village of Coyame on a chilly night, but a festival was in progress. There were lights strung all around the town square, and the sheriff and the mayor were out to lead us to witnesses. Local ranchers talked about cattle mutilations and how strange lights hovered over their fields at night. In the mornings they would find cows lying on their sides in a state of semiparalysis, clearly dead, but with no predators, birds, or even insects around them. It was as if nature itself recognized that something strange had happened to the cow and kept her other species away.

By far the strangest story we heard came from the mayor's wife, a tiny woman who explained that she was the repository of information from the local farmers and ranchers. She told us that at first she didn't believe what she was hearing. But then she saw an event with her own eyes that turned her into a believer. For months, she said, locals approached her with stories of flying saucers that seemed to arise from right out of the earth. Then one day when she was hanging her wash out on the line to dry, she heard a humming sound and turned around to look at the field outside her backyard. She saw a bubble in the earth, and then, through the bubble, a flying saucer, a disk-shaped saucer, emerged, hovered over the ground for a few minutes, and slowly ascended until it was hundreds of feet in the air and sped off in an instant. That, she said, turned her into a believer.

When all the interviews were completed and videotaped, we left the village for the drive to Mexico City, where we were scheduled to depart the next morning for Los Angeles, where we were to film the segments at the laboratories.

THE AIRPORT

The international airport in Mexico City was directly responsible for our coming together as a family on the road, as more than just a reality-television crew. A crew filming a television show starts out as a bunch of professionals, each doing his or her own job. But ultimately, you have to enjoy it and develop a trust for one another such that you're taking care of one another. The craziness at the Mexico City airport cemented us together during that first season and actually made *UFO Hunters* a stronger show.

We were dead tired when the bus dropped us off at the airport. One of the drivers was about to lose his job because he was sleeping at his post when a stranger walked past him onto the bus and stole one of our computers. We had spent over forty-eight hours on a converted tour bus, had been held at gunpoint by Mexican military units twice, had been chased out of a sugarcane field by Mexican police intelligence units, had weathered an unbelievable thunder and lightning storm that allowed us only one or two hours' sleep before heading back to film at Xilitla, and had crawled across areas of the Coyame desert looking for crash debris at two locations. We wanted to settle back into our airplane seats and sleep until we arrived in LA. But it was almost not to be.

We arrived at the airport early, saying good-bye to our drivers and making sure that all the equipment was unloaded. Our interpreter went looking for the appropriate customs officer to check our camera equipment through, making sure the entry manifest of equipment corresponded, piece by piece, with the exit manifest of the equipment. While the field coordinators and crew chief went over the equipment manifest for the exit visa, the rest of us searched for the customs officials to get our visas stamped. But there were no customs stands at our departure terminal. We went to the departure gate for our flight to check in, and the gate agent told us not to worry about the exit visas. He would take care of them as we boarded. So we sat down and stretched out until they called for preboarding. When we went up to present our tickets, the gate official was gone and another agent told us that we couldn't board without exit-visa stamps.

Panic. The plane was boarding, there were no customs kiosks open at this terminal, and this was the last flight out that night. Where's the customs kiosk? The gate agent pointed to a distant terminal accessible only by moving walkways that were out of service.

We began running, and running, and running. And we had to drag along our carry-ons. Computer bags banging, suitcases rolling, we ran across the terminal, sweat drenching us, until we came to the long line at the only open customs desk. Jumping up and down to catch the attention of the sleepy official robotically stamping paperwork at the head of the line, we used our best Los Angeles Spanglish to catch the guy's attention. Finally, our interpreter arrived and between him and the field coordinator, Dan Zarenkiewicz, they convinced the customs officer to rouse his dosing partner stretched out on an chair next to the booth to expedite our exit visas. As the sleepy official stamped away, not looking at us or at our passports, we sent runners back to the gate to hold the plane until we had our paperwork complete. Finally, at the end, he stamped the equipment exit manifest, stuffed it under the desk, and waved us off. One of our runners came back: the exit gate was closing. No time to run.

Alan LaGarde, our director and coexecutive producer, spotted an electric cart, more like a golf cart, sitting in a passenger area. "Grab it," he yelled, and we ran for the cart, piling aboard, even sitting on one another's shoulders as if we were characters in a Marx Brothers movie. "Hang on, we're off," he shouted, and we hung on for dear life as he gunned the electric cart, horn beeping away, through the terminal. "Perdón, perdón," we yelled at passengers frantically trying to get out of our way, mothers yanking children by the hand, terminal personnel looking at us in horror. Finally, one of the gate agents ran in front of us and pushed the passengers out of our path. Like a traffic cop, he waved us on, telling LaGarde to flatten the accelerator. Then he ran ahead and shouted to the gate agent to hold the plane.

LaGarde pulled the cart right up to the Jetway as the agent waved us on, telling us to drop our exit visas as we ran into the overly air-conditioned corridor. Flight attendants got us right to our seats and stowed our carry-ons forward, and we heard the cabin doors close behind us. "We're a family now," I heard LaGarde say, and the plane was pushed from the Jetway onto the taxiway as the engines whined in happiness.

Indeed, we were.

LAB WORK: CAPCO

Our first stop when we got back to California was to Capco Laboratories in Ventura for the testing of the ash and soil samples from Xilitla and Coyame. To break the ash sample apart, Capco used gas chromatography to analyze the components of the sample. They were also looking for the traces of petroleum in the soil samples in Coyame to determine whether the material we found in the mine shaft might have been the debris from an explosion and fire and thus comported with the story in the Deneb report.

The Xilitla ash sample, Capco determined, had much higher sulfur levels than it should have had, enough sulfur to show that whatever the core substance was, it had been subjected to an intense fire. But what might have caused that fire? With the results in hand, we drove to Tindall's lab to see if he could demonstrate any events that would have resulted in the amounts of sulfurous ash that we found. Moreover, because the ashes were not disintegrated, Ted wanted to know if Tindall could help us determine the nature of the ashes. Could they have resulted from a powerful explosive force rendering parts of a circuit into an ash?

First, Ted Acworth and John Tindall set out to demonstrate how an EMP event, whether it was the result of the propulsion system of a spacecraft or the result of the explosion of that propulsion system, could disrupt the police radios in Xilitla for over half an hour. And if such a powerful EMP event could also disintegrate electrical circuitry, turning it into ash, as well as kill anyone caught inside that EMP envelope.

John Tindall ran a powerful electric current through copper wire, and, in an instant, the wire turned into a long ribbon of ash. He did this a couple more times and the results were always the same. Powerful current applied to thin copper wiring rendered it an ash ribbon, much like the Xilitla ash ribbons Carlos Arillano gave us in Mexico. Then, as we suspected, when John tested how an EMP event would affect radio transmissions, such as police walkie-talkies and car radios, the EMP totally shut down any communication. It also interfered with electrical ignition systems such as spark plugs. Thus Tindall demonstrated that an intense EMP event would render copper wire into ash and at the same time shut down radio transmissions.

CAPCO'S TESTING OF THE COYAME DESERT SOIL SAMPLES

Using gas chromatography, the chemists at Capco discovered that the soil samples from Coyame, samples taken at four points from inside the mine shaft out into the area beyond the barbed-wire fence, contained levels of VOCs, the highest from the mine shaft itself. VOCs are volatile organic compounds, defined by the federal government as chemical compounds that easily vaporize into the atmosphere, such as methane, formaldehyde, and many simple household cleaning substances. The soil samples farthest from the mine shaft were completely free of volatile organic chemicals. However, the sample from the mine shaft and the one right near the hole contained measurable traces of hydrocarbons, which are petroleum products. These hydrocarbons, our lab analysts said, were actually typical motor oil.

Ted suggested that because the concentrations of volatiles seemed to increase inside the mine shaft, according to the lab analysis, this was consistent with the theory that someone had exploded something inside that shaft, infusing the soil with volatile chemicals from the force of the explosion. That would explain why there were no volatile chemicals at the two test points farthest away from the mine shaft and a measurable concentration from the mine shaft itself. It would also explain the dark color of the soil inside the mine shaft and the light color of the sandy soil outside the barbed-wire area around the shaft.

Considering what we found in the Coyame desert and the analysis of the soil from the desert, the results of our expedition supported the part of the Deneb report that talked about the two desert sites and the disposal of parts of an aircraft that a U.S. military ops team might have performed by digging a shaft and exploding or burning significant evidence not just of the aircraft, but of parts of the aircraft that might be toxic from any virus aboard an otherworldly craft.

With respect to the Xilitla incident, Ted suggested, it is intriguing that the reason we were able to obtain only a small amount of sulfuric ribbon ash was that the police had moved in right after the crash and collected all the ash they could find from the villagers, who originally collected it. As our informant from the Mexican intelligence services also said, his bureau clamped down a cone of silence around the entire event and filed his report away in a place where he would never see it again. Something had happened that the authorities didn't want anyone to know about. And we still haven't figured out why.

BILL'S BLOG

The Mexico trip was full of shocks. We were thrilled that our exploration of the Coyame desert yielded locations, and debris at locations, that coincided with the descriptions in the Deneb report. Did we prove that the Deneb report had described a real event? No. But did we find evidence that was consistent enough with what the Deneb report described that it substantiated, at the very least, that something took place in those locations? Yes.

In particular, we found a fabricated pit, not just a naturally occurring hole in the sand, but an actual shaft braced up with supporting beams that indicated someone was deliberate in digging it and then leaving it open for people to work in. Inside that pit we found petroleum cans and parts of what looked like a plane. The soil looked as though something had been exploded underground and the coloration of the soil indicated that a substance had been blown out from the hole. And the soil tests corroborated what we had eyeballed because volatile chemicals were in their highest concentrations inside the hole and diminished to zero in our control sample collected outside the barbed-wire fence.

And why would someone enclose that hole within a barbed-wire fence with wooden posts way out in the middle of a desert? Clearly that made no sense unless someone wanted to fence something in or out. Was this done to prevent whatever had killed the Mexican soldiers from infecting the local population?

In the village of Xilitla the local residents all corroborated one another's description of the event. And the heavy police response corroborated with the testimony from the intelligence officer that those in command took the Xilitla report very seriously. All of the ash, except for a small amount that we were able to recover from one of the officers, had been seized and locked away. What we were able to test returned results that were consistent with some sort of electrical circuitry that had been vaporized by a powerful EMP event. Such a powerful EMP event certainly would have knocked out the radio transmission in the area, and, in fact, it did.

Xilitla, high in a mountain and battered by a thunder and lightning storm that shook the earth like an angry deity punishing the residents of a tiny village, was out of a fairy tale. When we returned the morning after with only a couple of hours' sleep, the reactions of the villagers who offered us the best corn cakes we had ever had were a gift. And we got the story even as the rain storm that had lashed the mountain was drizzling away in the morning haze.

We also had the experience of being held at gunpoint, not a fun thing, but it was especially fearful when those holding the guns are so young you have to wonder whether they know what guns can do. These troops seemed to us to be just a tick up from boy soldiers. And when Ruben Uriarte jerked his thumb toward the machine gun nest behind a sandbag emplacement, we knew these teenage soldiers meant business.

The police chase after we interviewed the intelligence officer, the military checkpoints, and the trip on the bus itself—thirty hours across Mexico—were all events I'll never forget. Nor will I forget the sheriff of Coyame, a big Western lawman out of Hollywood central casting with two long-barreled six-guns in a double cowboy holster and wearing a ten-gallon hat, who showed me the hospitality of a Mexican jail. "See how cold it is inside?" he asked. "So be good." Didn't have to tell me twice.

Just when it was all over, when we believed we were finally heading home to where we could get some real rest in our real homes, it was a final marathon. The sleepy slow-motion customs officers had no urgency in getting us onto our plane, and the wild ride through the airport terminal on a hijacked golf cart from which we screamed at frightened travelers to get out of our way bonded us for the rest of the season.

In the ensuing years, we would have to encounter a gang of thugs in Poland wanting to steal our equipment, a federal police unit in Utah trying to seize our cameras and tape, and camo dudes outside Area 51 ready to challenge our presence, but our trip to Mexico following the path of the Deneb report would resonate in our collective memory as UFO hunters.

MILITARY VS. UFOS

The story of a UFO encounter over RAF Bentwaters and in Rendle-sham Forest in the United Kingdom in 1980 has become known as Britain's Roswell. Like the American Roswell, it was an inci-dent that, because of its strangeness, became the benchmark of what a UFO encounter is supposed to be. In December 1980, a strange glow-ing object flew over RAF Bentwaters, a secure NATO air base run by the United States, where nuclear weapons were stored. The incident involved the following:

- An actual UFO landing
- Landing tripod impression in the hard forest soil
- A USAF sergeant, named James Penniston, who actually touched the craft and copied in his notebook a set of sym-bols on the craft's hull
- A wild pursuit of the floating object through the woods led by the RAF Bentwaters deputy commander, who recorded the entire chase on his handheld tape recorder
- A spectacular light show in plowed farm field on the

perimeter of the forest that ended when the object, whatever it was, split into five objects and took off

- A heretofore undisclosed witness in an observation tower
who had seen the entire event

It is arguable that the mystery surrounding the incident might
have died away if the United States Air Force had gone to any lengths
to explain what had happened. But that did not happen. Instead, the
entire incident became entangled in a jurisdictional spiderweb. The
air force base was ostensibly United States territory staffed by American military personnel. However, the event took place in adjoining
Rendlesham Forest, British territory. Therefore, whose responsibility
was it to undertake the investigation, the U.K. Ministry of Defence or
the U.S. Department of Defense?

Neither agency wanted to handle this hot potato. As a result, the
case has never been fully investigated by the authorities even though
UFO researchers from both sides of the Atlantic have investigated
and extensively written about the case. Accordingly, with all the loose
ends dangling in the wind, the RAF Bentwaters and Rendlesham Forest UFO incident became the subject of our investigation on *UFO
Hunters*. But the case investigation and the episode actually began in
Washington, D.C.

THE NATIONAL PRESS CLUB DISCLOSURE CONFERENCE

In November 2007, the UFO community was abuzz with anticipation
because some of the most important witnesses to recent UFO encounters, all of them professional pilots or aviation officials, were
gathering at the National Press Club in Washington, D.C., to tell their
stories to the international and American press corps. The press conference, assembled by Leslie Kean and filmmaker James Fox, whose
film *Out of the Blue* was getting wide acclaim, brought together some
of the most important witnesses over the previous fifty years. We

were happy to have gotten an invitation to cover the event for the show and used footage that we shot there for three episodes in our first two seasons.

The first group of speakers comprised the witnesses to the December 1980 incident at RAF Bentwaters and Rendlesham Forest, an incident covered in Larry Warren's firsthand eyewitness account in his book *Left at East Gate*, with Peter Robbins (Marlow, 1998). Two of the speakers were former USAF Lieutenant Colonel Charles Halt, the deputy commander of RAF Bentwaters, and former USAF Staff Sergeant James Penniston, a member of Charles Halt's security detail investigating the strange lights over the base at the end of December 1980. In their dual presentations, Charles Halt described the entire incident and how he became involved when security personnel reported to him that they had witnessed a strange object penetrating restricted airspace over the base. James Penniston described that he'd been a part of the security detail accompanying Halt and what he saw in the clearing in the forest, that he touched the strange object that had landed, and that he saw writing or lettering on the side of it.

The incident, as Halt and Penniston described it, defied conventional attempts to explain it. Yet over the years, skeptics had come out of the woodwork to assert many conventional explanations for what the United States Air Force personnel say they witnessed, explanations that seemed even more anomalous than the possibility that the security detail on successive nights had witnessed an encounter with an unearthly craft. Because there were so many strange attempts at explaining these events conventionally, including a bizarre statement that trained air force personnel panicked and thought they saw something that wasn't there, *UFO Hunters* decided to go to Rendlesham; connect with our old friend, retired U.K. Ministry of Defence officer Nick Pope; and, along with Charles Halt, go through every plausible explanation for the RAF Bentwaters incident to see if science could separate myth from reality.

THE BENTWATERS INCIDENT

As intriguing and exciting as the Bentwaters incident was, investigating it was for us like unraveling a tangled ball of twine: there were so many witnesses observing strange sights from different positions and angles that it was almost as if different people saw entirely different events. Also, the Bentwaters incident took place over different nights so that depending on whom you're talking to, you get a different perspective. As we listened to the witnesses make their presentations at the National Press Club conference, we decided that the main throughline of the story was the experience of Charles Halt, the deputy base commander, because he recorded a running commentary of the entire event on the third night on his voice recorder. Nevertheless, the events began even before Lieutenant Colonel Halt became involved, when security personnel at Bentwaters responded to reports of strange lights buzzing overhead and a possible landing in Rendlesham Forest, an area that separates RAF Bentwaters from RAF Woodbridge.

The first sightings took place at 3 A.M. on December 26, 1980, when U.S. Air Force security spotted lights over the east gate at RAF Bentwaters. At first, according to Larry Warren in *Left at East Gate*, the security team thought it was an aircraft that had gone down, and a team went to investigate. But it was not a downed aircraft at all. Leaving the base and venturing into Rendlesham Forest, which was equivalent to leaving United States territory and entering the United Kingdom, the security team saw a series of lights in the sky moving through the forest. They came upon a glowing object, roughly the shape of an egg or a cone, hovering just off the ground. According to members of the team, the object then landed, leaving impressions from its triangular-shaped landing gear in the wet sand. Air Force Sergeant Jim Penniston, part of the security detail, said that he actually touched the object and made sketches of lettering he said he saw along the object's body.

Later that morning, just after daybreak, the servicemen returned to the spot in the forest where the object was reported to have landed and saw three landing impressions in the soft sand. Jim Penniston took plaster casts of the impressions, casts that he displayed to the audience at the National Press Club Disclosure Conference in November 2007. Penniston also posted on the Internet a copy of the graphics he said he saw on the object. Later that morning, local British police were summoned back to the site to see the landing impressions. The police had been there before dawn investigating the lights and believed them to be from the Orford Ness lighthouse, which is nearby on the coast of the North Sea. The police were reported to have said that the landing impressions in the sand were the marks of small animals. They were "rabbit scrapings," a local resident had said, which made no sense to us because rabbits tend to dig into the ground at an angle, and these impressions were relatively shallow and were straight down, as if they resulted from compression, not digging.

Colonel Halt told us that news of the strange events had circulated through the command structure, when, at a post-Christmas and pre–New Year's party, he was notified that the strange lights were back. Halt was a skeptic and believed there was nothing to the strange-lights story. He assured his boss, the wing commander, Gordon Williams, that he would investigate this incident himself and get to the bottom of whatever it was. It was, he told *UFO Hunters* in this episode, his intention to go out there and "put it all to rest." What he found out would effectively change his life.

With reports that the lights were back, Colonel Halt led a security team through the east gate of the base into Rendlesham Forest where, technically, the United States Air Force had no authority. But any threat to the perimeter of the base needed to be investigated, and that was Colonel Halt's job that night. In addition to his security detail, Halt had ordered up powerful lights to illuminate the area outside the base and, of course, a communications system to keep the different security details in contact with each other.

Charles Halt was, and still is, a very meticulous person. On December 27, 1980, Colonel Halt brought along his Lanier voice recorder to preserve a verbal memo of any incidents the security detail might witness so he could include all of them in a report he knew he would write. He assumed, being very skeptical about the appearance of strange things, that the incident he was investigating was much ado about nothing. But he also kept an open mind and figured that if his trusted security personnel reported something, there might be something there. He never expected to encounter what the team observed as they made their way into the forest.

On Colonel Halt's voice recording, he describes a light playing through the trees as his team entered Rendlesham Forest. Halt later said in his presentation at the November 2007 National Press Club conference that the lights he saw seemed to have affected the radio transmitters since they intermittently cut out, causing some confusion among the members of the security detail. Colonel Halt said that he and his team followed the lights deeper into the forest, where the rounded triangular-shaped craft that had been observed the night before led his men through the forest and to the edge of a clearing.

Staff Sergeant James Penniston, who was part of the detail the night before, had said in his presentation that when his team entered the forest to observe the lights, the object descended through the trees and touched down on the forest floor, its three landing pads making a triangular impression in the cold dirt. While the team watched the object in awe, Penniston carefully took note of its size and shape. As he told the gathering at the National Press Club, it was a "triangular craft" about nine feet long and six and a half feet high that had blue and yellow lights swirling around its surface.

"We started experiencing radio difficulties," Penniston said. "The air around us was electrically charged and we could feel it on our clothes, our skin, and our hair." Penniston approached it and laid his hands upon its surface. Although it was glowing brightly, the object, Penniston said, was cold to the touch. Penniston also noticed that there were designs, hieroglyphics almost, along the side of the object, the largest of which was a triangle in the center. He sketched these in a notebook he had brought along to record the events of the evening.

After what seemed to be almost forty-five minutes, the bright object lifted off the forest floor and shot away through the trees in "the blink of an eye," Penniston said. "And over eighty air force personnel witnessed the takeoff."

On the second night, the triangular object that led the pursuing security detail to the edge of the clearing touched down on the ground as if it were waiting. As Halt told us during his appearance in the episode, the object that landed in the clearing was so bright that its light reflected off the windows of a farmhouse at the other edge of the clearing, making the house look as if it were on fire. The air force detail didn't approach the object again because the object was now on private property, a farm that was off-limits to air force personnel absent permission from the landowner.

While Halt and his men watched the object from the edge of the forest, it seemed to grow brighter and suddenly split into five different lights, all of which suddenly took off and could be seen shooting over the treetops and into the sky. The men were still awestruck by the entire sequence of events. Some members of the detail were disoriented by the incident, but others were fully alert and wanted to report what had happened.

Halt kept a copy of his voice recording and wrote out a full report of the incident. He later signed an affidavit in which he said that he believed what he and his men saw was an actual extraterrestrial object. He wrote in his affidavit:

"I believe the objects that I saw at close quarter were extraterrestrial in origin and that the security services of both the United States and the United Kingdom have attempted—both then and now—to subvert the significance of what occurred at Rendlesham Forest and RAF Bentwaters by the use of well-practiced methods of disinformation."

Halt was referring to the fact that in the aftermath of the incident, both the United States Air Force and the U.K. Ministry of Defence were given copies of Halt's report and also eyewitness accounts of the entire incident. They also had access to James Penniston's sketch of the graphics on the object, but neither defense agency did anything. What made matters worse was that in the aftermath of the incident, investigators took radiation readings from the object's landing site and found that the radiation at the site was many times higher than the background radiation. And Penniston himself took plaster casts of the impressions made by the landing gear of the craft, casts that he showed at the 2007 National Press Club conference so as to corroborate, along with the radiation report, that there was physical trace evidence of the event he and Charles Halt described. In interviews, Penniston has said that the light was no illusion, nor was it the light from a nearby lighthouse. It was, he said at the National Press Club conference, "definitely mechanical in nature."

In summary, the object, in addition to having been witnessed by multiple professional service personnel, also left palpable and measurable trace evidence on the ground. But still, neither the British nor the Americans pursued any official inquiry into the incident. And this is what made Colonel Halt frustrated at the official lack of response.

The initial release of information from former USAF personnel, including the book *Left at East Gate*, by former air force serviceman Larry Warren and Peter Robbins, prompted a flurry of skeptical responses. Most of the responses centered on the nature of the light, such as claims that the air force personnel mistook the beacon from the Orford Ness lighthouse as the light that led them through the forest. Other debunkers, seeking to discredit the Bentwaters sighting reports even further, interviewed residents who lived by the base who claimed that the Americans misinterpreted the ground impressions of "rabbit scrapings." However, at least one of the residents, who was adamant about what he said was the Americans' lack of understanding about what they actually saw, also admitted that days after the incident he had been visited by plainclothes investigators from an unnamed British agency, who interrogated him about the incident and suggested he reject any speculation about UFOs. Who were these men asking about what had happened in Rendlesham Forest even before Colonel Halt had filed his report? How did they know there was an incident in the forest? How did they arrive on the scene so quickly?

One wonders whether the sudden appearance of these men and their immediate response to an incident that hadn't actually been reported yet was more of an intimidation than an information-gathering visit. The witness in question, one Vincent Thurkettle, whom Pat Uskert interviewed on *UFO Hunters,* admitted that he talked to the investigators and told them that he didn't believe the American service personnel saw anything anomalous. He said that he, too, believed they saw the light from the Orford Ness lighthouse and mistook holes that rabbits had dug for the impressions of the landing craft.

Colonel Halt, both on the record and on *UFO Hunters,* flat out rejected Thurkettle's characterization of the light in the forest and the skeptics' claims that the Americans mistook what they saw. Halt said on the show:

> "While in Rendlesham Forest, our security team observed a light that looked like a large eye, red in color, moving through the trees. After a few minutes this object began dripping something that looked like molten metal. A short while later it broke into several smaller, white-colored objects, which flew away in all directions. Claims by skeptics that this was merely a sweeping beam from a distant lighthouse are unfounded. We could see the unknown light and the lighthouse simultaneously. The latter was thirty to forty degrees off where all of this was happening."

Could Halt and his men have seen the lighthouse beacon and the light from the object simultaneously? That was one of the statements that special-effects producer John Tindall and Dr. Ted Acworth set out to test.

In order to facilitate this test and absent a UFO making its way into the clearing, we did two things to simulate the effects. First, we spoke to the lighthouse keeper at Orford Ness and asked whether it was possible for the beam to reach into the forest and to thus be confused with an illuminated flying object on the ground. This, the lighthouse keeper said, was impossible because a metal bar across the lighthouse lens, in place in December 1980, would have kept the beam from sweeping the forest floor. Also, he suggested, even if it weren't for the metal barrier, service personnel from RAF Bentwaters would have recognized the lighthouse beacon because they would have regularly seen it. In this case, the appearance of the light was completely anomalous and didn't resemble the lighthouse beacon in the least.

As for the simulation test itself, to see whether Charles Halt was right about having been able to see the beacon and the object in the clearing at the same time, Tindall and Acworth took GPS readings that comported with the positions Colonel Halt gave us. With each waypoint, Tindall and Acworth mapped out the locations of Halt's team, the location of the object, the location of the beacon, and the location of the farmhouse where the windows reflected the light from the object. Tindall then constructed a scale model of the entire landscape area, farmhouse and all. He then positioned the beacon and the object according to the GPS waypoints and demonstrated what would happen were the beacon and the object to be visible at the same time.

Tindall demonstrated that the beacon from the lighthouse and the light from the unidentified object in the clearing would have been clearly visible to Halt and his team at the same time. The beacon was to the right of the object, and the object itself as well as its reflection would have been visible as separate lights. Thus, Halt's explanation that he and his team could not have mistaken the Orford Ness lighthouse beacon for an unidentified object was accurate and was substantiated by our experiments on *UFO Hunters* as well as by the lighthouse keeper himself. Moreover, as Colonel Halt explained to the November 2007 audience at the National Press Club conference, the personnel at

RAF Bentwaters were well aware of the presence of the Orford Ness lighthouse and are certainly able to distinguish the very familiar beacon from any anomalous light in the forest.

THE HALT REPORT

Six months after the incident in Rendlesham Forest, Charles Halt wrote a full report to the United States Air Force. The report, which Colonel Halt affirmed for *UFO Hunters*, set forth his full description of the incident. It read as follows:

Department of the Air Force
Headquarter 81st Combat Support Group (USAFE)
APO NEW YORK DY735

13 Jan 81
Reply to Attn of: CD
Subject: Unexplained Lights

To: RAF/CC

1. Early in the morning of 27 Dec 80 (approximately 0300L), two USAF security police patrolmen saw unusual lights outside the back gate at RAF Woodbridge. Thinking an aircraft might have crashed or been forced down, they called for permission to go outside the gate to investigate. The on-duty flight chief responded and allowed three patrolmen to proceed on foot. The individuals reported seeing a strange glowing object in the forest. The Object was described as being metallic in appearance and triangular in shape, approximately two and three meters across the base and approximately two meters high. It illuminated the entire forest with a white light. The object itself had a pulsing red light on top and a bank(s) of blue lights underneath. The object was hovering or on legs. As the patrolmen approached the object, it maneuvered through the trees and disappeared. At this time

the animals on a nearby farm went into frenzy. The object was briefly sighted approximately an hour later near the back gate.

2.   The next day, three depressions 1 ½" deep and 7" in diameter were found where the object had been sighted on the ground. The following night (29 Dec 80) the area was checked for radiation. Beta/gamma readings of 0.1 milliroentgens were recorded with peak readings in the three depressions and near the center of the triangle formed by the depressions. A nearby tree had moderate (.05–.07) readings on the side of the tree toward the depressions.

3.   Later in the night a red sun-like light was seen through the trees. It moved about and pulsed. At one point it appeared to throw off glowing particles and then broke into five separate white objects and then disappeared. Immediately thereafter, three star-like objects were noticed in the sky, two objects to the north and one to the south, all of which were about 10 degrees off the horizon. The objects moved rapidly in sharp angular movements and displayed red, green and blue lights. The objects to the north appeared to be elliptical through an 8-12 power lens. They then turned to full circles. The objects to the north remained in the sky for an hour or more. The object to the south was visible for two or three hours and beamed down a stream of light from time to time. Numerous individuals, including the undersigned, witnessed the activities in paragraphs 2 and 3.

Charles I. Halt, Lt. Col. USAF
Deputy Base Commander

If Charles Halt had hoped that his very inconvenient memo would stir those in both the USAF and RAF, as well as in the Ministry of Defence higher command, to investigate this entire incident, he was to be disappointed. The immediate result of the Halt report was complete silence. His own commanding officer believed that Halt had overreached by writing the memo and thought that the events the security team encountered were completely conventional. Skeptics and debunkers attacked the witness stories about unidentified flying objects landing in the forest, and the air force personnel witnesses, according to witness Larry Warren, were subjected to hostile and aggressive debriefings.

Former U.K. Ministry of Defence spokesperson Nick Pope, a respected author and UFO researcher (*Open Skies, Closed Minds* [Pocket, 1997]), has said that there were a number of reasons why the U.K. Ministry of Defence shied away from getting involved in the case. First, he said, higher-ups at the ministry believed that because American servicemen were involved at what was essentially an American-staffed NATO base, it was the U.S. Department of Defense that should have investigated the incident.

For their part, the Americans seemed to argue that because the actual event took place on U.K. territory—Rendlesham Forest—and not on the RAF Bentwaters base itself, authority to investigate belonged to the British, therefore removing the burden of dealing with Colonel Halt's report from the U.S. defense establishment. This was convenient, Nick Pope said on *UFO Hunters* and in a number of radio interviews, because it allowed each side to push the burden of the investigation onto the other side. Accordingly, neither side actually investigated the incident, and the personnel who witnessed the events are still left wondering what really was behind the whole thing.

"YOU CAN'T TELL THE PEOPLE"

Pope also pointed to two other interesting postincident developments as independent researchers in the U.K. pursued their inquiries. First, British journalist and UFO researcher Georgina Bruni, in her book *You Can't Tell the People* (Sidgwick and Jackson, 2000; rpt. Pan Macmillan, 2001), reported her brief conversation with U.K. Prime Minister Margaret Thatcher in which she asked the prime minister about the 1980 RAF Bentwaters / Rendlesham Forest incident. The prime minister was said to have replied that, when it came to UFOs, "you had to get your facts straight." And that there are some things, presumably relating to UFOs, that "you just can't tell the people." This quote is for many UFO researchers one of the most telling statements imaginable because, without admitting to anything, Prime Minister Thatcher admitted to everything. Were there no secrets regarding UFOs, indeed were there no UFOs at all, the prime minister would have simply dismissed the question or laughed it off. However, because, as those of us in the UFO research field believe, the entire subject of the reality of UFOs and what their existence implies is so secret, Margaret Thatcher (not one given to outright lying) simply admitted that the subject can't be talked about because the people, presumably all of us, can't be allowed to know the truth.

While Margaret Thatcher's statement is a piece of dynamite for me, for Nick Pope it was a series of statements by former Admiral of the Fleet Lord Peter Hill-Norton that caught his attention. Lord Hill-Norton, the former defence chief of the United Kingdom, was a member of the House of Lords when he asked the government whether there was any involvement of the U.K.'s Special Branch in the investigation of the Rendlesham Forest incident. He was told that because there was no threat to British national security, there was no investigation. However, Lord Hill-Norton said, "Either large numbers of people were hallucinating, and for an American Air Force nuclear base this is extremely dangerous, or what they say happened did happen, and in either of those circumstances there can only be one answer, and that is that it was of extreme defence interest" (quoted by Nick Pope on his Web site, http://www.nickpope.net/rendlesham_forest.htm).

Admiral Lord Hill-Norton's comment is as logical as it is insightful. He correctly assumed that for a group of American servicemen, including the deputy base commander, to have been so deluded about what they were seeing and yet, at the same time, to have been the service personnel in charge of nuclear weapons on British soil, would certainly be an issue of national security worth investigating. On the other hand, if a hallucinating custodian of nuclear weapons is a threat, what is a far greater potential threat is the presence of an otherworldly craft interfering with the routine of a NATO nuclear weapons facility. And he believed that the Americans were far from deluded and traipsing through the woods on a winter night in pursuit of a hallucination.

To this day, the fundamental truth of what happened in Rendlesham Forest has not been established. Charles Halt, James Penniston, Larry Warren, and others to this day assert that they know what they saw. Their case is bolstered by the four prongs of UFO evidence: multiple credible witnesses, documentary substantiation, physical trace evidence, and bizarre government or quasi-government reaction to the event.

Multiple Credible Witnesses

Charles Halt, James Penniston, Larry Warren, Sergeant John Burroughs, and others all said that they saw strange and anomalous lights in Rendlesham Forest on the 26, 27, and 28 of December 1980. All of these individuals were United States Air Force command and security personnel serving at a highly classified and secure NATO nuclear weapons storage base during the Cold War.

Documentary Substantiation

Not only do we have the report filed by Colonel Halt, but we have documentation in the form of the "Halt tape," the voice recording that Charles Halt made on his Lanier device while the actual incident in the forest was unfolding. This ongoing commentary, which was played on History Channel's "*UFO Files*: Britain's Roswell" as well as on *UFO Hunters* is probably some of the best documentary evidence available because, to this day, it is the only moment-by-moment description by a highly credible witness in a classified military facility of an anomalous event affecting the security of that facility. Remember, Charles Halt did not go out into the forest to find a UFO. He went out into the forest on a security detail to, in his words, "put a stop" to all the nonsense about a light in the forest. Accordingly, he assembled a highly qualified security detail, complete with powerful Light-Alls (intense lights) and secure radio transceivers. What he discovered was not at all what he expected.

When Charles Halt reported in writing on what he encountered in the forest, he was ignored by the higher-ups, criticized by his commanding officer, and excoriated by skeptics and debunkers. Yet throughout, Charles Halt was only doing what he was ordered to do: provide for the security of RAF Bentwaters and the United States Air Force personnel under his command. On December 28, 1980, he was investigating a possible security threat to the base, which was his job.

The other piece of documentary evidence, which Nick Pope characterized as "chilling," was the official Ministry of Defence corroboration of the high radiation levels in the three landing impressions made by the craft. Because the ministry acknowledged the high radiation levels at the landing site, that acknowledgment, and other documents in the Rendlesham file, amount to nothing less than an "audit trail," as Nick Pope described it, of a UFO encounter. The investigation of the Bentwaters incident is all documented and the evidence memorialized in official memos and reports, setting forth one of the most complete paper trails of a UFO encounter in any official archive.

Physical Trace Evidence

Perhaps the most important form of evidence of UFO contact is physical evidence, evidence that conforms to Locard's theory of transference, in which when an object comes into contact with another object, each leaves trace material on the other. In the Rendlesham Forest case, when the object was observed by Colonel Halt and his detail to have landed, James Penniston touched the object and copied certain designs on the side of the object into his notebook. The landing area also tested positively for radiation, and plaster casts were taken of the landing impressions in the forest floor. Nick Pope reminded *UFO Hunters* that because this event took place in the dead of winter, the ground was hard. Thus the object had to have been very heavy to have made those impressions.

The physical evidence and the reports thereof still exist today and are strong substantiating evidence that an event took place where the witnesses said it took place.

Bizarre Government or Quasi-Government Reaction to the Event

We have often said on *UFO Hunters* that if you look at the images of a black hole you will see that light bends around it, swirling into its complete darkness. So it is with reality around the black hole of a lie. Reality, the rational behavior of individuals, institutions, and even governments, contorts and bends around the center of a lie. The bigger and more massive the falsehood, the more reality bends to conform to covering it up. This phenomenon is most apparent around the riddle of the existence of UFOs. Find a strong UFO case, and you will find that rational people, especially those in bureaucracies, go to great lengths to find ways to deny the reality of what happened even when their denials are completely implausible. In the case of Roswell, the military denied what had happened through preposterous explanations, even distorting time by claiming that crash dummies, used first in 1953, turned up in 1947.

In the case of Rendlesham Forest, even in the face of science that proved that the Orford Ness lighthouse could not be the source of the light in the forest, the skeptics still hung on to the lighthouse explanation. The diehards claimed that the plaster casts from the dirt were rabbit scrapings when rabbits burrow down at an angle and throw the dirt behind them, creating holes in the ground not at all like the landing impressions from the craft. And to this day no one can account for the radiation except to deny that measurements were ever taken. As for Penniston's sketches, they were explained away as the hallucinations of a disoriented individual.

The air force simply maintained a rigid silence. Had they not debriefed Larry Warren and others so harshly, forcing them to recant their descriptions of what had happened, the event might have simply disappeared with time. But the military's continuing harassment of members of its own personnel who had the misfortune to see something anomalous gave away its true intent.

When government and the truth give way to lies to cover up a secret, those lies become obvious to those whose minds are not preset to deny.

WHAT WE LEARNED FROM THE EPISODE

The various stories from witnesses and the facts they attest to have been available for years, in some cases over a decade. Charles Halt's assertion that the Orford Ness light could be seen at a different location and at the same time as the light from the object has also been available to researchers for years, as has his audio recording of the events on the night in question. However, *UFO Hunters* did manage to piece some new information together not only from what we gleaned from the record but also from new interviews.

We ascertained from another one of our guests on the episode, former RAF police officer and the publisher of the U.K.'s "Police Reports of UFOs," Gary Heseltine, that RAF Bentwaters housed nuclear weapons. According to Heseltine's experience, there had to be some on-duty personnel in the base watchtower with a view of the entire area. And Charles Halt confirmed that the RAF Bentwaters watchtower was staffed on the successive nights in question and that a sentry in that tower witnessed the entire incident in the forest. In fact, Halt revealed, not only did the sentry see the events unfold in the forest, he also saw other lights in the sky shining their beams directly onto the "hot line," the areas where nuclear warheads were stored. Therefore, if there was a mission that the UFOs were carrying out, one of the craft led the security detail out into the forest and away from the base while one or more other lights surveyed the storage facility for nuclear weapons. Or was that all they were doing?

Could it be, given the stories about UFOs interfering with the missile-launch-control systems at Malmstrom and other nuclear missile sites both in the United States and in the former USSR decades ago, that whoever is flying these UFOs into heavily guarded military airspaces is testing their ability to shut down our ability to launch nuclear weapons? Might it be that we have been prevented, ever since 1947, by some otherworldly presence from engaging in nuclear war? We certainly have come close on more than one occasion. But the truth is that for over sixty years the world's nuclear powers, despite the provocation, have managed not to obliterate themselves. Is this entirely our own doing? The witness description from RAF Bentwaters is indeed tantalizing.

The other fascinating piece of new information we learned in this episode came from Keith Seeman, the lighthouse keeper at Orford Ness, whom we interviewed, regarding the lighthouse beam. We learned that despite all the claims from journalists and skeptics that Halt and his men were only chasing a lighthouse beam, no one had ever asked lighthouse keeper Keith Seeman for his opinion about how far that beam could have reached. We took it upon ourselves to visit Orford Ness, a bleak but magnificent spot on the coast of the North Sea, evocative of *Beowulf* and Vikings and even Count Dracula sailing to England from Transylvania.

Keith Seeman told us that it would have been impossible for the lighthouse beam to have played across Rendlesham Forest and onto the clearing because of a metal plate that kept the beam from hitting the land. Besides, the beam was a bright white and not red. We could see the metal plate with our own eyes, and had anyone investigated the Orford Ness explanation, he or she would have seen it, too.

And finally there were the aptly called "men in black." Most people who had interviewed forester Vincent Thurkettle knew that he had been interviewed by two strange men shortly after the incident but before Charles Halt's report to the U.K. Ministry of Defence. However, what we learned was that it was not only Thurkettle who was the subject of the interview. The strange men also interviewed other residents of the area and were very specific in asking those residents whether they had seen the "red light." How did those men know not only that U.S. Air Force personnel had seen a light in the forest but that it was red? The more we probed, the mystery about RAF Bentwaters only deepened. Our job was to peel away the layers of conventional explanation by holding each skeptical argument up to the light and the rigor of scientific testing to see if it stood up to scrutiny. And as each one peeled away, what we would be left with was the nugget of truth, even if that nugget was not itself an explanation.

RENDLESHAM, THE MONSTERS, AND THE CRITICS

In my taxonomy of UFO evidence, one of the four prongs that usually helps establish the existence of an anomalous event that those in power don't want you to know about is the reaction of those in power to the event. In other words, to what lengths will those in power go to make the unexplainable seem explainable even if the explainable arguments defy not only plausibility and evidence but logic itself?

In the case of the Rendlesham incident, this fourth prong became most prominent. The principal attacks against the witness testimonies were based on a number of assertions, all of them false:

- The RAF Bentwaters USAF base commander, Colonel Conrad, thought that his deputy's testimony was inaccurate.
- The story Staff Sergeant James Penniston told Colonel Conrad was different from the story he told in public.
- The USAF personnel mistook the Orford Ness lighthouse for a UFO.
- There never was any radiation reading of significance at the alleged landing spot.
- The landing impressions on the ground were only mild indentations.
- There was never any radar contacts on the nights the UFOs were alleged to be over the base.
- The British investigated the case and found no credible evidence that anything had happened.

- It was only a fireball that initiated the entire incident, not a UFO.
- The USAF never investigated the case because they believed nothing happened.
- No other witnesses saw the event, especially Colonel Conrad, so the event never happened.

What's astounding is that the real story behind these skeptical arguments is that the people making them seem to have failed to check their sources and even disregarded compelling evidence contradicting their arguments. For example, skeptics made the argument that Colonel Ted Conrad seemed to deny that any real incident took place, that the description of the incident James Penniston gave differed so much from the description Penniston gave publicly that it was hard to believe, and that there was no radar or independent corroboration that the event took place. The real facts are that Colonel Ted Conrad never denied that anything had happened. He simply told one of the skeptics in a letter, which he didn't want made public, that he thought that Colonel Halt's comment in his official memo about the craft the air force security team said they saw in Rendlesham Forest was less than professional given the lack of conclusive evidence. But Colonel Conrad never said he doubted that incident occurred. In fact, he said just the opposite, that he believed an incident occurred. He just didn't know what it was.

When it came to Colonel Conrad's statement that Jim Penniston told different stories to different people, Penniston himself said that it was true on the surface but that there was a deeper explanation. Penniston explained that immediately after the incident, plainclothes agents from the Air Force Office of Special Investigations (AFOSI) descended upon the personnel who witnessed the events in the forest, interrogated them thoroughly, and told them to report only that they saw a light in the forest. They instructed them not to tell any stories of touching the object or approaching it. They were only to tell others that whatever they saw they saw from a distance and not close up.

And this is exactly what James Penniston told Colonel Ted Conrad, that he saw the light from a distance. He didn't tell him that he touched the object or sketched it into his notebook—a fact he also withheld from AFOSI investigators—but only the official cover story. This is important because, first, he reveals that the air force took this event seriously enough to investigate it immediately and come up with a cover story. Second, it reveals that the AFOSI investigators had the authority to tell Staff Sergeant Penniston to withhold the truth from his commanding officer. They superseded the command structure at the base.

Penniston also revealed that other agencies got involved in the investigation, saying that even before Halt's report, U.S. intelligence agencies were investigating the event. In fact, Penniston believes that the NSA became involved not only because of the potential security threats but because they had their own field office at Orford Ness. This fact will become important later.

As for Colonel Conrad's statement that no one else saw the events unfold at the base except for the security personnel in the forest, this, too, is inaccurate. In fact, Lieutenant Colonel Halt as well as James Penniston and additional witness John Burroughs, who was on security detail with Penniston, stated that objects were picked up on radar and that it was that radar contact that alerted the security detail on the first night to go to the east gate to investigate. In addition, sentries in the observation tower above the base saw the entire sequence of events, the lights in the sky, and an object focusing a beam on the nuclear storage facilities. Even the RAF, according to the witnesses, saw the event unfold, but refused to comment about it to the Americans. Thus, the arguments of the skeptics pointing to the statements of the then American base commander Colonel Ted Conrad are inaccurate at best, certainly incorrect, and probably disingenuous.

The Orford Ness explanation for the mysterious lights in the forest still lingers on today, even though all of the witnesses reported that anyone who worked at the base for even a brief amount of time could recognize and identify the beacon at Orford Ness. John Burroughs has explained in his many radio interviews that the beacon was visible from the end of the runway and that new personnel were instructed to observe and recognize it so that there was no mistake about mysterious lights. Therefore, the security detail investigating the mysterious lights caught on radar would not have misidentified the light. Colonel Halt himself said that he was able to see three lights at the same time: the bright light from the object in the clearing, the light from the object reflecting from the farmhouse windows, and the beacon from Orford Ness. Moreover, the lighthouse keeper himself said that the light was blocked from scanning along the ground. And finally, if the NSA had a base at Orford Ness, why would they investigate a mysterious light if they already knew what it was? So much for the Orford Ness argument.

When it came to the skeptics' argument that there never was any radiation reading of significance at the alleged landing spot, the witnesses flatly denied it and pointed to documents from the Ministry of Defence stating that they verified the heightened readings at the landing site.

The argument that the landing impressions on the ground were only mild indentations was also debunked by the witnesses, who said that the forest floor had already become frozen during December. It was a hard surface and the impressions, the plaster case of which I saw with my own eyes, were too deep to be animal scrapings or footprints.

It is also a myth that the British investigated the case and found no credible evidence that anything had happened. First of all, any activity in Rendlesham Forest by American personnel would of necessity arouse some interest, even if only by the police. They'd want to know why an American detail was patrolling into British territory. But, according to witnesses James Penniston and John Burroughs, the British authorities, particularly the RAF, were notified. Might that explain the interview that plainclothes British investigators had conducted with Vincent Thurkettle? If it is a fact that the British were indeed investigating the event because they had been contacted by the Americans, it explains how the British knew enough to contact Thurkettle even before Charles Halt's report was sent to the ministry. Insofar as the British were concerned, therefore, an incident did occur in the forest, and they were gathering facts and evidence.

The argument that it was only a fireball that initiated the entire incident, not a UFO, simply falls apart when the witnesses reveal that British radar did, indeed, pick up radar targets over the Bentwaters/Rendlesham area, particularly on the first night. The skeptics' contention, based on what they're saying Colonel Ted Conrad said, is incorrect.

Another false argument, raised by the skeptics, who may or may not know the full story of the involvement of AFOSI and the NSA, is that the USAF never investigated the case because they believed nothing happened. As James Penniston and John Burroughs have said, the air force aggressively investigated the happenings at Bentwaters even from the very first and concocted a story that they ordered Penniston to give to his commanding officer, Ted Conrad, a story that deviated from the story Penniston told AFOSI investigators and even deviated from what Penniston later revealed to the public. Thus, the impression was that the USAF was not investigating the case, when, in fact, they did. And the air force was joined in the investigation by another intelligence agency, possibly the NSA or the CIA.

Were you to go by the letter from Colonel Conrad that British folklorist and professor of journalism Dr. David Clarke released—Professor Clarke investigated the Rendlesham case—you might get the impression that no other witnesses saw the event, especially not the base commander, Conrad. But that would be a false impression. The former debuty base commander, Charles Halt, revealed on *UFO Hunters* that sentries in the observation tower saw the entire event unfold, that they saw the lights and saw beams of light, just like searchlights, shining down on the nuclear storage facility. There was also an RAF officer present, according to some witnesses, who saw the event, too. But that officer would not report the event.

Try as they might, the skeptics' arguments remain far from convincing. In fact, the disingenuousness of their arguments and the contorted explanations only make the witnesses' stories of what happened at RAF Bentwaters and Rendlesham Forest even more convincing.

BILL'S BLOG

I have to confess that when I first began to read about the strange events at RAF Bentwaters, my first thought was that this was some kind of test of either a new weapon or a readiness test performed upon unsuspecting air force personnel. It came at a time just after the Soviets had invaded Afghanistan and when Ronald Reagan had just been elected president. President Carter had pulled the U.S. team out of the Olympics in protest of Moscow's invasion of its neighbor to oust an unfriendly president and replace him with a puppet. Would Jimmy Carter's strong reaction and Ronald Reagan's election serve as the backdrop for the Soviets to press an advantage in Europe? Would bases like RAF Bentwaters be ready if someone pushed the wrong button?

This is what I thought when I first heard about the Rendlesham Forest incident.

Was the object that landed in the forest some kind of drone? Might it have been a holographic projection?

Our trip to the United Kingdom to investigate this incident blew away any prior suspicions I held about the Bentwaters case. First of all, it couldn't have been a holographic projection if James Penniston actually touched the thing. And its triangular shape comported with the sightings of other triangular-shaped objects over the years.

Some skeptics contend that witnesses were too quick to jump to a conclusion that it was otherworldly. It could have been an American or British test aircraft used to assess the security responses to a perceived airspace intrusion. However, skeptics also tend to have a particular bias. Whenever they react to reports of UFOs, they almost always judge those who report it as claiming that the craft is otherworldly. In point of fact, most witnesses, including some of the witnesses at Bentwaters, don't claim that at all. Rather, most witnesses simply say that they've never seen anything like it, believe it is nothing that any armed service has, and leave it at that. It's the skeptics and the media who scream that witnesses are claiming to have seen flying saucers from outer space. And so it was with the Bentwaters skeptics. By laying a straw man out in front of the witnesses and then attacking it, skeptics believe they have proved a point. But they haven't.

Nancy and I were living on our boat in Santa Monica Bay back in 2007, in the weeks before Thanksgiving, when *UFO Hunters* set out for the United Kingdom, and the opinions and arguments of the skeptics were ringing in my thoughts as the van pulled up at the international departure gate at LAX. I, personally, really wanted to tackle the issues surrounding RAF Bentwaters, and was anticipating with delight the prospect of meeting retired Ministry of Defence officer Nick Pope at the base.

Nick and I had our first UFO books published by the same company back in 1997 and had become friends through *UFO Magazine*. In 2007, with the release of Ministry of Defence UFO files, including files on RAF Bentwaters, I had hopes that we would be able to come to some understanding of the mysteries surrounding the U.K. and U.S. military agencies' refusal to investigate scientifically and seriously the facts in evidence of the RAF Bentwaters incident.

As Nick had pointed out previously, the RAF Bentwaters, RAF Woodbridge, and RAF Lakenheath bases had prior histories of UFO incidents dating all the way back to Operation Mainbrace in 1952, the first joint NATO naval exercise of the Cold War. Pilots and sailors in the fleet reported UFO and USO sightings, particularly from the aircraft carrier USS *Franklin D. Roosevelt*. In 1956, aircraft from RAF Lakenheath had encountered UFOs over the North Sea, which had been observed visually by the pilots and on radar both from the Lakenheath tower and from the cockpits of the two RAF Venom fighters sent to intercept them. The east coast of Britain, therefore, was no stranger to UFO sightings, and the RAF Bentwaters / Rendlesham Forest incidents fell into a pattern of strange events in this area. Among the long history of UFO incidents in this area of Britain, RAF Bentwaters / Rendlesham Forest was among the strangest because it was here that someone not only saw and copied into a notebook aspects of a UFO sighting but also actually touched the object and analyzed trace evidence left by the craft.

In November 2007, while on our way to complete our NASA episode, the news that James Penniston, Charles Halt, and Nick Pope would be appearing at the National Press Club in Washington caused us to stop what we were doing and retool our schedule so that we could meet them at the press conference. And from there, after our interviews with the witnesses and Nick Pope, covering the Bentwaters/Rendlesham story went to the very top of our list. And, thus, as the crew assembled at the departure gate at LAX for what would be a very long flight across the continental United States and the Atlantic Ocean, I was very, very excited.

And I wasn't to be disappointed. Charles Halt had brought

along his Lanier voice recorder to give us a demonstration of why his narration of the events on the second night of lights in Rendlesham Forest seemed to coincide with the pulsations of the light at Orford Ness. He demonstrated that because the minitape had only twenty minutes of recording time on it, he was simply sliding the recorder to "off" every few seconds to conserve valuable tape space. That mystery was solved. Halt also showed us what real rabbit scrapings looked like. And they weren't what he and Penniston described at the National Press Club.

The highlights of the episode filming, however, were the discovery of a brand new witness—who chose to remain nameless out of fear that he would violate a national security oath—who had observed the entire interaction between air force security and the strange lights from his observation tower. The same individual also observed that objects overhead were shining beams down on the nuclear storage facilities. This was an astounding revelation, and in all the hoopla surrounding the skeptics' reemergence to challenge the Rendlesham witnesses it has never been discussed. Imagine that. While all the skeptics and debunkers go after the witnesses and the experts, we don't hear of any of them talking about what the sentry on his guard observation tower witnessed.

Our interview with Orford Ness lighthouse keeper Keith Seeman was also a revelation for me. Had any of the skeptics talked to him? Had any of the debunkers actually looked at the lighthouse beacon itself? We didn't need circumstantial evidence to destroy their argument that U.S. Air Force personnel saw only the lighthouse beacon. We had the visual evidence from our videotaping the lighthouse tower and talking to the lighthouse keeper.

It was a very fulfilling episode. Of course, as Ted Acworth pointed out, we never established that what the air force witnesses saw was a craft from another world. But that wasn't our

EPISODE 101 "THE UFO BEFORE ROSWELL" Pat Uskert looks for pieces of slag on the sea bottom off Maury Island.

EPISODE 104 "CRASH AND RETRIEVALS" Hidden from view in a sugarcane field in Mexico, we interview a federal police officer who brought what he believed was UFO debris to Mexico's intelligence bureau.

EPISODE 104 "CRASH AND RETRIEVALS" Noe Torres discovers the site of plane wreckage in the Coyame Desert, thus substantiating the Deneb report.

EPISODE 101 "THE UFO BEFORE ROSWELL" Our special effects producer, John Tindall, in his workshop.

EPISODE 102 "USOS"
John Tindall demonstrates how a particle beam of electrons can interrupt the ignition of an airplane engine.

EPISODE 105 "MILITARY VS. UFOS"
Colonel Charles Halt (USAF, Ret.), former deputy base commander of RAF Bentwaters, addressing the press at the UFO Disclosure Conference in November 2007. This was the precursor to our episode in the U.K.'s Rendlesham Forest.

EPISODE 105 "MILITARY VS. UFOS"
(l to r) Jeff Tomlinson, John Tindall, Dr. Ted Acworth, and Charles Halt take a GPS reading in the clearing adjacent to Rendlesham Forest to determine whether the light Halt's Air Force security detail saw in the clearing in December 1980 was the Orford Ness lighthouse beam or a different light.

EPISODE 105 "MILITARY VS. UFOS"
(l to r) Sitting: Dr. Ted, Jeff Tomlinson, Pat (behind the desk), and me. In the beginning of the episode, we are watching the video of the National Press Club UFO Disclosure Conference and discussing the RAF Bentwaters/Rendlesham Forest case.

EPISODE 103 "ABDUCTIONS"
Witness and abductee Tim Cullen
describing his UFO encounter
in an open field.

EPISODE 106 "COPS VS. UFOS"
Witness and abductee retired police
constable Alan Godfrey (l) describes
his UFO encounter to Pat Uskert and me.

EPISODE 108 "VORTEXES"
Pat Uskert (c), Bruce
Cornet (r), and I talk
about the energy
vortex right beneath
our feet in Pine Bush,
New York, in the heart
of the Hudson Valley.

EPISODE 107 "REVERSE ENGINEERING"
This is the Internet photo of a device, referred
to as the CARAT craft, that was supposedly
reverse engineered by a California company
from extraterrestrial technology. Our guest,
former MUFON Director James Carion, told
us that he believed these photos were hoaxed
for the purposes of official government
disinformation.

EPISODE 111 "UFO DOGFIGHTS"
Former Iranian fighter pilot and member of the Iranian Air Force general staff General Parvis Jafari explains to me what happened when he got into a dogfight with a large UFO over the Tehran airport in 1976 when the UFO turned off his weapons panel in his F-4 Phantom jet.

EPISODE 110 "INVASION: TEXAS 2008"
UFO Hunter Jeff Tomlinson listens to Dr. Ted explain a proposed scientific experiment.

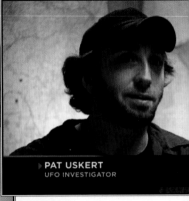

PAT USKERT
UFO INVESTIGATOR

EPISODE 110 "INVASION: TEXAS 2008
Pat Uskert, in an OTF interview, explains what the team is doing to gather evidence from witness to the Stephenville lights.

EPISODE 110 "INVASION: TEXAS 2008"
In our Stephenville, Texas, office, Jeff Tomlinson (l) and Pat Uskert (r) high-five over the successful setting up of our UFO sighting data board.

EPISODE 109 "ALIEN CONTACT"
Witness and contacte Terrell Copeland (c) describes his sighting of a giant UFO to Pat Uskert (l) and me.

EPISODE 109 "ALIEN CONTACT"
[Te]rrell Copeland (l) describes to Pat and me [h]ow a strange person outside his apartment [c]ommunicated with him telepathically, a person [w]ho wanted him to embrace what she called [h]is "star seed." This was the famous "you are a [h]ybrid" episode.

EPISODE 109 "ALIEN CONTACT"
Terrell Copeland shows Pat and me the videos of a UFO he captured on camera.

EPISODE 112 "CODE RED"
Retired USAF air traffic controller Chuck Sorrells describes to former NSA and USAF officer Bill Scott— retired Rocky Mountain bureau chief of *Aviation Week*—what happened in 1965 when a UFO entered the secure airspace over Edwards Air Force Base in California, prompting a Code Red Intruder Alert.

EPISODE 213 "AREA 51 REVEALED"
[Jo]hn Lear (r) sets up the model of the UFO [p]ropulsion system to show me how [el]ement 115 operates.

EPISODE 213 "AREA 51 REVEALED"
John Lear demonstrates the working of the element 115 UFO propulsion system as explained to him by Bob Lazar.

EPISODE 213 "AREA 51 REVEALED"
(*above*) Looking through the telephoto lens set up at the top of Tikaboo Peak at Area 51 at dawn.

EPISODE 213 "AREA 51 REVEALED"
Looking at the large hangar at sunrise from Tikaboo Peak at Area 51.

EPISODE 213 "AREA 51 REVEALED"
A Janet Airlines flight from Area 51 landing at McCarran Airport in Las Vegas.

EPISODE 213 "AREA 51 REVEALED"
The surveillance cameras we set up around the perimeter at Area 51.

PISODE 213 "AREA 51 REVEALED"
give an OTF interview at Area 51.

EPISODE 213 "AREA 51 REVEALED"
John Lear and I talk about Bob Lazar and reverse engineering at Area 51.

purpose. Our purpose was, as it continued to be in every episode, to look at every conventional explanation for an event
and put that explanation to the test. What was left was what we
had to investigate further. In the case of Bentwaters what required further investigation, and still does, is the rationale for
the U.S. Department of Defense's refusal to reveal any of its information about the case.

We caught a predawn flight back to Los Angeles, taking off
from Manchester and transferring at Heathrow with a dead-
tired crew. We had only gotten a few hours' sleep the night before, wrapping up the shoot and prepping the equipment for
the flight. When we reached the airport in the dead of darkness, we discovered that the Manchester airport baggage crew
couldn't transfer the equipment onto our flight because of size
and weight restrictions. And we couldn't ship the equipment
separately as freight on a different flight. Nor could we leave it
behind or stay with it for another day.

The only solution was to repack, in the hour or so remaining before the flight to London had to board, all of the equipment to meet the size and weight requirements as well as to
obtain special dispensation from the baggage handlers for
them to lift luggage over fifty pounds per piece. It wasn't pretty.
However, in one of the most amazing feats of equipment re-
packing, our crew of Director of Photography Kevin Graves,
Assistant Camera and B Camera Operator Brian Garrity, and Assistant Camera Linh Nguyen took apart all the equipment they
had prepped and packed the night before and repacked it so
that it would conform to the baggage requirements at the airport for the local short hop to London. Never in the course of
reality television had so few done so much for so many in so
little time.

I don't remember much of the flight back home. British Air-
ways flight attendants kept on pouring drinks, and in the weeks
before Christmas with a vacation looming before the next

episodes' schedules were to begin, I was reveling in the happiness of a more than successful shoot. Sometimes you're lucky enough to nail it. And sinking back into my seat on the plane and thinking of our interviews at the Orford Ness lighthouse and at the RAF Bentwaters observation tower with episode guests Charles Halt and Gary Heseltine, I knew that even though the ensuing years may never point to what we were able to show, I had at least proved to myself that whatever happened in Rendlesham Forest was real, not an illusion and not a fabrication.

SEVEN

COPS VS. UFOS

I have to admit at the very outset that episode 106—which was partially filmed in the United Kingdom while we were there for the Bentwaters episode and partially in Florida with video from the pilot for *UFO Hunters* that never aired—contains my absolute favorite UFO story. Sure, Roswell is Roswell, the mother of all American UFO incidents just by its very nature of being one of the first completely documented encounters. And certainly the Phoenix lights, with the state's governor as the eyewitness and the military's turning itself inside out, and then failing, to prove there was a conventional explanation for it. And there are hundreds of other incredible UFO incidents and stories that captured my imagination.

But there is one story that we covered in this episode that held everything for me: a strange death on a lonely coal heap that a lone police officer saw as a murder when his superiors didn't, a UFO encounter and abduction that actually left trace evidence, and an official response that amounted to nothing less than a complete cover-up. This was the story of police officer Alan Godfrey of West Yorkshire, and I was thrilled to have met and interviewed him for this episode.

The premise of this episode was that police encounters with

anomalous objects, especially multiple witnessed encounters, held a greater credibility than ordinary encounters because the police, as part of their job, are trained to be reliable witnesses. In fact, police testimony in court is so powerful that unless the credibility of a police witness is completely compromised on the stand—and we all remember F. Lee Bailey's cross-examination of Mark Furman in the OJ Simpson trial—refuting it can be an insurmountable burden. When police see UFOs or, worse, videotape UFOs, you know there's something there. And that's the level of credibility that we were after in this episode. In fact, when we'd finished shooting, we were so happy with the information we'd obtained that we revisited "Cops vs. UFOs" in our ensuing two seasons.

THE FIRST STORY: MYSTERIOUS OBJECT CAUGHT ON VIDEO IN DAYTONA BEACH

This was the story we covered in our pilot for the network, the March 1, 1991, story of two Volusia County Sheriff's Department employees who, while on a routine nighttime helicopter patrol looking for narcotics traffickers, caught a strange-looking object on their helicopter-mounted forward-looking infrared camera, or FLIR. This is a camera sensitive to heat, wavelengths invisible to the human eye.

Mark Patterson, a sheriff's sergeant, and Jim Della Rosa were on patrol over the New Smyrna Beach Municipal Airport in 1991, surveying the area with their infrared camera when they picked up a strange object. The two men didn't know they had captured anything on video because they couldn't see the object with their naked eyes. It was invisible to them but gave off a heat signature that the camera was able to capture.

They had taken off from New Smyrna Beach heading south along Route 1 to cover the sea routes when Mark Patterson noticed that the FLIR screen, the monitor inside the cockpit that displays the images on the infrared camera mounted beneath the helicopter, had picked up an object on the right of his craft. Mark said that he couldn't identify it. It was a "round egg-shaped object that seemed to be producing a great heat signature." He looked out his window to get a visual, but, he said, "there was nothing there to see." Perhaps because it was a dark and moonless night the officers' visibility was very limited and they could see nothing in the air alongside them. But for the next thirty-three seconds, the FLIR camera saw the barbell UFO with the egg-shaped bow as it appeared to track the police helicopter on its way south.

The FLIR monitor was just that, a monitor showing a real-time image of what the camera was picking up. Although the FLIR was also laying the image down on tape, the helicopter couldn't play the tape back until they got to the hangar where the playback machine was located. So all they could do was watch the object on the monitor as they called out to local radar air controllers to see if anyone had the object on radar as well. FLIR camera operator Jim Della Rosa said that Mark Patterson called the Daytona Air Traffic Control (ATC), who told them that they did not have the object on radar. Very strange, Mark and Jim thought, because they could still see it on their FLIR monitor seemingly pacing them.

Jim Della Rosa said that in all of his experience, flying under many different weather and light conditions, during hundreds of hours using the FLIR unit, he had never seen anything like this on a FLIR monitor. This was an unknown object, resembling nothing either officer had ever encountered before. First of all, Patterson pointed out to Ted Acworth, the object had two distinct heat sources: a mushroom- or egg-shaped nose and a rotating tail assembly. But, Patterson also said, there was a white band separating the nose and tail, which meant that that particular section was not generating any heat. Jim Della Rosa was convinced that the object was not a helicopter because there was no distinctive tail or fuselage that resembled a helicopter, no top or tail rotor-blade motion, no heat signature of an engine.

At first, the UFO Hunters team thought that the object on the monitor might have been something out of focus, a blur. But as Patterson pointed out, the images of the ground picked up by the FLIR showed that everything was in perfect focus. Therefore, the mystery object wouldn't have been the display of a defocused lens.

What was also spooky about the object's maneuvers was that whenever Mark Patterson changed the direction of his helicopter, the object matched his course change. It descended to his altitude and seemed to mirror every move he made. And as it got closer, Mark and Jim tried to see if they could make out the outline of a traditional helicopter on the monitor. But they could not. In all his years of flying, Mark said, he could not recognize the shape of the object that was almost pulling up alongside him.

My own opinion, which I bounced off Mark and Jim, was that the object was a gyrocopter, a very early design of a vertical take-off and landing craft, made for a single pilot, that had a large conventional in its rear to propel it and a large rotor up top, which was not driven by an engine. Hence, the top rotor should have no heat signature. But Mark knew exactly what a gyrocopter was and said that its top rotor would have appeared on the FLIR monitor because of the heat rising up the rotor mast. This craft, he said, had to have been something else.

We brought the footage from Patterson's and Della Rosa's FLIR video to United States Navy photo analyst Dr. Bruce Maccabee, who is well known in the UFO field for his methodical approach to deconstructing photos and videos. Bruce would be a frequent guest on *UFO Hunters*, helping us figure out the Ed Walters Gulf Breeze photos. Maccabee was also well known for his important detective work on the very famous Trent photos from McMinnville, Oregon, perhaps one of the best flying-saucer photos ever taken.

Maccabee resolved the issues very quickly. He pointed out that if the object in the FLIR video had been a conventional helicopter, we would have seen the heat signature of the top rotors. Also, the rear rotor was rotating the wrong way for a helicopter and was rotating too slowly for a gyrocopter. In fact, the shape was all wrong for any conventional aircraft. But when pressed to identify the object, all

Bruce Maccabee could say with certainty was that he knew what it wasn't. Beyond that, it was unidentifiable from the video that we brought him.

One of the issues that Ted Acworth raised actually popped up on the FLIR tape. When Patterson and Della Rosa scanned the ground area at nearby Massey Ranch Airpark to the south of New Smyrna Beach, they picked up a person loading something into a vehicle. Ted tracked him down and learned that he was retired NASA engineer Mike Holloman, who corroborated that he was the person in the FLIR video. We called him to confirm where he was and what he saw, and he said, "I know that I stepped out and actually saw the helicopter circling the airfield." Asked whether he saw any other craft or helicopter besides the Volusia County Sheriff's Department helicopter, Holloman said that he never saw any other craft in the sky that evening. Moreover, Holloman told Pat Uskert that he had never seen any aircraft flying without showing any lights in the area around the airport.

We also asked Patterson and Della Rosa whether they could have picked up another helicopter so far away from them that the defocused lens on the FLIR would have distorted the heat signature it was imaging. But both sheriff's officers said that wouldn't have been possible. Even if we were able to duplicate that image with another helicopter far in the distance, they suggested, the fact that the image on the FLIR seemed to be tracking their every move made it unlikely that it was a distant object. And while neither officer went so far as to call the object a flying saucer or a dumbbell-shaped otherworldly craft, they also said that until someone could figure out what it was, it would have to remain unidentified. They even dismissed the idea that they could have been picked up by some sort of government drone—possibly on antinarcotics surveillance—because the unmanned aerial vehicles circa 1991, and even today, look more like conventional fixed-wing aircraft than unconventional aircraft.

In a final attempt to prove Ted's theory that a FLIR camera could become defocused on an object far in the distance but emit an intense heat signature, we traveled to Corona, California, to set up an experiment with a helicopter unit from the Corona Police Department. We filmed a Corona PD helicopter with our FLIR camera as the craft moved far from the field and then circled around. As the FLIR became defocused, it began to smudge the image, losing the defined shape of the helicopter until, at a certain point, the image on the FLIR depicting the Corona PD helicopter was almost identical to the image on the FLIR camera from Mark Patterson's Volusia County Sheriff's Department helicopter back in 1991. That image was, according to Sergeant Reynolds of the Corona Police Department, just another helicopter, even though both Mark Patterson and Jim Della Rosa strongly disagreed because they said that the other images on their FLIR showed that the camera was always in focus.

Since Bruce Maccabee and the Volusia County Sheriff's Department deputies said that the Florida FLIR image was a UFO and Corona Police Department's Sergeant Reynolds said it was simply a defocused image of another helicopter, we logged the Florida sighting as inconclusive. A helicopter perhaps, but a UFO by definition. In other words, the craft caught by the FLIR could have been conventional or not. And since neither Patterson and Della Rosa in the air nor Mike Holloman on the ground could see or hear anything, the image was simply a mystery.

The image the sheriff's officers picked up on their helicopter-mounted Forward Looking Infrared Camera was an interesting phenomenon and certainly an encounter, but it was time to see if we could get some more solid evidence of police encounters with UFOs. We turned our attention to the United Kingdom and to a document called "Police Reports of UFO Sightings," compiled by former RAF security police officer and West Yorkshire constable Gary Heseltine. Heseltine's reports, going back to 1901, contain one of the most compelling sighting reports, a report from North Yorkshire, which was not only attested to by a police officer on patrol but also caught on his dashboard video camera.

AN UNKNOWN BRIGHT OBJECT

In May 2003, at 9:30 P.M., a police officer in North Yorkshire spotted a bright object in the distance shining through his windshield. The object seemed to move across his line of sight from right to left. As he drove off along Route 59 from Skipton to Bolton Abbey, he slowed down to get a better look at it. It was something strange, something that he probably couldn't identify, and he wanted to take his time as it passed across his windshield.

Our consultant, former NASA imaging expert physicist Dr. Jack Kasher, said flat out that it was not an astronomical object, even though, he determined from the car's direction, the object wasn't moving on its own. It was stationary. Ted Acworth, never one to be impressed by strange sightings in the sky, said that the obvious explanations didn't match up the way he would have expected them to. It clearly wasn't astronomical. It wasn't a conventional airplane.

Ted suggested that even though this light might seem undramatic, the fact that it wasn't a plane or a fixed beacon or radio tower and that it was clearly so unconventional to the police officer who slowed down to get a better look and capture it on video met all of his criteria for a UFO. Ted and Jack Kasher also eliminated a plane traveling away from the police car. One of the keys to that argument was that, even though the object was relatively low to the horizon, there were no airports in the area from where it could have been taking off or landing.

ALAN GODFREY, POLICE CONSTABLE

This is one of my favorite cases on *UFO Hunters* and, in fact, in all ufology. The Alan Godfrey case is actually composed of three separate incidents: reports of UFO appearances and orbs witnesses saw during the week that a body was discovered on top of a coal heap; Godfrey's discovery of that body lying near the top of a coal heap in the town of Todmorden on June 11, 1980; and Godfrey's reported sighting of a diamond-shaped craft spinning in the road and his abduction by the inhabitants of that craft.

The Zygmunt Jan Adamski Discovery

In his own words, Godfrey described the body-discovery scene as a "murder on our hands." From the outset, he saw the entire scene as strange. The deceased, a Polish coal miner named Zygmunt Jan Adamski, was wearing a string vest and a topcoat, but no shirt underneath. He had disappeared five days earlier from Tingley, near Wakefield, when he told his wife he was going out to buy some potatoes for dinner. The fifty-six-year-old miner simply vanished, but he turned up on top of a twelve-foot coal heap, dead of heart failure, but with no indication that he had approached the coal heap on foot. That was one of the initial mysteries that so intrigued Police Constable Alan Godfrey. There were no footprints around the coal heap, nothing to indicate that someone had walked around there or up to the heap. How did Adamski get there without leaving any tracks, and why did he wind up there, over thirty miles from Tingley near Wakefield, where he lived?

Adamski's topcoat had been buttoned irregularly, as if someone had dressed him but didn't know exactly how to do it. The fly on his pants was undone, as if he had been naked and someone put his pants on but didn't know that the fly had to be closed, and his shoes looked like someone had put them on for him and didn't know how to tie the laces properly. In short, PC Godfrey said, in the absence of any clear explanation, it looked as though Adamski had been redressed by someone who didn't know how people should be dressed.

Godfrey followed up to find out when the body was discovered and when it turned up on the coal heap. He learned from interviewing a coal-yard security guard and the owner of the yard that Adamski's body had only been there a few hours, yet he had been dead for over eight hours when the body had been discovered. That meant that he died somewhere else, not on the coal heap, and that somehow his body was transported there. This comported with the fact that Adamski looked as if he had just taken a shower. There was no coal dust on his body or on his clothing. As Godfrey explained it, "it had been raining that day and the coal dust should have stuck to him like glue." But the body was clean. Therefore, he did not seem to have climbed up the heap.

A medical examiner doing a routine workup to present a preliminary cause of death report to the coroner for the inquest explained to Godfrey that he believed Adamski died of shock. Shock caused his heart to fail, as Godfrey explained to us, "something had really, really terrified him." But of particular interest to the doctor and to Godfrey were the burn marks around the back of the victim's head that had occurred approximately two days before his death. Medical testing of those burn marks revealed the burns were probably caused by the application of a corrosive agent. There was also the presence of a strange green ointment on the burn wounds, Godfrey said, but it was an ointment that no amount of medical and chemical testing could identify. But of particular mystery to the coroner himself was the fact that Adamski, though missing for five days, had only one day's growth of beard. There were no reports of his having been taken to a hospital. Where had he been and where had he shaved if, as his widow believed, he'd been kidnapped and tortured? It was the most puzzling case that the coroner had ever seen in twenty-five years.

Ultimately, the coroner's inquest ruled that Adamski had died of natural causes, a shock that stopped his heart. But, Godfrey learned, the victim had a very weak heart, a heart so weak that had the victim attempted to climb the coal heap himself he would have probably died before he reached the top. What did that mean? It meant that Adamski, the lack of coal dust or soot on his body and lack of footprints around the heap notwithstanding, physically and medically could not have climbed that pile of coal. He had to have been put there. But by whom?

The Diamond-Shaped UFO and the Abduction

On November 28, 1980, six months after having discovered Zygmunt Adamski's body and one month before the UFO incident at RAF

Bentwaters and Rendlesham Forest, Alan Godfrey, on his way to investigate a case of cows that had gone missing without a trace, encountered a large blue object in the middle of the road, an object sporting flashing blue lights. At first he thought that it was another vehicle, a double-decker bus that had skidded sideways. But, he said, "whatever it was, it was blocking the road."

As he approached the object, however, he remembered, "It was a sight I had never expected to see. It wasn't actually sitting on the ground; it actually was hovering over the ground, five feet." He tried to contact his dispatch on his car's VHF radio, but the radio was simply out of commission. He tried and tried, even as the blue lights swirled hypnotically across his windshield, but he couldn't raise his dispatcher to report the strange thing blocking the road. Then he tried his UHF personal radio, but, again, no one answered. Both radios were completely dead. Godfrey said that he tried to maintain a professional demeanor as he keyed his mike to report what he was seeing, but, in reality, he told us, he was really seeing an object twenty-five yards ahead of him and simply hovering as it rotated that resembled something out of *Close Encounters of the Third Kind* more than anything else. He knew it was real because, in addition to the rotating lights on the craft, the craft itself was reflecting the lights from his police car. He had never seen its like before. "It just didn't register with any of the training I'd been given as a police officer.

"It was obvious that what I was looking at was a UFO, a nuts and bolts craft," Godfrey said. "There was no emitting of noise or heat from it." However, Godfrey realized, because the trees around him were shaking violently as if the ground were vibrating, it seemed that there was some kind of force emanating from the object, which he now could see was actually spinning as it hovered. With his radio not working and thus out of contact with dispatch and all alone on the road in front of the strange object, Godfrey took out his clipboard and began to sketch the shape of the object and take notes about his observation. He told us that it was what he was trained to do in any situation, and he fell back on his procedure.

"But then," he said, as he sketched the object, "there was a sudden bright, white flash, and then a very strange thing happened. There was a jump in time. After I had made the drawing, I suddenly found myself twenty or thirty yards up the road driving the police car." He was on the other side of the object, which had simply vanished. To make matters even more mysterious, Godfrey realized that more than forty minutes had passed, forty minutes that he couldn't account for. Nor could he remember what had happened to him. He then turned the car around and went back to where he'd seen the UFO.

"I was a bit gob-smacked at this," he said. "It had been raining all night so the road surface should be completely wet through. Yet, the place where the object had been the road surface was bone dry." He also discovered the leaves on the road around the edge of the object had been swirled out as if they had been spun around a vortex or in a whirlpool. And there were broken twigs and limbs from the trees around the dry area on the road. It was inexplicable. In order to get some other eyeballs on the physical trace evidence of this strange presence, he drove back to the town center to get two of his colleagues to come to the scene so they could get a look at the road. They confirmed that the spot in the road where Godfrey said he saw the object was dry while all around the spot it was still wet from the rain.

As for the object, "it had disappeared." Godfrey then resumed his search for the herd of cattle that had disappeared from their pasture. "The only way it could get into the park was over the bridge and through a locked gate. We got into the gate and saw a herd of cows. How did the cows get there?" he asked. These were the same missing herd of cows he had been looking for earlier in the evening when he saw the flying object in the road. But, like the body of Zygmunt Adamski, the cows seemed to appear out of nowhere because there were no hoof prints on the ground and no indication of how the cows got over a bridge and through a locked gate that only the police could open with their keys. The only way the cows could have gotten into the park, Godfrey said, was if they were lowered there.

Godfrey reported the events of that night, the UFO sighting and the cattle, to his superiors, who told him that the mysterious object had been seen by police officers twelve miles away from his location on the moors in Halifax and between five and six miles away in Littleborough. And Godfrey also noticed that, although he couldn't account for forty minutes of his life the previous night, he did have one physical reminder that something had happened. He discovered that the sole of his boot was split horizontally, a split that he had not noticed before. Also, when he took off his socks, on the bottom of his foot where the boot had been split, he had a bright red spot, which was itching furiously. It was a sore whose presence he could not explain because he had no memory of having received it.

Godfrey was ridiculed by some fellow officers for his UFO story, even though his superiors took the sightings as something worth reporting. However, a newspaper reporter who noticed that it was the same Alan Godfrey who had discovered the body of Zygmunt Adamski and had experienced the UFO sighting published an article linking the two stories that suggested that Adamski had been the victim of a UFO abduction. The notoriety made Godfrey the butt of jokes inside the police department, causing the department to remove him from police-car duty and to put him on a bike. His encounters had begun to damage his credibility as well as his career in law enforcement. All the while, at the core of Godfrey's concern was, what had happened to him during those missing forty minutes, and how had he wound up in his car driving along the road on the other side of the object?

A friend of his, in talking with him about the events that had befallen him and his worry over the missing time, suggested that he undergo hypnotic regression to attempt to recover the memories of that missing time. During the session, Godfrey shielded his eyes, presumably from re-experiencing the bright light, and then described being floated out of his car and into the craft. After repeated sessions, which the therapist videotaped, Alan Godfrey came to understand that, for some reason, he had been abducted by the entities aboard that craft, entities he later sketched from memory as looking like small grays. Was there a purpose to this abduction? Godfrey doesn't know. Nor can he say with any certainty that it was connected to his discovery of Zygmunt Adamski's body. But he did recover memories that he was the subject of some type of medical experiments aboard that craft, experiments that could have led to a remarkable cure for an injury that he had suffered over a year earlier even though, in a subsequent radio interview, Godfrey said it was probably the result of his body's healing.

A miraculous recovery

Over a year before Godfrey's discovery of Adamski's body on a coal heap and his subsequent report of an encounter with a UFO, Godfrey was investigating a case of three felons, whom the local police were trying to find. He saw them sitting outside a pub, stopped his police car, notified his dispatch he'd located the suspects, called for backup, and approached them to make an arrest. However, even though he tried to handcuff them, they overpowered him, knocked him to the ground, gave him a severe beating, and kicked him viciously in his testicles. As a result, Godfrey lost a testicle and was told that he was infertile and would never have a child. It had a devastating impact on his life.

Over a year later, while Godfrey was still adjusting to the possibility that he had been abducted by entities in a UFO and subjected to some sort of medical experimentation, Godfrey's wife was awakened one night by a strange whirring noise. It was a similar noise, she said, that Godfrey himself had remembered under hypnotic regression. She tried to awaken her husband, but he was fast asleep. When he did awaken, the two of them made love, something they hadn't done since Godfrey's beating and resulting impotency. Months later, when Mrs. Godfrey had been told she was pregnant, Godfrey himself asked his doctor how that could be. After a test of Godfrey's semen, the doctor told him that, although he couldn't explain it, he was completely recovered from his impotency and that he was capable of fathering children. It was an amazing recovery and the last strange fact in the pattern of events that marked Godfrey's life since discovering

Adamski's body and encountering the unidentified object outside the town of Todmorden.

A suspected murder, a police officer not willing to go along with a coroner's judgment that a victim died of natural causes, and a series of UFO sightings, one of which involved the very officer who discovered the victim's body, all pointed to the possibility of a connection among all three. Such a connection was ultimately made not by the evidence itself or by the testimony of PC Alan Godfrey, but by the British government, who forced Godfrey to sign an Official Secrets Act letter, which linked all of the incidents. Why would the discovery of a body, whose death, the coroner ruled, was from natural causes, and an encounter with something that the skeptics called a bus stuck in the road require a police officer's signing an Official Secrets Act letter forbidding him to speak about it? What was the mystery of those events, linked not by Alan Godfrey's claims or the claims of UFO researchers, but by a local newspaper and then the British government?

The skeptics, even skeptics in the UFO community, may argue that the discovery of Adamski's body and the UFO story have no relation to each other, but what's clear is that Godfrey's superiors and some agency in British national security thought otherwise. The Adamski case, though treated as a natural death, is still a mystery just because the circumstances of the body's location and its condition simply don't lend themselves to any rational explanation. And Godfrey's UFO experience, the evidence of his split boot, the corroborating witness reports of other police officers, and Godfrey's strange recovery are still unexplained to this day. Whatever the underlying story is, whatever the relation may be to Zygmunt Adamski, and whatever issues rise in a debate about that relation, all we are left with until real evidence can be unearthed is pure speculation. But sometimes it's worth speculating.

With no dispositive or even substantive evidence, I speculated that there was a relationship among Godfrey's discovery of Adamski's body, the nature of Adamski's death, the disappearance and reappearance of the cattle herd, the strange diamond-shaped object whirling in the middle of the wet road in front of Godfrey's police car, and Godfrey's abduction by some form of otherworldly beings. Whatever evidence I have to go on is purely circumstantial, but it is suggestive enough to point to some underlying decision by Godfrey's superiors in the police department to make connections that most UFO researchers would not make. Perhaps individuals in Godfrey's command structure or even at Whitehall determined that there was a relation between Adamski and Godfrey's abduction because even though the coroner ruled that Adamski died of natural causes, a heart attack brought on by shock or trauma, Godfrey thought Adamski's death was a homicide and pursued his arguments even in the face of a legal determination.

Godfrey's arguments against the coroner's decision probably rankled his superiors, who, it seemed, sought to put the matter to rest. Maybe because the case seemed unsolvable or maybe because the police command was reacting to pressure from other agencies in the national security network, they seemed anxious to close the books on the Adamski death. Pushing for a ruling of natural causes took the police out of it because it was not a homicide that needed to be investigated.

Godfrey, however, was the problem. He pointed his fingers at the obvious disconnects in this case, such as the impossibility of a man with Adamski's cardiac condition being able to climb a twenty-five-foot-tall coal heap, the absence of footprints around the coal heap, the lack of coal dust on a person who allegedly climbed a coal heap, the strange burn marks around his head and neck, and the unidentifiable ointment. Adamski's wife believed her husband had been kidnapped and tortured, hence the burn marks and the ointment. But there was nothing in Adamski's background to suggest a reason for the torture. If it involved organized crime, why would the police cover it up? If Adamski was a spy, why would British intelligence cover it up? And, most important, why would a national-secrets letter connect the Adamski case with a UFO sighting and abduction, especially since Adamski's death was ruled due to natural causes? And why was Godfrey then forced out of the police department? Nothing connects these events except the national-secrets letter.

Could it be, I asked myself, that Adamski himself had been a victim of an alien abduction, an abduction gone horribly wrong because those who took him did not know until it was too late that he had a serious cardiac problem? In their experiments on Adamski, and even in their attempts to restart his heart through some sort of electrotherapy, his otherworldly abductors found themselves with a corpse instead of a subject. They redressed him, not really knowing how, of course, and simply dumped his body on a convenient coal heap. However, when a lone patrol officer refused to buy the party line and accept the findings, the Adamski abductors—perhaps even with the complicity of some agency in government—took Godfrey and shook him enough that the police could simply get rid of him while at the same time forcing his silence under national security. Far-fetched? Obviously, but still very convenient.

The scariest part of this for me isn't really the UFO or what happened to Adamski, although that was certainly tragic. It is the possibility that somewhere in the British government, as in our own, there is some entity in touch with or even working for the entities inside that strange craft. Just what kind of deal have they struck, and why aren't we in on it?

I would love to discover a conventional explanation for Adamski's death, even one on the margin of plausibility so we can go over the forensics. However, in the absence of such an explanation, the Alan Godfrey case is still one of my favorite, if not my very favorite, of the UFO cases.

STONEHENGE

Between 2 and 3 A.M. on June 21, 1987, officer Phil Hutchings and a group of police officers were standing guard over Stonehenge during a summer solstice ceremony attended by modern-day druid cele-brants when the officers spotted a strange light in the sky. The light came shooting over the horizon and flew directly across Salisbury Plain when Hutchings and the other officers noticed that it suddenly took a ninety-degree turn without ever slowing down. It maintained its speed. It flew back and forth as if, Constable Hutchings said, it were mapping the area—almost like a surveillance aircraft flying a grid pattern. The police officers did not file a formal report, Phil Hutchings said, because they would be held up to ridicule by their fellow police officers and looked at very critically by their superiors.

If the light the police saw was flying a grid pattern, why would that be? If we assume for the sake of argument that the light was a real ob-ject and that the light was emitted by an intelligently piloted craft, we might ask what was its intent? Special-effects producer John Tindall, who was with us at Stonehenge, took a number of GPS measurements and diagrammed the pattern of megaliths at Stonehenge. His goal was to see whether we could speculate as to the intent of what might arguably have been an intelligently piloted craft seen by police at Salis-bury Plain on the summer solstice.

Tindall began by building a scale model of the original Stonehenge to determine what its geometry might have been. He discovered that the relation among the megalithic stones was a series of equilateral triangles. By shining a laser through the scale model, built out of acrylic, Tindall was able to highlight those triangles. Then, in order to get a UFO eye view of what some pilot in the object overhead might have seen, he fixed a mirror to his workshop ceiling, reflecting the laser-demarcated triangles of Stonehenge. But Stonehenge is just that, stone. It isn't illuminating and doesn't reflect light. Therefore, light reflecting off an acrylic model only indicates one form of energy. What if the UFO were able to pick up another form of energy as it zigzagged across the sky over the site?

Hypothetically, Pat Uskert suggested, the UFO could be picking up some form of electrical energy, mapping it or even tapping into it as it followed the lines from stone to stone. Was Stonehenge generating an energy that we couldn't measure with our modern instruments but that the ancients could perceive and the UFO could receive? To suggest an answer to that question, Ted Acworth and Jeff Tomlinson, along with professional dowsers, experimented with mapping out lines of energy that human beings using dowsing rods could pick up. In repeated tests, our dowsers and even Jeff were able to mark areas where lines of energy crossed from stone to stone across the circle, which allowed us to outline the equilateral triangles that John Tindall measured. Therefore, as Pat speculated, if the lines of energy picked up by the dowsers were perceivable by a UFO, then the configuration of those energy lines might explain the odd zigzag pattern that the object seen by the police skirmish line was flying over Stonehenge on June 21, 1987.

BILL'S BLOG

Doing an episode on police UFO sightings was one of the highlights of the first season, as it would be in seasons 2 and 3, because of the very high credibility of police officers. It is also an interesting avenue to pursue because of the strange dichotomy between the police command, often administratively responsive to the demands of government policy, and the public's demands for full disclosure when police officers do report seeing UFOs. Consider this: when a police officer files a complaint or a witness report, a finder of fact in court takes it very seriously. More often than not, a police-witness report alone is enough for many juries or judges to convict. But take that same police officer and have him admit to seeing a UFO, and he will be subjected to ridicule to the extent that his credibility will be challenged even later in his career. In the case of Police Constable Alan Godfrey, his report of an abduction and subsequent investigation into what happened to him was considered such a breach of protocol that he was ordered to cease any regression therapy and ultimately forced out of the police.

Of particular note in the Godfrey case was the British Official

Secrets Act letter. If one is looking for some documentary evidence that the British took the UFO sighting seriously, all one has to do is consider the letter itself that orders Godfrey not to talk about the UFO he saw. Alan Godfrey described the contents of that letter to us on *UFO Hunters*. If there was no UFO, why would the letter make mention of it? And in the case of Phil Hutchings and the police skirmish line at Stonehenge, why would multiple witnesses admit to seeing the strange object but not report it to higher command? Again, the ridicule factor suppresses UFO reporting.

At Stonehenge, Pat and I were able to walk among the megaliths at dawn. For me, having taught medieval English literature and researched the Arthurian legends as a graduate student and college professor, just walking among the stones and standing on Salisbury Plain was thrilling enough. It recalled to me the thrill of reading Sir Thomas Malory and contemplating the majesty of the mystical court of Camelot for the first time. Britain's druidic past, the remains of the prehistoric beaker folk and barrow people, and the expanse of the plain itself as the first rays of the sun played through the architecture of Stonehenge made real for me what had only been faded folios of decayed manuscript. UFOs notwithstanding, this was Stonehenge. And in that cold gray dawn, the spirits of King Arthur, Sir Lancelot, and Sir Gawain walked among its ruins. For a magic moment, as the sun's first rays peeked from behind the stones, the crew, the cameras, the entire episode faded away and I was there in the rapture of sixth-century Britain experiencing my private and personal "realms of gold."

REVERSE ENGINEERING

Reverse engineering, in its simplest form, is the development of or copying of a technology from an existing technology. Although Philip Corso made the term famous to the UFO community in his book *The Day After Roswell* (Simon and Schuster, 1997), which I wrote with him, reverse engineering in its purest form is not automatically connected to alien technology. The Soviets, for example, reverse engineered a version of our B-29 bomber, the United States reverse engineered the machine gun mounts on helicopters from seeing the French gun mounts, and, during World War I, aircraft manufacturers copied one another in developing the firing mechanisms of machine guns on fighter planes. Reverse engineering, or back engineering, as it is sometimes called, has been around for a long time.

In this episode, the team investigated claims that much of our modern technology was reverse engineered from crashed UFOs. Real evidence to substantiate any claims of reverse engineering from alien technology was not only elusive, it was downright invisible. However, there was certainly no shortage of circumstantial and anecdotal evidence. At the same time, some of the claims of reverse-engineered technology that we covered in our investigation were not only doubtful but, we found, downright fraudulent. People, we discovered, can be quick to jump on board attractive claims of ET proof, but the evidence to support it is inconclusive at best. We did find some real compellingly suggestive testimony, however, as well as evidence that one of the most widely circulated Internet stories of a reverse-engineered alien craft was nothing more than an elaborate hoax.

THE EPISODE

Our first segment took the team out to Littleton, Colorado, to meet with MUFON's then director James Carrion to talk about a UFO flap that was getting a lot of attention on the Internet. It was a strange-shaped object that looked as if it were somehow alien that had been photographed in the skies over Bakersfield, Capitola, and then Lake Tahoe, California. Photos of the object were circulating around the Web, folks were talking about it on the various UFO discussion lists, and questions were abounding. What was this thing that was hoop shaped, had no wings or propellers, and had a series of spires on top of it? Were it not for the spiked spires and the narrow arms attached to the hoop, you might think it was a flying doughnut. How did the thing stay aloft?

There were three different sets of photographs, the last of which was sent directly to the MUFON Web site, thus coming to the attention of James Carrion. Most of the locations of this craft were near Saratoga, California, in addition to Capitola, locations near Moffett Field, which houses NASA's Ames Research Center, Carrion explained. Was that significant? It could be, speculation went, because at least one theory was that the craft was a NASA–air force creation reverse engineered from alien or otherworldly technology. This theory was rampant even though many people asked why, if this was secret government technology, were its creators flying it during daylight hours over populated areas?

James Carrion pointed out that the craft in the photos bore cryptic symbols along the arms, symbols that did not resemble the letters of any known alphabet. However, Carrion said, in June of 2007 a gentleman named Isaac had come forward, saying that he recognized the symbols because he worked on a project in the 1980s called the CARET Program. This individual claimed that he was an engineer who had worked on a government program called the Commercial Applications Research for Extraterrestrial Technology, or CARET, and posted a number of documents on the Internet about this device and the program, saying he had taken them from the government.

Among the claims that Isaac made, Carrion explained, were that the craft used invisibility technology and that the reason this craft was observed in the sky—plain as day—was that the invisibility cloak was disrupted by nonhuman technology. It was alien technology that enabled the craft to fly, to levitate, and to be under intelligent control without any visible evidence of a conventional propulsion system. Simply stated, the craft had been reverse engineered from otherworldly technology. As outrageous as these claims were, it was certainly not the first time either the team or I had heard of reverse engineering being used on otherworldly technology.

Carrion said he had strong reservations about the authenticity of the CARET images. They seemed too staged, too clear against the sky background, and awkwardly out of place. He pointed to the clarity of the photos and the fact that the object was in perfect focus against the perfect focus of the background, meaning there was no distinction between the object in the foreground and the background focal plane. That focus made it tough to gauge the object's size from the photographs. It looked as though the object had been photographed separately and then dropped or Photoshopped onto an existing background. The other problem that we noticed was that the object gave no indication of motion. Was it hovering or moving in any direction? Simply stated, according to Carrion, the object and the information supplied by the mysterious Isaac seemed like a hoax.

Dr. Ted Acworth also reviewed the CARET object photographs

with a U.S. navy photo expert, Dr. Bruce Maccabee. They noted, as Carrion did, that the object was completely unaerodynamic from a conventional perspective. In order to fly it had to be using a physics unknown to us or it had encased itself in some kind of antigravity envelope. But Dr. Maccabee also noted that the photographs seemed to have evolved from the first Internet postings to the photos sent to MUFON. The object grew more parts to it, which Ted suggested could have meant that the object was still under development or that whoever was posting this was adding more features to the photos.

Ted Acworth also conducted detailed frame-by-frame image analysis of the CARET craft and determined that not only was the lighting all wrong because sunlight was shining in one direction while the object itself was lit from another direction, but the craft always seemed to be photographed near, but not in, wooded areas. It looked as if someone was building a digital composite photo by placing the craft near straight lines in order to position it. It made no sense, Ted surmised, because someone photographing a strange-looking object would most certainly have snapped off a series of photos, one or more of which would have captured the craft behind the trees. But in a composite, it would have been difficult to position the image digitally on an existing background if one had to put it behind trees.

The other problem is that the craft seems stationary even though it is depicted as moving across a tree line, seeming both stationary and moving at the same time. The photograph seemed to be contradicting itself. If the craft is indeed moving, the camera should have picked up something called "motion blur," a slight blurring effect around the edges that occurs because the shutter isn't fast enough to hold the image in place. In these photos, there is no motion blur, no indication that the craft is moving even though the series of photos indicates motion. Therefore, it is plausible to suggest that the craft is simply an image digitally dropped onto a preexisting background. Ted ultimately concluded, along with Bruce Maccabee, that the CARET image is a hoax.

But why? Why would someone go to such elaborate lengths to create such a hoax? For fun?

James Carrion believes that the CARET hoax was a piece of disinformation, an intentional setup to cover up some real secrets that the government—or private industry—felt were in jeopardy. What that secret was we may never know, but Carrion felt it was important enough to warrant the level of deception that CARET offered.

The other suggestion we raised to explain CARET, assuming for the sake of argument that the object was not real but covering up something else, was that reverse engineering of ET objects was being contracted out to corporations outside the government to protect the secrets from Freedom of Information requests. This would comport with the theory that aerospace companies such as Lockheed were given pieces of alien technology from which to develop new types of aircraft. Was the SR-71, whose advanced design and composite fabrication were far ahead of anything flying when it was created in the mid 1960s, the result of Lockheed's Kelly Johnson seeing a UFO flying over the Pacific or of Lockheed's getting a piece of alien technology?

NASA'S HIDDEN UFO SIGHTINGS

If the CARET object was a hoax, what did it say about reverse engineering in general? We asked one of the country's living experts about it, MUFON's national director and its cofounder, former NASA employer John Scheussler, whom, like Carrion, we also visited in Colorado. Scheussler's interest in NASA's involvement with UFOs began with the unmanned January 19, 1965, *Gemini* mission around Earth, during which radar operators picked up two unidentified objects following the craft on its first suborbital pass. By the time the *Gemini* came around the second time, the objects had disappeared.

Six months later, *Gemini* 4 astronaut Air Force Major James McDivitt reported a sighting of a cylindrical object through his window as the space capsule passed over Hawaii. He radioed the sighting and

took photographs of the object. McDivitt said in subsequent interviews, some of which were cited in *UFO Magazine*, the object was
white and "had a long arm that stuck out on the side." UFO debunker
Phil Klass later showed McDivitt a photo of *Gemini* 4's Titan II booster
to see if, perhaps, McDivitt observed the booster and was unable to
identify it as such. But McDivitt wrote back to Klass, telling him that
the booster was definitely not the object he saw in space near the
Gemini 4 capsule. Scheussler said that McDivitt was serious when he
claimed that the object he saw "wasn't ours." He went on to become a
high-ranking officer in the air force and never tried to hide the fact
that he'd seen an object in space that he couldn't identify.

While Scheussler was at NASA, he told us, he began compiling
astronaut-UFO-sighting reports. This caught the attention of others
at NASA, and Scheussler was finally called into a meeting in which he
was asked to present his findings about the descriptions of UFOs. It
turned out, Scheussler said, that the group seeking this information
was an advanced design group, developing the concept for a stealth
fighter. The group was seeking to reverse engineer, from Scheussler's
information, a configuration for the new fighter. And before long there
was a stealth fighter on the drawing boards, which later saw action in
the Gulf War.

Scheussler explained that the early crashes of UFOs in the late
1940s provided Pentagon researchers and scientists with a wealth of
hardware from which they could reverse engineer new technologies.
He said that one of the most important of those technologies was fiber optics. These glass wires through which observers could see the
passage of light weren't called fiber optics at first. Another technology
was invisibility.

"We had lots of reports," Scheussler revealed about his days at
NASA and the Mutual UFO Network, "that UFOs were flying along,
being chased, when they suddenly disappeared." Maybe the idea of a
cloaking device to create the sense of invisibility came from the reported abilities of UFOs to cloak themselves. Scheussler pointed to
the recent development of cloaking technology by the British mili-

tary. They were able to make a tank disappear by using cameras on one side of the tank to project an image on the opposite side of the tank of the background. To the observer, the tank itself was invisible because all they saw was the landscape on the other side of the tank. Scheussler said that the idea for this has been around for some time and might well have come from a cloaking device that UFOs used to make themselves disappear while they were being chased by military fighter jets.

Inside NASA, Scheussler explained, there existed a "special access community." This was a close-knit group through which all UFO secrets were passed and shared among similar groups inside other government entities. Pat Uskert asked him straight out, "Can you tell us who had what?" in terms of what secrets were shared. And Scheussler responded, "I would not say anything about that on camera." When Pat pressed him about it, Scheussler said, "You wouldn't want me shot."

Reverse engineering from UFOs was also responsible, according to our guest aviation historian Bernard Thounel, for the design and development of the SR-71 Blackbird. He told us that it was a well-known and often-told story that Lockheed president and head of the secret Skunk Works division Clarence "Kelly" Johnson once revealed that he saw a Roswell-type UFO, a flying crescent.

THE CLARENCE "KELLY" JOHNSON SIGHTING

Although in UFO lore many believe that this was simply a sighting of an unidentified craft, the incident goes much deeper and actually wound up in Project Blue Book, although it was later explained away as a lenticular cloud. The sighting, which Johnson made from the window of his home overlooking the navy air station facility on Point Mugu on the Pacific Ocean, took place around 5 P.M. on December 16, 1953. Johnson saw a cylindrical object seemingly floating over the sea. At first, by his own admission, Johnson thought he was looking at a lens-shaped cloud formation. The flat clouds, because of their

disk shape, can easily be mistaken for UFOs or as a cloud cover for
UFOs. This is what Johnson thought he was seeing at first, until he got
a closer look through his binoculars and saw that it had begun to
move, climbing and accelerating away from him and against the direction of the other clouds in the sky. These clouds were floating with
the wind and the object was moving against the wind. It was clear to
him, when he saw how the shape was moving, that it was not a lenticular cloud—which would be dependent on the air currents—but
an object navigating under its own power. As for what it was, Johnson
couldn't say at first.

As Johnson watched the craft ascend at a very high speed, one of
his Lockheed test craft, the prototype of what would become a fleet of
navy and air force early-warning radar-surveillance planes, was flying off the coast of Long Beach, California. The plane, soon to become
part of the radar defense system in the 1950s and 1960s, was flying at
about fourteen thousand feet when one of the Lockheed pilots, Roy
Wimmer, noticed a circular-shaped object off to the west. It was almost 5 P.M. Wimmer determined that the object was not moving, just
hovering, and was a flying object, not a cloud. He actually told his
copilot, Rudy Thoren, perhaps jokingly, to "look out for the flying
saucer." Thoren turned the aircraft toward the object, which simply
sped away from the oncoming plane.

The following day at a meeting between Johnson and the crew,
Thoren told his boss about the encounter with the unknown object,
thus confirming Kelly Johnson's own sighting at the same time and
in the same position. Although Johnson, now believing that he and
his test crew had seen the same object and that it was not a conventional aircraft, was reluctant to make a formal report because he believed it would injure his credibility with the air force, for whom he
was developing advanced aircraft, he did make a report of what he
and his crew saw to air force general Donald Putt, who had helped
develop the B-29 bomber during World War II.

Putt might well have been in the loop of those who were studying

UFOs in the air force. He had reviewed the Canadian Avro flying saucer, which was like the flying wedge, or crescent, that Kenneth Arnold reported seeing over Mount Rainier in June, 1947, and Putt's visit to Canada to see the craft made the newspapers. Putt had been identified with investigations into the nature of UFOs. Putt, eventually, sent the Lockheed report to the air force, a report that wound up in the files of Project Blue Book even though it was dismissed as simply a sighting of lenticular clouds.

His sighting impressed on him the possibility that a craft shaped like the Avro saucer could fly, and as a result he ultimately designed the body for the SR-71 Blackbird to match it. The SR-71, as aviation historian Bernard Thounel told us on *UFO Hunters,* mirrors the shape that Johnson drew of a UFO he said he had seen. The SR-71, with its blended wing design, its body shaped to provide lift, and a huge tail section for stability, looks almost exactly like the Roswell craft. And, as Pat Uskert asked when he saw Kelly Johnson's sketch of the UFO, "Was his sketch of a UFO the first blueprint for the SR-71?" If so, it would have been among the early attempts to reverse engineer an aircraft from a flying saucer.

Modern stealth aircraft technology, the Stealth Fighter and the B-2 bomber, employ the blended wing shape of the SR-71. We also have had our own terrestrial history of a flying wing, including the Northrop flying wing and the Nazi jet-powered flying design in 1944. The U.S. Air Force shut down its own flying-wing program in 1948 after two test pilots were killed in a crash of that aircraft. Ted Acworth argued that the development of the flying wing here on our planet could have completely accounted for today's flying-wing warplanes without any help from extraterrestrial technology. His point was that, even if we got the geometry of the alien craft accurately, the functionality and underlying physics of an alien craft would have been almost impossible to duplicate given that society's advanced culture. A point well taken if we assume that the alien civilization was at the time of development thousands of years ahead of us. However, if, just for the sake of argument, we assume that some alien civilizations are not thousands of years ahead of us, but only a few hundred—or less—then suddenly a lot of new possibilities open up.

For example, UFO researcher and author Stanton Friedman has suggested that visiting aliens not only might be just a few hundred years ahead but also might be already living in our own interplanetary neighborhood. In that case, they are not traveling hundreds of light years just to grab a gallon of fresh water or to observe the dating habits of human beings in New York and San Francisco nightspots. They might have bases right here on planet Earth, as hidden from our view as duck blinds are from game, so that they can move about without the necessity of long-distance travel. In that case, their technology might be more mundane than we think. And if our secret technology is much more advanced than we think, perhaps the distance that had to be traversed by reverse engineering was far from insurmountable.

Among the areas where this reverse engineering might have been taking place, we surmised in this episode, was the top-secret base at Area 51 near Groom Lake in the Nevada desert. It was here, according to one of the most celebrated UFO whistleblowers, that alien craft were brought for research and development on back engineering an alien reproduction vehicle.

THE BOB LAZAR STORY

The Bob Lazar story has been circulating for almost twenty years. It has been talked about on television, on radio, and on the Internet. Bob has been featured on *UFO Hunters* as well as interviewed by Art Bell, George Noory, and George Knapp on *Coast to Coast AM*. Yet the debate about his background and his story still rages among UFO researchers. What we found when covering Bob Lazar's story on three seasons of *UFO Hunters* was that very credible and reputable people vouched for it and found documentation to show that Lazar was not fabricating or confabulating what he saw and did.

Robert Lazar first went on the air with George Knapp to reveal that he was an expert in propulsion systems who had been asked by the United States Air Force to take up employment at Area 51 to participate in a reverse-engineering program involving the propulsion of extraterrestrial craft. His mission was to figure out what made these things fly long distances, perform extreme maneuvers in Earth's atmosphere, and defy conventional aerodynamics.

The arc of Lazar's story—the discovery of what powered extraterrestrial craft; his marital problems over his long disappearances from home, during which time he said he was working at a top-secret base; and his hubris in revealing what he did to his wife and friends—has been at the center of the UFO controversy ever since his story was first broadcast. Lazar explained that he saw reverse-engineered flying saucers, watched them fly, and took his friends out to the Nevada desert to show them how these craft maneuvered through the sky. But his story became even more compelling when he told friends that he actually witnessed an energy beam that could, it was explained to him, freeze time. That beam, he explained, was part of the secret of alien vehicular propulsion and was something he was assigned to reverse engineer to a terrestrial craft.

Lazar's violations of his security clearance were discovered by those he reported to, and his job at the base was terminated. He, too, was almost terminated and has been wary of going public again for almost a decade. His story, however, goes to the very heart of reverse engineering, because if it is true, then he was a firsthand witness and participant in the air force's most secret back-engineering program.

DULCE

We also examined the possibility that some form of reverse engineering might have been taking place in the New Mexico town of Dulce, underground beneath or inside the Archuleta Mesa on the Jicarilla Apache reservation. It was to this facility, first constructed by the United States Army in 1936–37 in a series of old mining tunnels, that alien technology was brought for research purposes.

The lore, which has been proved to some extent, is that the western United States is riddled with underground tunnels, most of which were enlarged from nineteenth- and early-twentieth-century mining tunnels, that connect various bases across the West and Southwest. Understandably, after the Soviets launched their first space satellite in 1957, it became obvious that soon orbital surveillance would become a fact of life. Nothing on the surface could be hidden from cameras in space. Therefore, both sides in the Cold War began moving their assets underground. And because the surface of the planet was vulnerable to surveillance, even using highways or private roads to move material was to give away secrets. Thus, the United States began an intense tunneling operation to allow all types of materials to be moved from place to place without the scrutiny of cameras in space. Dulce, and the tunnels connecting it to other bases, was just such a facility.

We visited the Dulce area in our third season, but in this episode, we introduced the idea that if reverse engineering of alien technology were taking place, including research into recombinant DNA for the purposes of hybridizing the human and alien races or even for the purposes of studying ET DNA, Dulce would be a likely candidate for that type of research. In 2009, we would discover photographic evidence that genetic research at Dulce might well have been taking place.

THE CHINESE STEALTH FIGHTER

You don't need to go to Area 51 or Dulce to see reverse engineering in action. You only need to go to the nightly news or the Internet, where you'll find the reports of the Chinese stealth fighter, the J-20. If we think that we're the only ones in the stealth business, think again. Even if stealthy might have originally come from UFOs, it's now very conventional and very terrestrial.

Both the Chinese and the Russians, not challenged aeronautically, received a tremendous gift of technology from us when one of our

F-117 Nighthawks crashed over Bosnia during the Kosovo war. The pilot was rescued, but the plane that broke up when it was hit by a missile and crashed became a treasure trove for those trying to catch up to us. Not only were parts of the plane retrieved by the Serbians and put up for sale to the highest bidders, but parts of the plane were collected by souvenir hunters and local residents, who also sold them off. Thus, both the Chinese and the Russians, public bidders for these parts, benefited by seeing how our technology worked. And the Chinese People's Liberation Army tested the J-20 as a show of defiance, even while the secretary of defense at the time, Robert Gates, was hobnobbing with his Chinese counterpart and President Hu Jintao was visiting the White House. But stealth was all our technology originally, maybe ET technology before that, and was reverse engineered from our crashed F-117 in the same way, perhaps, that the transistor, integrated circuitry, fiber optics, and even Kevlar were reverse engineered from the flying saucer that crashed at Roswell in 1947.

THE TESLA FLYING SAUCER

Although wound up in all types of myth and lore, the story Ralph Ring tells about the Tesla/Otis Carr is a fascinating tale of a saucer-shaped flying machine invented by Carr, which Carr patented as an "amusement device" in 1959, which actually took off and flew seven miles. The craft, as far as Ring knew, had no conventional engine or propulsion system and, when Ring flew in it, presented no feeling or sensation of flying. It was at one moment stationary, according to Ring, and the next moment seven miles away. Ring said he could never explain it satisfactorily to himself.

Otis Carr claimed to have been a protégé of the great inventor and discoverer of alternating current, Nikola Tesla. Tesla also conducted the first experiments in the wireless transmission of electricity, invented the wireless radio, and claimed he could develop deadly particle-beam weapons. Carr believed, and convinced a number of investors, that he could build a working flying disk based on Tesla's theories of antigravity. Ralph Ring told us on *UFO Hunters* that despite what people have said about Carr—who died in 1982 and was once convicted of stock fraud—he really believed that he had the technology to build a flying disk, and, after meeting Ring, Carr wanted him to be a member of his team. This was in 1958, when Carr was building a device that he called the OTC-X1, which, he claimed, would be able to levitate, hover, and move so quickly that those inside would have no sense of motion. Carr could accomplish this feat, he told Long John Nebel on Nebel's radio show in 1958, because he had been shown the secret theories of motion by Nikola Tesla.

Carr was inspired to create this craft, he said, because he had personally witnessed the flights of three UFOs. Seeing these craft suggested to him that Tesla's theories of energy were correct, and he set about to build his own flying disk. Ralph Ring and two engineers were the first to test-fly this device, Ring told us. It was an experience he said he will never forget. Carr had told him that he was going to vibrate the craft to a particular frequency that was the color of aquamarine. And, indeed, Ring said that when Carr turned on the propulsion system, he and the two other engineers were surrounded by a "beautiful color of aquamarine." And then, that was it. Carr told them the experiment was over and to exit the craft.

According to Ring, the entire experiment lasted only fifteen seconds. But, Carr told the crew, during those fifteen seconds the craft when downrange for a distance of ten miles and then came back to the starting point. "You resonated here for about five seconds," Carr told the crew. "But for you it might have seemed like fifteen minutes." Then he asked Ring and the crew to check their pockets. What they found in the pockets of their jumpsuits were pieces of debris, rocks, stones, twigs, and grass that supposedly came from the landing spot ten miles away. "There was something," Ring told us, "we didn't have when we entered the craft."

"Were there any external witnesses extrinsic to the entire event?" I asked. "Yes," Ring said. "There was a police officer in Apple Valley and he and his buddy saw this craft." He had contacted Ring and asked if he and his crew had jumpsuits on. He said that he saw the craft and crew there for a few minutes and that then they left.

Ted Acworth was fascinated by what the propulsion system might have been and asked Ring what he thought was the power source. Ring explained that from what he understood from Otis Carr, the craft reached a specific frequency and the crew became resonant with it or, in Ring's words, "You become one with it." There is a science behind this, of course, if you consider what happens when two tuning forks, both in the key of C, are set side by side. If you strike one tuning fork, the resonant frequency will oscillate the other tuning fork because they are frequency entangled in the same key.

In our own experiment, John Tindall proposed that if he, in an isolation chamber, could strike the right frequency, the sound waves would actually levitate an object. In this case, John was using a paper cup, a very small-scale version of a cylindrical craft. Tindall tuned the three speakers feeding sound waves into the chamber to the resonant frequency of the chamber itself. In that way the chamber amplified the sound waves. When the speakers were turned on and balanced, the sound waves themselves made the cup levitate. Then, by directing the speakers, Tindall was able to navigate the paper cup around the chamber. It was an intriguing performance that showed that on a small scale, some of Otis Carr's theories about resonant frequency were actually demonstrable under laboratory conditions.

Pat Uskert wanted to know how Tindall related this laboratory demonstration to Ring's claims of riding a craft powered by some sort of resonant frequency device. Tindall explained that if Carr had managed to discover the resonant frequency of the ether in the atmosphere, Earth's energy, he would have been able to use that frequency, amplified and directed, to propel the craft.

Ring told us that the crew had no sense of movement other than a vibration. They were surrounded by an aquamarine color. They had no memory of traveling to another location, exiting the craft, and then returning. And they couldn't account for the passage of time. That element alone—missing time—sounded to me very much like an alien abduction. Could this mean that as part of their tool kit, the ETs are able to use resonant frequency not only as part of the propulsion system of their craft, but to levitate and to navigate their abductees into the craft? This was one of the tantalizing, but ultimately unanswerable, questions.

BILL'S BLOG

Ever since I met the late Lieutenant Colonel Philip Corso in 1995 and wrote the *New York Times* bestseller *The Day After Roswell* with him, I have been fascinated by stories of reverse engineering. Of course, Corso never claimed that there was anything exclusively extraterrestrial about reverse engineering, a process that has been going on ever since technologies from one culture were discovered by another culture. William Congreve's rockets, for example, deployed by the British against Napoleon and against us in the War of 1812 were reverse engineered from Chinese rockets. Corso explained that the Foreign Technology Division of army research and development also reverse engineered the machine gun mounts from French helicopters to allow American helicopters to use guns in the Korean War without the recoil from the rapid-fire weapons shaking the helicopter apart.

The stories about Clarence "Kelly" Johnson's UFO sightings were legend among the UFO community and were supported to an extent by another Lockheed Skunk Works executive, Ben Rich. Rich once told a gathering that "we"—either the United

States or Lockheed—had the technology to "send ET home." Parsing that statement, one can either construe it to mean that there is an extraterrestrial and we have actually sent it home, because we know where its home is, or that we have technology that could transport an ET to its home planet if we truly had an ET and knew where its home planet was situated. You can be the judge of that. But the interesting confluence here is that both heads of Lockheed Skunk Works addressed the ET question from the perspective of technology in a very knowing way.

One of the theories that has consistently permeated the UFO community is that, from the very beginning of human civilization on planet Earth, extraterrestrials have been slowly seeding communities with specific technologies to jump the communities' advancement ahead by decades or centuries. Discoveries of devices, gear-driven calendars and time pieces, in ancient shipwrecks; advanced structural engineering in ancient ruins atop unscalable mountain peaks; massive undersea monoliths arranged as shipping docks—all point to some sort of seeding of technology with the local cultures, which those cultures were able to reverse engineer. Therefore, when we proposed a reverse-engineering episode to the network, they were enthusiastic about seeing the evidence. And one of the guest experts that we invited, although his segment was not in final cut, was theoretical physicist Dr. Jack Sarfatti, whose story of intellectual-technological seeding was downright hair-raising.

Sarfatti described an experience he had in his Brooklyn home back in the 1950s when he was twelve and received a strange phone call. A thin, metallic voice was on the other end of the line, promising him that if he agreed to meet other intellectually gifted children a spaceship would soon arrive to pick him up. There were other children in this group, children he probably met later in life as adults. It was the strangeness of this phone call and his meeting up with other scientists such as Fred Alan Wolf that made up most of this segment and set us

REVERSE ENGINEERING ◆ 233

up for meeting Ralph Ring and his story of the Otis Carr/Tesla-driven flying saucer.

The Tesla segment was also something I had been looking forward to because the technology that Tesla researched and then proposed to the U.S. military was decades ahead of its time. Tesla proposed robotic soldiers, guided missiles, advanced radio-directed torpedoes, and even antigravity to the Department of War as World War II storm clouds gathered over Europe. In fact, when the United States refused to fund his antigravity development, Tesla offered it to the Soviet Union, who gave him a $25,000 grant for the development. This caught the attention of the American authorities to the point where, after Tesla's death, the Office of Alien Properties seized Tesla's notes and gave his antigravity notes to General Nathan Twining at the Air Materiel Command at Wright Field. It was to Wright Field that the Roswell flying saucer was finally brought for analysis.

It has been suggested by some Tesla researchers that Tesla reverse engineered some of the ET technology for particle-beam weaponry, and wireless energy, and antigravity from those extraterrestrials, with whom, he claimed, he had been in contact. That's why stories of gifted individuals have always fascinated me. Their out-of-the-box thinking and stunning inventions suggest a kind of inspiration that doesn't come from schoolrooms alone. In Tesla's case, perhaps his claims of extraterrestrial contact had a basis in reality.

I can only imagine what else might be out there. What other technologies have we developed besides invisibility, cloaking devices, propulsion systems that could bend time and space, and others that we're keeping under wraps lest they find their way into the hands of those who would use them for destruction? Or maybe, as some UFO researchers have suggested, it is ET himself who is keeping the most dangerous technologies under wraps so we don't destroy ourselves.

VORTEXES

I t's actually "vortices," but since everybody on the set was stumbling over the word, we settled on "vortexes" and figured whoever wanted to admonish us would probably do so for many other reasons besides our use of the word. Whether it's "vortices" or "vortexes," the premise of the episode was that there are places on the earth where it seems as though there is a portal to another reality. It's easy to dismiss this idea of portals or vortexes as a fantasy out of a Harry Potter story, but there is science behind this and at least some mathematics to reinforce the prospect of portals as a theoretical possibility. For our purposes, consider the idea of parallel universes or even a "multiverse" created at the first nanoseconds of the Big Bang. Theoretical physicists suggest that there could be an infinite number of universes created when the singularity inflated. Imagine that some of these universes exist on different planes that criss-cross, creating portals where the realities intersect. If so, what can pass through these portals? Are these other universes populated by life-forms just like us or are there completely different life-forms that can exist in a multitude of realities?

If you can consider all these possibilities, consider the further possibility that there are places right here on Earth where elements from one or more universes can pass through into ours. Might this explain everything from ghostly apparitions to extraterrestrials to flying saucers? That was what we set out to investigate in this episode, seeking evidence from eyewitnesses and possibly from scientific testing that there are places where portals exist between our reality and another.

THE EPISODE

We began by listing some of the great UFO hot spots in the United States, places that have a preponderance of UFO sightings or reports of strange creatures. There is no shortage of these. Places like the Skinwalker Ranch, in Utah; the Dugway Proving Ground, in Utah; Dulce, in New Mexico; Sedona, Arizona; and the site of one of the most intense UFO flaps twenty years ago, New York's Hudson Valley.

Portals, as first defined by one of our guest experts, Chris O'Brien, meet four major criteria, which require that the area in question be a sacred or hallowed site, have an energy presence in it that differs from the ambient energy in areas surrounding it, have a military presence, and have a history of UFO sightings. Each of the areas we visited in this episode qualified as a portal because it had these four elements.

LEY LINES

First explored by Alfred Watkins as a series of ancient pathways crisscrossing the English countryside, pathways used by Bronze Age Britons, ley lines have come to mean lines of low energy that traverse the planet. Whether these lines are paths of electrical energy or hydroelectric energy generated by underground streams, when they cross, they form a nexus of energy. The pattern of ley lines, also called the earth's grid or magnetic grid, seems to connect ancient monuments and megaliths.

It is at the sites of these megalithic monuments, huge multi-ton stones seemingly transported to these spots by prehistoric societies, that ley lines intersect and highly strange phenomena also occur. Ley-line intersections have been known to be flying-saucer hot spots, or places, as we investigated on *UFO Hunters,* where there may be natural portals to other worlds. Other researchers have said that the intersection of ley lines also results in "stargates," portals that connect different realities or different levels of the multiverse to one another.

HUDSON VALLEY

The best-known flap of UFO sightings in the lower Hudson River valley just north of New York City began in December 1981, according to the records. But one of the first sightings/encounters took place over Ossining, New York, in June 1962, when balls of light passed over cars on the road, causing them to stall and their radios to go silent, only to restart by themselves after the lights had gone. A year later, an enormous craft moved silently through the skies over Newburgh, New York.

On December 31, 1981, thousands of witnesses in the Hudson Valley area saw strange lights in the sky, flying in a formation. This sighting began with a retired police officer's sighting in Kent, New York. He'd stepped into his backyard that night for a breath of fresh winter air when he saw a cluster of red, green, and white lights floating overhead in an organized pattern. At first, he thought they belonged to a formation of helicopters. Odd though it seemed, it was still conventional. However, as the lights came toward him from the south, he realized, to his astonishment, that these were not helicopters at all. He could not see the flashing navigation lights. Instead, he saw steady colored lights flying in a huge V formation.

Nevertheless, at first—and this is typical of most witnesses—he believed the lights were the navigation lights of one or more airplanes. As it turned out, one of the explanations for the lights was that a group of private pilots were flying in formation over the Hudson Valley and this group of pilots did hoax the phenomenon once it hit the news. But on this night, the first witness really did believe he was looking at conventional aircraft until the lights grew closer.

If these were conventional, the witness told himself as the lights approached, he would be hearing the whine of engines or the roar of jets. Yet there was nothing but silence. Then, as the lights came closer, the witness said he realized that he was not looking at a formation of aircraft because the lights didn't move with respect to each other. If they were military aircraft, he thought, jets flying in a tight formation, he would have long since heard the sound of jet engines. But these lights were low to the ground, and he could see that they didn't move independently at all. He believed that he could actually see a rigid structure connecting the lights, thus making it a single craft. It was shaped like a triangle, perhaps with softly rounded edges, he reported later.

As the object passed almost directly overhead, the witness said it emitted something like a soft electrical hum, as if he were listening to a pulsating electric engine. It sounded as if something was generating a powerful field that throbbed with each surge of energy. He could also see that the triangle shape was more like an arrowhead with a clearly distinctive body. He was watching a shape, whether extraterrestrial or a new air force craft, that would appear regularly over the Hudson Valley and the west side of Manhattan for the next few years and that would reappear over Phoenix, Arizona, and parts of Nevada fifteen years later.

From 1982 to 1983, even before claims of hoaxes filled the newspapers and airwaves, the same type of craft would be seen up and down the Hudson Valley and across the river into Connecticut. The sightings all involved a V-shaped string of lights or a triangular-shaped object. These ongoing reports of sightings, shared informally among friends and neighbors, transmitted to 911 dispatchers, and appearing regularly in local newspapers prompted local UFO researchers to seek investigative help from national sources. Among those who became curious about the reports, particularly the mass sightings and the uniformity of the descriptions, was Dr. J. Allen Hynek, the astronomer, who had been the official skeptic/advisor to the U.S. Air Force's Project Blue Book. Blue Book was at first thought to be the military's honest attempt to compile and investigate UFO sightings dating back to the late 1940s, but years later it was determined to be a simple cover-up. It debunked most sightings, reserving the most troubling reports to more secret files before being shut down in 1969. Dr. Hynek, once freed from his official role as the skeptic, then came forward with a change of perspective. He became an advocate of UFO research and sought explanations for just the type of incidents that folks in the Hudson Valley were reporting.

Working with local researcher Phil Imbrogno, with whom he wrote the book *Night Siege* (Llewellyn, 1987), along with Bob Pratt, Dr. Hynek, who died in 1986 before the book's completion, encouraged local researchers to collect as many sighting reports as they could. With hundreds of reports describing the same object, sometimes well over two hundred a night, the team of researchers was able to come up with a pattern not only to the object itself, but to the ongoing sightings. The silence of the object, its slow-moving progress across the night sky, and its vast size—"larger than two or three football fields," many witnesses said—all suggested to the researchers that so many witnesses couldn't be deceiving themselves into believing they were seeing something highly strange. Ironically, on one of the very same nights in March 1983 that the researchers were at work on compiling the data, the object was observed by motorists driving along the Taconic State Parkway. In this famous group sighting, reminiscent of scenes from *Close Encounters of the Third Kind,* drivers pulled their cars over to the shoulder of the parkway and simply watched in awe as the huge object noiselessly floated over them. The 911 switchboards that night lit up with so many calls that the dispatchers were overwhelmed. Afterward, some said that if there had been a true emergency it would have been doubtful whether enough open lines existed to handle the emergency and the calls coming in about the unidentified flying object.

One of the most dramatic and possibly threatening episodes in the

Hudson Valley sightings was the appearance of a giant flying triangle over the Indian Point nuclear power plant in 1984. Then editor in chief Vicki Cooper reported in *UFO Magazine* that interviews with sources, who refused to be named because they were afraid for their jobs and their reputations, revealed that in June 1984, in the midst of the UFO flap, a huge craft appeared over the Indian Point nuclear power plant on two separate occasions. These incidents also occurred not only within the context of the ongoing sightings but also just about five years after the motion picture *China Syndrome* and the release of radioactive-contaminated water at the Three Mile Island nuke in Pennsylvania, an incident that, coinciding with the movie, just about shut the nuclear industry down in the United States and put the East Coast in a panic. Therefore, a strange craft reportedly hovering over a nuclear power plant just north of New York City was a major incident.

According to *UFO Magazine*, the two appearances occurred just ten days apart. The first one, on June 14, amounted only to a sighting by security officers at the plant as a craft flew over the area. In the light of the subsequent UFO event, one might assume that the first flyover might have been simply for surveillance purposes, presaging a later appearance of the UFO. The second incident was far more extensive.

On the night of June 24, according to Vicki's story, one of the security guards who noticed the large triangle approaching the plant yelled out, "Here comes that UFO again." He alerted the other guards as the craft seemed to hover about three hundred feet over the number 3 reactor, the only reactor online that evening. The thousand-foot craft—that was the estimate the security guards gave—spent at least ten minutes over the active reactor. The length of time the craft spent and the ability of it to hover at such a low altitude prompted some of the management personnel at the plant to consider calling the Air National Guard or the air force to confront the object.

Some investigators said that the appearance of the object and its flight characteristics fit those of a blimp. But a thousand-foot blimp intruding over restricted airspace and staying there for no other purpose than to draw attention seems very unlikely. Moreover, researchers after the event contacted facilities that handled blimps or large balloons, and none of them reported having any craft in the air that night. Moreover, the shape of the craft itself, a flying V, wasn't like any conventional blimp anyone had ever seen before. The craft was clearly a mystery.

Night Siege coauthor Phil Imbrogno said that after the UFO incident, a crack developed in reactor 3, but New York Power Authority employee Carl Patrick denied any damage to the reactor. Further, Imbrogno has said, the UFO appearances continued over Indian Point even after the July 24, 1984, incident. Carl Patrick denied this as well and said that, despite claims to the contrary, there were no fluctuations in power at the plant, the security system was not disabled, and no upgrades to the security system were installed after the incident. Records from the Nuclear Regulatory Commission also do not show any irregularities in the plant's operation, but UFO researchers who've spent years searching government records and interviewing government spokespersons say that when it comes to talking about UFOs, government people simply deny, deny, and deny.

What is especially fascinating about UFOs over nuclear facilities is that there seems to be correlations between UFOs and their interest in our nuclear plants, nuclear weapons, and the bases that house nuclear weapons. RAF Bentwaters, the site of the 1980 UFO incident, was a nuclear weapons base, storing nukes for use by forward squadrons of NATO and U.S. Air Force warplanes in Germany. The 1947 Roswell, New Mexico, incident was also noteworthy because the Roswell base, called Walker Field, was the first Strategic Air Command facility and was a base where nuclear weapons were to be stored in the event of a deployment. It was also the base from which the atomic bomb was loaded onto the B-29 that dropped it over Hiroshima to end World War II. Were UFOs sniffing out our nukes, or were they simply observing them or drawing power from them? That is still an unknown.

Author Phil Imbrogno has said that by 1987, residents of the Hudson Valley had filed so many reports of UFO sightings that it was clear that no formation of planes could account for all of it. In fact, many of the residents had come to believe that their area was the object of some kind of nonhuman surveillance. To collect data and bring many of the witnesses together, Imbrogno and New York attorney Peter Gersten held a conference, also attended by the author of *Communion*, Whitley Strieber; alien abduction researcher and author Budd Hopkins; and researcher Ellen Crystall, who investigated the Pine Bush sightings.

At the conference, some of the witnesses revealed that they not only saw strange craft but also were abducted and taken aboard the craft, entered into some kind of telepathic communication with an intelligence aboard the craft, or had an actual face-to-face meeting with an alien life-form. These were incredible reports that, if true, indicated the Hudson Valley sightings were far more than they were first assumed to be and encompassed a much broader scope.

The sightings of craft were not limited to New York State, but were actually recorded by researchers in Connecticut as well until 1989. Local residents spotted the craft from their cars as they were driving along local country routes and state routes all the way into eastern Connecticut. There were also accompanying sightings in the late 1980s in northern New Jersey on the western side of the Hudson River. These continuing sightings across three states amounted to one of the longest UFO flaps in the history of American ufology. According to some researchers, the flying triangles, at least one of which was reported floating over the West Side Highway in Manhattan in the late 1980s, are still going on today and, even though no longer in the headlines, can still be seen occasionally at night.

All of this being said, it would be inaccurate not to mention that a group of pilots, calling themselves the Stormville Flyers, claim to have been behind the early 1980s Hudson Valley sightings all along. They claim to have flown routes over the Hudson Valley in very tight formations to give the impression to people on the ground that it was a single craft sporting a V-shaped formation of lights. They also say they were able to change the colors of the lights on the planes they were flying, convincing some observers on the ground that they were looking at a craft with lights changing colors. And, finally, they said that they were able to fly so proficiently in a tight formation that they were able to turn their lights off to give the illusion that the craft disappeared. As for the hovering nature of the craft and its humming noise, the pilots claim that they were flying at such low speeds that from a distance it looked as if the craft was actually creeping along. And the humming sound? It was actually the sound of their propeller engines cruising at low speed.

If the Stormville Flyers were responsible for every sighting, then even experienced pilots on the ground, who were among the witnesses, and police officers, generally excellent observers, would have had to have been fooled by the formation of planes. Moreover, the Stormville Flyers' account does not explain the reports from the security guards at the Indian Point nuclear power facility, reports that suggested that guards saw a single craft. In addition, as happy-go-lucky as these "bored" private pilots might have been, it is, thankfully, a very rare private pilot reckless enough to chance flying over the restricted airspace of a nuclear power reactor and to thus alarm security personnel so much that they would consider calling in the Air National Guard to intercept the intruder. Bored pilots are not so bored that they want to lose their licenses and perhaps spend time in federal custody.

Most of the UFO researchers investigating the Hudson Valley sightings have long since become aware of the claims of the Stormville Flyers during the years 1983–1984. However, researchers say, the sightings in the Hudson Valley began in 1981 and continued for the following year. Yes, they ramped up during the middle 1980s, but they continued into the latter part of the decade. Did that mean that private pilots flying in formation were responsible for all the sightings? Were they responsible for the sightings across the state line in Connecticut or over Indian Point? The answer they come up with is no. At best, they concede, private pilots may have been responsible for some of the sightings, and certainly other people, influenced by reports in the newspapers and on television, might have duped themselves into believing that they were witnesses as well. Nothing would have prevented that. In fact, at the conference of Hudson Valley sighting investigators convened by Phil Imbrogno, they eliminated or discounted the majority of the reports as explainable by other means. It was a core minority of reports they focused on that defied explanation by conventional means.

Finally, it is unlikely that a respected scholar and U.S. government analyst like Dr. Hynek would have become involved in investigating a phenomenon that could have been explained away so conventionally. Wouldn't Hynek's and Imbrogno's reading reports from local airfields, searching for flight plans, and talking to witnesses at least put Hynek and Imbrogno on alert that this could have been a hoax from the beginning? It is more likely that the early reports of something strange in the skies prompted a group of pilots to mimic or re-create what folks on the ground were already seeing and thus to compound the situation with their actions. That's not far-fetched, and it does account for the Stormville Flyers' claims, the claims of witnesses, and the reports from the investigators.

As in all UFO investigations, the best investigators can get, after they methodically eliminate as many conventional explanations as they can, is that the object remains unidentified. Accordingly, even if the Stormville Flyers were responsible for some of the sightings during the most intense weeks of the Hudson Valley flap, the witnesses who were unable to identify the planes because they were camouflaging themselves by turning off their navigation lights or changing the colors of their lights were correct in saying that the objects they saw flying in the sky were unidentifiable. And that was the point of the investigation in the first place.

The Hudson Valley sightings weren't an isolated occurrence in the area, and sightings in the area date back to the 1960s and continue into the twenty-first century. Historically, the area was depicted by author Washington Irving as a place where ghosts and goblins ran

244 ❖ UFO HUNTERS

free, where the Headless Horseman terrified local residents, and where the spirits of the Native Americans held sway. But might there be a physical explanation for these phenomena? Are these just folk tales leading up to a mass sighting of small private aircraft misidentified as a UFO? One of the most reputable and important scientists involved in UFO research, Dr. J. Allen Hynek, says no; the Hudson Valley sightings, at the very least, were verifiable and credible.

Was there something about the extent of the Hudson Valley sightings that made them one of the longest flaps in American UFO history, stretching over twenty years and continuing, sporadically, into the present? UFO investigator Phil Imbrogno, who wrote *Night Siege* with J. Allen Hynek and Bob Pratt, suggested that there is a curious relation between Native American ruins and the prevalence of UFO sightings. He thought that the entire Hudson Valley area, with specific hot spots, is a portal between different realities, alternate universes, or even dimensions.

Science producer John Tindall states categorically that the earth is a dynamo. There is a theory that because the electrical energy generated by the earth's core reaches the surface in different intensities as a result of inconsistencies in the earth's crust, points along the earth's surface resonate with a greater energy. This might be another definition of an energy vortex. If so, it might explain why the ancients, at a time before the industrial generation of electricity, were more sensitive to low-level energy in the ground than we are today.

If UFO hot spots are connected to the ancients because the hot spots are energy vortexes, we would expect some correlation between ancient ruins or ancient altars and modern UFO activity. There are four criteria for identifying these potential hot spots:

1. The area had to be considered sacred by ancient peoples and is marked by monuments considered to be religious in nature.
2. There is a detectable energy field in the area that differs from the ambient energy in the surrounding areas.

3. There is a history of regular and ongoing UFO sightings or other anomalous experiences.
4. There is always a military presence nearby.

We found that all these criteria were present in the Hudson Valley area, particularly near the town of Pine Bush, New York, where geologist Dr. Bruce Cornet had conducted his research. Cornet said he investigated the nature of the area that might have attracted UFOs north of New York City and had been a hotbed of activity since the first Dutch settlers came to the Hudson Valley in the seventeenth century. This location has energy pulses so strong that the energy wave sometimes causes airplane instruments to fail. Cornet's readings, the result of his use of magnetometers and other energy-sensitive devices, centered on a property owned by Congregation Beth Hillel. It was the synagogue's cemetery.

Cornet began his research in 1992 by locating a grid of magnetic anomalies through the Pine Bush region. Then, by calibrating the locations of the UFO sightings over the years, he discovered that the magnetic anomalies on the ground, the anomalies that interfered with airplane instrumentation, were the same locations where witnesses spotted UFOs overhead, especially during the 1981–1986 Hudson Valley flap. Thus, two of the criteria are satisfied: the area has anomalous energy readings and it has documented UFO activity.

In April 1993, Cornet set up cameras around the area near the Beth Hillel cemetery to see if he could capture any images of UFOs on a time-lapse shutter. What he found astounded even him. He captured a strange light source moving across the sky, a light source that didn't move in a straight line, the way an airplane on course or even a helicopter would move, but that seemed to be spinning as it crossed the frame. We asked Cornet specifically why he thought the light was not a conventional aircraft. He said that there was no trace of navigation lights on the image he captured and that because the light source was spinning, he determined that no conventional aircraft could have made that image. This was not, he said, either an airplane or a helicopter. It was a completely different type of craft. He believed he caught a UFO on film.

As further evidence, Cornet cited the way the images seem to be making impossible hairpin turns, turns of 180 degrees that are so sharp, aircraft could not make them. The lights also seem to wink out on the film and then reappear a few beats of time later. These, also, are not the signatures of conventional aircraft, which form a steady line. And for those skeptics who said that Cornet was bouncing the camera, vibrating or shaking it, Cornet reminded us that the cameras were on tripods and set up automatically to film the night sky. There was no human handling of the equipment other than to set it up and leave it in the field. Moreover, the light itself, when the stream was measured and calculated across the frame of the photo, seemed to be moving at 35–40 miles per hour, far slower than any conventional aircraft could fly. This was another piece of evidence, Cornet argued, that showed the object was unconventional.

The strangest thing about the photographs, however, is the odd funnel-shaped portion of the stream, repeating itself every few frames. This seems to indicate that the craft, whatever it is, might be dissipating and reappearing, winking out and winking back into reality, as it travels. If this is the case, it might constitute photographic proof of the object's interacting with the energy field over Pine Bush. But, Cornet admitted, this is all speculation based on how one interprets the photograph.

One expert who worked on interpreting the photograph along with Dr. Ted Acworth and Dr. Bruce Cornet was Dr. Bruce Maccabee, the U.S. Navy and CIA photo analyst and one of *UFO Hunters'* most respected photo analysts. Maccabee, a highly regarded expert inside the UFO investigations community, said that even if the camera—which Cornet assured us was on a tripod the entire time—were being vibrated, the oscillations would be regular or symmetrical. These oscillations in the stream of light were asymmetrical, indicating that they were not the result of camera vibration but of something inherent in the object itself. This also intrigued Ted, who said that the breaks in the stream of light came from a damped harmonic motion. Because the camera was not moving, the harmonics were in the object, and that also made it difficult to call "conventional." Maccabee said that whatever it was, and he could not identify it, it had to be judged anomalous.

We further corroborated that there were no strange weather patterns that night, no thundershowers or lightning. We also checked with local air traffic controllers and learned that during that period there were no aircraft in the area. The sky was clear and no planes were flying through Cornet's camera's field of vision. There were no comets or meteor activity in the area. Accordingly, as Ted put it, Cornet's photograph was one of the best pieces of evidence we've been able to collect indicating the presence of vortexes.

Bruce Cornet's photograph establishes two criteria of vortexes: an intense energy field and the presence of UFOs. The third criteria, a military presence, is also a factor here because Stewart Air Force Base, now the Stewart Air National Guard Base, was at the time only sixteen miles away from Pine Bush. But what about the fourth criteria, the presence of ancient hallow ground? Is the Beth Hillel cemetery evidence of that? Probably not. However, as Dr. Phil Imbrogno showed us, there is another piece of evidence in support of the fourth criteria, the Native American obelisks.

"This is an area," Imbrogno said, "where there are structures dating back to probably 2000 BCE." Enigmatic stone chambers, built with great precision, and standing stones dot the entire valley. If they were built by early Native American inhabitants, they don't fit the type of structures built by the Algonquins, who populated the lower Hudson Valley. Another theory is that the stone chambers were root cellars built by early European settlers or colonists. But these chambers are aboveground and thus could not function as root cellars because the vegetables would freeze. Root cellars have to be dug beneath the frost line. This left us with the questions, why and by whom were these chambers constructed?

Imbrogno suggested that they were built by ancient Celtic

inhabitants of the area. He surmised that the Celts were temporary dwellers in North America and that the stone chambers were laid out according to a strict plan to form a line across the area that comported with the energy grid. They were all the same approximate size, six feet by eight feet high by fifteen feet deep, and constructed from medium-sized stones. The ceiling stones, however, are ten feet long, and, like England's Stonehenge, they seemed to be aligned to the position of the setting sun during winter solstice.

Pat asked Imbrogno, "So what's the connection between these stone chambers and obelisks and the UFOs?"

Imbrogno explained that when he was plotting the sights of UFOs across the Hudson Valley area, moving from town to town—Kent Cliffs, Peekskill, Brewster, Fishkill, North Salem, and Lake Carmel—he noticed that, one by one, each location had an obelisk standing in front of a stone chamber. At first, Imbrogno told us, "that was interesting, seeing a chamber and an obelisk at a UFO sighting location." Then at the next location he found the same thing. And at the next. And at the next. "Finally," he said, "after the fourth location it was obvious that this was more than a coincidence. The location of the chambers and the obelisks has something to do with UFOs." Is it the chambers themselves that draw the UFOs? Probably not, Imbrogno says. It's the locations. Something about the locations determines the way the stone chambers are aligned and the alignment also correlates to the UFO-sighting hot spots. These hot spots are places on the earth's grid where crossing lines of energy form a vortex.

One theory we talked about was the possibility that the UFOs are able to pull energy out of the earth's energy grid almost like plugging in an electrical device to a wall socket. Wireless transfer of energy was one of the successful experiments conducted by Nikola Tesla early in the twentieth century and particle-beam weapons are becoming a staple of the U.S. military's nonlethal weapons inventory.

Another possibility, raised by anomalous activities at Skinwalker Ranch in Utah, as described by authors George Knapp and Colm Kelleher in their book *Hunt for the Skinwalker* (Paraview Pocket, 2005), is that these energy vortexes are actually portals, portals to another reality or dimension, through which craft or even entities may pass. These portals, dangerous though they may be, would have been sacred sites in ancient religious ceremonies, especially if only shamans or seers were able to peer into them to see what might lie on the other side. If entities on the other side trusted the seers to keep their secrets and keep onlookers away from the portals, there might have been a sympathetic relationship between the human shamans and the entities in the other dimension. This is why the final criteria for a portal might be that it exists on sacred ground.

STONEHENGE

Of all the celebrated ancient sites in the Western world, Stonehenge is perhaps the best known. Not only because it figures so much in Celtic and druid legend or because it sits in the area where some of the stories of King Arthur played out, but because the huge stones, not native to the immediate environment and placed the way they are, remain a mystery to scholars and archaeologists. What was the function of this architecture? Why the specific arrangements of the stones, and how were they balanced? What were the builders trying to do?

A henge, of course, is a circular earthwork with a ditch inside the earthwork, possibly built as a ceremonial site during the Neolithic period. The modern word "henge," a back formation from Stonehenge, comes from the Old English verb meaning "to suspend" or "to hang," which may suggest that something was suspended from the stones inside the circle. Stonehenge is the best known of these structures, the intent of whose builders might have been purely ritualistic for the purposes of conducting seasonal ceremonies. Legend has it that the structure, possibly built by a community known as the barrow or beaker folk because they buried their dead in long earthen barrows, predated the Celts and the druids and was used as a place where human sacrifices were performed. Something about the particular area attracted the initial builders, and once the site was constructed other cultures used it for their own purposes, adding stones to the original arrangement.

Modern theory says that the arrangement of the stones served as a calendar marking the solstice. That might have been its original purpose, serving more for sacrificial rites than for anything else. Gradually, though, ancient sacrifices might have been associated with fertility rites to celebrate the passing of seasons in an agricultural society. Hence, the site might have been modified to mark the solstice by seeing where the sun's shadow or early rays fell inside the circle or through the stones. Today, modern new agers and celebrants reenacting druidic festivals congregate around Stonehenge at the summer solstice.

Historically, Stonehenge certainly qualifies as a sacred site. We also learned from police officers who guard the site during new age celebrations that it is a place where witnesses, mainly police, have seen UFO activity. In fact, in May 1990, music producer David Tickle, driving across Salisbury Plain to Guilford and passing Stonehenge and the barrow burial mounds that surround the site, was astonished to witness a flight of white circular objects, lights in the sky, blinking in and out of existence in synchronization with black objects on top of the barrow also winking in and out of view. Were the white blinking lights simply a function of the camera shutter or the lens aperture? Because the Tickle video we saw was a late generation poor copy of an analog video, we could not do much analysis except to comment on the possibilities. However, even if we discounted the white lights as being objects themselves, the black objects sitting on the barrows and winking in and out in concert with the white lights were hard to explain away. I speculated that if these lights were UFOs moving across the Stonehenge ley lines, the blinking—disappearing and reappearing in the same places—might represent their method of propulsion, drawing space and time through them so that they had a skipping motion.

The third criteria of a vortex hot spot is a military presence in the area. Stonehenge sits on Salisbury Plain at the center of over twelve military complexes. In fact, even while we were filming at the site we had to pause because of the sounds of military helicopters overhead and the intermittent thundering of artillery fire from one of the base's practice ranges. Thus, the third criteria for a vortex and hot spot was certainly satisfied.

We also wondered whether there was any energy vortex present at Stonehenge that might have attracted the original builders. The standard theory from local dowsers and folklore historians is that Stonehenge sits on a nexus of several ley lines, streams of low-level energy that, when crossing each other, become a swirl or vortex of energy.

How can modern science approach such a theory? Certainly there are instruments that can detect all types of electrical or magnetic energy, but in an age of cell phones, power grids, satellite transmission, and microwave towers populating the landscape, would there be interference blocking our ability to use instruments to detect very low levels of, for want of a better term, "Earth energy"? We can hypothesize that in an age before industry, before electricity, and even before large cities and the infrastructure necessary to support them, there existed intuitives among prehistoric cultures who were able to pick up these streams of low-level energy and the vortexes where they met with their own bodies. They might well have used certain implements to focus their abilities to receive these energies, implements that today would be called dowsing rods.

THE DOWSING EXPERIMENT AT STONEHENGE

Before we laughed it off, we were reminded that dowsers played an important part in the American West by finding places where settlers could dig wells for a water supply. In modern times, we were told by former army remote viewer Dr. Paul H. Smith, dowsing is still considered a way to focus attention on surroundings, that is, to block everyday sensory input, called analytic overlay, from flooding one's perception in order to receive a form of an energy signal. If those signals are the resonance of energy, harmonics that vibrate because of the interaction of ley lines, then it might validate scientifically the practice of dowsing. It was worth an experiment.

Dowser Maria Wheatley was our guide through the Stonehenge structure. Her job, she told us, would be to detect intersecting lines of energy through her dowsing rods, lines that would evidence the vortex nature of the structure. She knew that she could do it, but she also wanted to show that Pat could dowse as well. She explained that dowsing rods are not talismans or instruments with powers intrinsic to themselves. Rather, she said, it is the person who is sensitive to the very low levels of energy and responds by involuntary muscle movements. The dowsing rods merely react to those muscle movements and point in the direction of the energy flow.

Maria said that the altar stone was the center of the original ancient site, a stone where human sacrifice took place. She said that because it was at the center, it would make sense that she would be able to sense intersecting energy lines with her dowsing rods. She stepped into the circle demarcated by the stones, dowsing rods in position, and, sure enough, as she crossed the center line the rods swung to align themselves with the invisible energy field. She kept walking to the next stone in line with the altar, and again the rods swung. She told us that she was not dipping her hands or moving her hands. It was the rods that moved by themselves in response to her intuiting the energy field.

To prove her point, Maria suggested that Pat Uskert use the dowsing rods and walk the same path she did. Her argument was that if Pat experienced the same sensations and the rods moved in the same way, that would indicate two things: that Pat was intuitive and that the same dowsing path would return the same results. Then, with Ted Acworth as the referee, making sure that Pat didn't consciously move his hands to get the rods to swing, Pat walked through the circle. At the same spot where Maria sensed the energy stream, Pat's dowsing rods also swung, aligning themselves with the altar stone at the center of the henge. Pat said that he deliberately tried to hold the rods steady, forcing his hands not to drop. "They moved by themselves," Pat said. "And, I have to say, I was really weirded out by it."

Now it was time for Ted to see if he could validate Maria's and Pat's readings by retracing their steps, this time with a magnetometer to see if Maria's and Pat's perceptions of energy with the use of their dowsing rods matched what Ted could read from his magnetometer. With Maria holding the dowsing rods and a magnetometer, Ted and Maria retraced Maria's path through the circle. This time, however, even though the rods reacted in the same way, aligning themselves with an invisible energy field, the dial on the magnetometer remained motionless. Nothing. "Maybe it's not a magnetic field at all," Ted said, leaving open the possibilities that there was a force that our instruments were incapable of registering or that there was no real energy field at all, only the motion of the dowsers' hands and body that made the rods move. Maybe Maria, having dowsed this area before, simply reacted to an old pattern. For his part, Pat, seeing the rod motion Maria experienced, may have simply done the same. It was time for another test, this time a blind one.

Ted led our science intern Jeff Tomlinson, who had not been a part of the initial dowsing-rod testing, to the edge of the circle without telling him what was about to happen. We had kept Jeff away from the set for the entire dowsing demonstration. Ted blindfolded Jeff, put the dowsing rods into his hands, and then walked him toward the spots where both Maria and Pat had dowsed. Without any prompting or explanation, as Ted and Jeff walked the same path as Pat and Maria had moments earlier, the dowsing rods in Jeff's hands reacted, aligning themselves with the streams of energy. You could see the shock on Ted's face. At first he could not explain it.

To Ted's credit, however, he wanted to make sure that he could prevent Jeff's small, almost unconscious hand movements from tilting the dowsing rods. To accomplish this, Ted fashioned a pendulum device to steady the L-shaped rod Jeff was holding, thereby separating it from his direct control. Jeff held the pendulum, not the rod. This time, when Jeff walked Pat's and Maria's path, there was no dowsing-rod reaction. Ted said he believed that during the first test, as exciting as it looked, Jeff's hands were moving and that caused the dowsing rods to react. Nevertheless, the blind test with Jeff Tomlinson was very intriguing because Jeff said that he never moved his hands and did not realize what was happening. Was Ted's separating the dowsing rod with another instrument simply interfering with Jeff's intuitive transmission of his impulses to the dowsing rod? After all, Jeff did not know where he was as he walked the path, yet his dowsing rod turned at the same point as Pat's and Maria's. We left the explanation up to the viewers.

OBJECTIVE EVIDENCE OF MAGNETIC-FIELD INFLUENCE ON BIRDS

We know that birds use the earth's magnetic field when migrating. Recently in 2011, shifts in the magnetic field, also called polar shifts, resulted in large numbers of bird deaths, possibly because of loss of navigation abilities that confused them. If birds can detect low levels of magnetic energy to use in navigating, do human beings also have this ability? We know that many people are affected by electrically charged particles in the air. You can smell ozone. We also know that heavy static electricity fields can be extremely disorienting, creating feelings of temporal and observational distortion in human beings. Perhaps at a time before the crush of urbanization and industrially generated electricity, sensitive individuals could receive signals from low-level lines of magnetism and react to them, a reaction objectified by the use of instruments such as dowsing rods.

Our conclusion was that Stonehenge satisfied all four major criteria for a vortex. It was a sacred or hallowed site with ancient roots. There was a significant military presence in the area. It certainly demonstrated some form of low-level energy that our dowsers were able to sense. There was also a long history of documented UFO sightings, at least one of which was on video, in the area.

SEDONA, ARIZONA

Sedona has had a long history of UFO sightings. In fact, the area has the highest per capita rate of UFO sightings in the United States. Ringed by high and steep hilltops that are red from a heavy concentration of iron, Sedona is a haven for new age experiencers and retirees who relish the dry, warm air and the many golf courses and resorts. In addition to the year-round population, tourists flock to the area to climb Bell Rock and camp near Castle Rock to see UFOs and claim that they've had encounters with alien beings.

Our guest expert in Sedona was Chris O'Brien, who had originally formulated the four criteria for defining a vortex or a portal: a sacred or hallowed area revered by the ancients, an area where an energy field exists that differs from the surrounding countryside, a military presence in the area, and a long history of UFOs or other anomalous phenomena in the area. In this segment, we brought Chris O'Brien to Sedona for a general conversation about the nature of portals, even though, specifically, Chris was describing his particular area of expertise, the San Luis Valley in Colorado, which Chris wrote about in his book, *The Mysterious Valley* (St. Martin's, 1996).

In the Sedona valley, there is an intense magnetic field up to five times greater than the surrounding countryside. Like the San Luis Valley in Colorado, which Chris O'Brien described, the Sedona area has a heavy presence of UFO activity. Often, as in the case of the San Luis Valley, the UFO sightings directly correlate to the lines of greatest magnetic force. Ted Acworth thought that particularly noteworthy, because O'Brien was using two different data sources, witness sightings and geological maps, to show that the two criteria were present in the same spots.

In Sedona, there is a strong military presence, made even more formidable by the federal government's acquisition of Bradshaw Ranch, often referred to as a portal itself. Bradshaw Ranch is reputed to be the busiest site for anomalous sightings in the area. Once the government bought the land, the area was immediately posted, prohibiting anyone from entering onto the land, and guards turned visitors and sightseers away. Why would a small, out-of-the-way ranch draw so much government interest? Local residents say that the ranch is a portal to another reality and that the forestry service, which acquired the land, is actually a front for the U.S. military, whose presence they want to keep a secret. But the presence of UFOs, people in the area say, gives that secret away all too well.

To see if they can capture UFOs on video for themselves, Ted and Jeff set up a two-camera system just beneath Castle Rock, one camera for video, the other for stills. The still camera was on an automatic time delay, snapping a photo every sixty seconds. Many of the witnesses, Ted explained, said that they only saw images of UFOs when they reviewed camera footage or stills they had taken. They hadn't seen craft with the naked eye, only in photographs. Therefore, Ted hoped that by leaving the cameras running all night, they would capture images of UFOs digitally and on tape.

While the cameras were running, Ted, Pat, and I gathered in the living room of a witness, William Watson, with a group of other local witnesses to hear their stories about sightings and the kinds of encounters they had. The session became very intense because for many of these witnesses this was the first time they had shared their stories outside their local group. As they explained to us, most people who don't see the phenomena around Castle Rock and Bradshaw Ranch think that people who do see anomalous sights are simply crazy or making things up, replacing everyday reality with a fantasy. However, listening to the stories, we were hard-pressed to discount the veracity of their experiences. One witness said that he saw a big flash. He had his camera with him and snapped thirty stills in quick succession. When he reviewed them, he said that what he thought was a single white flash was in reality a stream of colors with a blue tail on it. In previous discussions, Ted has suggested that when a camera lens is forced to an extreme close-up on night shutter, it will sometimes break up the colors in an image, especially if the shutter stays open, thereby blurring the subject of the photo.

Ted was curious about the phenomena, however, and asked, "Do you think the energy is stronger around the specific vortexes or is it constant through the entire Sedona area?"

"When you're in Sedona," one of the witnesses responded, "you can feel the energy all over, not just near the portal hot spots."

Another witness said that she saw an object over Sedona that was round, disk-shaped. "Then it tilted toward me and I saw that it was ringed by lights," she revealed. "But as I was staring at it, it just collapsed in on itself as if it folded into darkness." Did its disappearance before the witness's eyes resemble the winking out and into existence on Bruce Cornet's photographs and on David Tickle's video?

And still another witness described his sighting of a large black triangle, similar to the triangles that have been seen all over Europe and England. He said that as he watched it float, it suddenly shot out of his line of sight at an incredible speed.

We asked the assembled group whether anyone had seen anything other than craft, possibly life-forms or incarnations or manifestations of intelligent energy. One witness described his having seen two "crimson" orbs that, to him, were more than simply craft or robot probes. "They were spheres," he said, "about fifty feet across. These things were alive." If alive, we wondered, could these be actual life-forms, balls of sapient energy manifesting themselves through portals from another dimension into our reality? In subsequent seasons we would come to learn that orbs, bright white or colored balls of light that seemed to operate as if they were intelligently controlled, quite possibly were not just from another planet but from another reality. Sedona was our first introduction to this possibility.

We saw lots of video taken by the witnesses in which the cameras picked up images that the photographers did not see with the naked eye. Was this simply an example of anomalies created by the camera or the lens, or were there really objects moving through the frame? In some cases, we could not see an object on the video until the video was played back in slow motion. At that point, strange objects appeared. It could be that the objects in the video were moving so quickly that they could only be spotted when the video was played back in slow motion. But, as Ted pointed out, unless the video was played back and analyzed professionally frame by frame, all we were doing was simply speculating.

Could we say that Sedona satisfied the requirements for a portal?

Certainly one of Chris O'Brien's four criteria, that there has to be an intense energy presence in the area, is satisfied because there are strong magnetic fields in the area, whether the result of the heavily ferrous rock or because the area lies on the earth's energy grid. Literally thousands of witnesses in the area prove a second one of Chris's criteria: that there must exist numerous sightings of UFOs. The Native Americans from the area have said that the area is sacred. Thousands of tourists each year also say that they make the journey because of the ancient spiritual nature of Sedona. Thus a third criteria, hallowed ground, is satisfied. And finally, Chris's point that an area must have a military presence is satisfied, even if that presence is the strange government purchase and occupation of Bradshaw Ranch. At the ranch, people have claimed they have been driven off by guards in military fatigues and that at least one researcher was shot and killed. What is going on at Bradshaw Ranch?

As for Ted's camera array, it, indeed, captured several lights traveling through the sky periodically through the night in the area of Castle Rock. Ted said that there was nothing about these lights to eliminate the possibility that they were commercial aircraft flying their routes out of the local airport or Sky Harbor. There were no hairpin turns, no sharp zigzags, no winking in and out of existence, and no maneuvers that the witnesses described in their sightings. The results were inconclusive, but we must presume these were conventional aircraft unless irrefutable evidence proves otherwise.

Our nighttime camera experiment notwithstanding, the record of Sedona UFO sightings—official sightings reported to public safety officials such as the police and fire departments as well as to Peter Davenport's National UFO Reporting Center—reveals scores of sightings over the previous years. The number of sighting reports was so great that even Ted, who tried, but could not, capture an image of a definable UFO on camera, admitted that Sedona does seem to be an anomalous sighting hot spot. "There is, statistically," he said, "more evidence here in Sedona than anywhere else. That is a matter of fact."

As for the nature of portals in general, Pat Uskert was more circumspect in his opinion. "What we don't know," he said, "far out-weighs what we do know. We don't have a full understanding of the universe yet. And our knowledge of the planet is still in its infancy. There could be forces that we don't currently recognize."

Ted acknowledged, though, despite our failure to capture a UFO image on camera, that "we've lent a certain amount of credibility to the possibility that there are places which are conduits of energy lead-ing electricity to the earth's surface." Whether these conduits of energy coincide with specific places we were calling portals, he said, is an open question. "They may or may not coincide with these positions."

We did determine, however, that, at least based on witness testi-mony and one dowsing experience, the claims that people made about areas we call portals or vortexes have a basis in reality. There were simply too many witnesses describing the same thing, too many sighting reports, and too many videos and photographs to discount the possibility of portals.

"It is clear, though," Ted pointed out, "that whatever these energies are or are not, they are simply unmeasurable by today's scientific in-struments thus far. Certainly our instruments couldn't measure them. But, if these energies exist, they are only measurable by people."

It is interesting that for all the science we brought to the investiga-tion of portals and vortexes, at the end of the day, comparing what witnesses and their videos suggested with what we saw, we were left with the same wonderment as the ancients. Strange things did and probably still do happen at these sites, things that modern measuring instruments cannot display but ancient tools probably could. How far have we come, we wondered, from the ancients, who seemed far more certain about the nature of portals than we are? If we consider, how-ever, what Native Americans have said about the existence of portals and the stories of beings who abide behind the portal doors, how much of that lore is actual truth, and if it is true that beings reside within these portals, then what do these otherworldly creatures want?

BILL'S BLOG

Originally, there were two episodes, one on vortexes and one on portals. As the producers and their assistants researched the field, they kept crossing paths with the same material. We had talked about portals as time portals, gateways that—and I do believe they exist on Earth—opened up to a different time or a different time continuum. Also, we looked at the various stories of portals to different dimensions such as Bradshaw Ranch and the Skinwalker Ranch. At both those locations, the Bureau of Land Management was the property manager of record. However, the BLM was actually a cover organization for the military presence at Bradshaw Ranch or the private corporation that owned Skinwalker and was refusing access to all who asked. Another location, Marley Woods, which we talked about in a subsequent season, was also off-limits because the residents of that area wanted nothing to do with the media. In all these instances, the phenomena were so strange, so bizarre, and, let's face it, so downright scary that it went beyond any horror movie.

There were instances at all three locations where witnesses

described exotic creatures, winged creatures, wolflike creatures who stood up on two legs, and actual unidentified flying
objects we could not identify from witness descriptions seemed
to slip into our world with impunity. At Marley Woods and at
Skinwalker Ranch, orb creatures that behaved like sentient and
sapient beings floated in the faces of human beings, frightening
them. Worse, the orbs sometimes attacked people and, in more
than one instance, exploded large animals as if they had been
microwaved. Sometimes when you hear a voice saying, "Get
out," you get out. Also, because we had no access, there was no
point in setting up an episode where there was no firsthand or
direct information. So the producers decided to combine portals with vortexes to make a single episode.

One of the highlights of this episode for me was our visit to
Stonehenge, getting there before dawn at the winter solstice,
and watching the sun rise just over the horizontal stones. You
can imagine what it was like for a former professor of medieval
history and literature to stand, at dawn, on Salisbury Plain
imagining the ghosts of King Arthur and his knights in the
early morning mist. It was as exhilarating as it was chilling. Indeed, even as the crew was setting up cameras, I wandered off
through the stones wishing with all my might, if this were indeed a portal, that I could slip through a seam in time and see
Stonehenge as it really was, truly was, when the ancients first
set the monster stones in place.

Our trip to England was also the first time I got to direct a
segment. It didn't actually make it into the final cut, but it had
to do with one of our guests who had claimed that she's been
abducted by extraterrestrials and had implants in her ear. The
other segment I directed that didn't make it in was set in Sedona, where one of the witnesses to the UFO phenomena, a
trance channeler, said that her spirit guide wanted to talk to us.
The spirit guide, a man who died in the 1920s, told his subject
that in the reality where he abided, extraterrestrials wanted to

communicate with us. I thought it was an interesting segment, and I was glad that our show runner, Al LaGarde, gave me the opportunity to set up the segment. Unfortunately, the segment wound up being way off topic and thus didn't even make the first cut.

The Sedona segment gave us the opportunity to meet William Watson, a retired Special Forces sergeant whose stories of being sent out on UFO retrieval operations were thrilling. He was very convincing and told of being sent to remote locations where he'd been sworn to secrecy on pain of dire punishment if he ever revealed the truth publicly about what he'd been ordered to do. If true, it supported other stories I'd heard about military operations to retrieve downed UFOs and the entities that flew them.

I still want to do an episode on portals. Maybe someday.

ALIEN CONTACT

The idea of alien contact, in whatever form it takes, is one of the aspects of today's ufology that dates all the way back to ancient people and to prophets in biblical times. Whether one defines "alien" as a spirit, angel, extraterrestrial biological entity, or even a ghost, human beings have reported contact with otherworldly beings almost since the first civilizations. Contact, even in the form of sighting strange beings, has been depicted in the Sumerian glyphs, on the walls of Mayan temples, in ancient Egypt, in the Bible, and throughout classical literature. Even George Washington at Valley Forge reported a contact with an unearthly being, who predicted the future course of the American Revolution and the challenges the new republic would face. Washington also said he saw a green floating orb in the woods at Valley Forge.

After the Roswell incident in 1947 and throughout the 1950s, various individuals came forward with vivid claims of alien contact. George Van Tassel and George Adamski both said that they were contacted by creatures from Venus, who emerged from spacecraft and made predictions about the future of humankind. Howard Menger also claimed to have met creatures from Venus, first when he was a young man in High Bridge, New Jersey, and later on when he was in the military. The ongoing and celebrated Billy Meier case, about a Swiss farmer who has claimed alien contact dating back to the 1970s, is another example of reported alien contact, as is the Ed Walters Gulf Breeze UFO encounters in Florida. The idea of alien contact has fascinated modern UFO historians for over sixty years.

Alien contact, as ufologists see it, is more than an abduction scenario and almost goes into the realm of good ETs vs. bad ETs. Bad ETs abduct human beings, run experimental medical tests on them, retrieve sperm and ovum for the purposes of hybridization of the species, and deposit their abductees back on Earth to deal with loss of memory, missing time, physical discomfort, and varying degrees of post-traumatic stress. Good ETs communicate with selected contactees, predict future events, empower them with a message of hope, and, for a few, instruct them in how to broadcast their message to the rest of humanity.

Early in our first season, we dealt with alien abduction, focusing on the Barney and Betty Hill and Tim Cullen cases. We revisited the alien-human contact later in the season in "Alien Contact." Our intent in this episode was to show, by focusing on two cases, that there is another side to the picture of alien-human interaction that witnesses talk about, a side that is based on human empowerment rather than human victimization. It was with this sense of excitement that we traveled to Ohio and Virginia to interview two subjects who had taken extraordinary videos of the craft that they said were shadowing them.

Of all the episodes in season 1, it was the "Alien Contact" episode that, I believe, defined the show. It was for me when I heard Terrell Copeland's story of what he believed was his alien contact that time seemed to freeze in place. There was a sense of truth here, a moment of private revelation. The "Alien Contact" episode became the essence of UFO Hunters. Also, ironically enough, it was that same moment in episode 109 that got the series renewed for a second season. If you watched the show, you know what I'm talking about: the moment I turned to Terrell Copeland and suggested he was an alien hybrid. At which point Pat Uskert freaked out.

The premise of this episode was straightforward enough. We had videos from both our guest contactees, Terrell Copeland and Michael Lee Hill, in which they had photographed lights in the sky over their respective locations. Michael lived in Ohio, right near Lake Ontario, and had some incredible footage of UFOs over the lake. Terrell lived in Suffolk, Virginia, and had videos of UFOs over his house. But the episode took a startling turn midway through, and the stories we wound up telling were far more intriguing than just a set of great UFO videos. It was a story of close encounters of the fourth kind.

THE EPISODE

We began with a reminder that on September 5, 1977, *Voyager* 1 was launched on a mission that would take it to the planet Jupiter and beyond. On that spacecraft was an encoded disk, prepared by astronomer Carl Sagan and others, with messages in fifty-five languages to whatever alien life-form might encounter the craft. There were instructions on the disk for how to play it to retrieve the information, a mathematical formula for extraterrestrials to use to find planet Earth, natural sounds from Earth's weather and from the animals that live here, and information about who we are as human beings and how we live. *Voyager* continues to travel into deep space. Meanwhile, here on Earth, the Search for Extraterrestrial Intelligence (SETI) continues to search the distant stars for a radio signal carrying an intelligent message from some extraterrestrial life-form out there.

TRIP TO SETI

To meet with SETI director Dr. Seth Shostak, we traveled to the newly installed Allen Telescope Array in Hat Creek, California. The Allen Telescope Array is a collection of radio telescopes designed to scan specific points in space to locate and ideally identify what might be an artificial signal, not simply space noise or signals bouncing back and forth from our own satellites to our receivers. In the process of discriminating different signals and discarding those from artificial satellites, the array also must be able to flag what seem like false alarms, signals that seem genuine, but are not. For example, on August 15, 1977, SETI picked up what is now referred to as the wow signal, a signal noticed by the SETI project at Ohio State, where one of the observers noticed a sequence that looked intelligent. He circled it on the printout and wrote, "Wow." The signal lasted for seventy-two seconds and seemed to have characteristics that were not consistent with Earth-originated signals. However, at that same moment another receiver on the same antenna looked at the same spot in the heavens and found no signal at all. If the test of scientific proof is repeatability, Shostak explained, then the wow signal was not an artificially generated signal from an intelligent source in space.

On the other hand, what if the wow signal was simply intermittent? And if intermittent, what if it repeats itself every hour or every Earth month, or even every Earth century? Unless the antenna is pointed at the exact same spot of origination constantly it wouldn't receive a repeat of that signal and would miss something that is a true transmission from an extraterrestrial source. Could it be that we actually had a hailing message, but we missed the return call?

All of the individual telescopes, Dr. Shostak told us, act as one, a single "metal ear" aimed at a relatively nearby star to pick up a radio signal. He explained that from all that we've learned about the nature of the universe and nearby stars that might hold Earth-like planets in their orbits, life might not be the singular miracle we think it is. Life, he suggested, might well, and probably does, exist out there on other planets. Seth Shostak, we pointed out, says that life probably exists somewhere out there in nearby star systems. We say that alien life might have not only visited Earth but may remain here on Earth, watching or monitoring us. Ideally, Seth and the team agreed, we might just meet in the middle. Regardless of any potential ET encounters we might have in space as our robotic probes orbit or land on other planets, Shostak predicted that with additional telescopes being added to the SETI arrays, SETI hopes to make contact with an alien civilization by 2025.

CLOSE ENCOUNTERS: THE J. ALLEN HYNEK PARADIGM

J. Allen Hynek, who was the scientific advisor and resident skeptic to Project Blue Book and later revealed that he had come to believe that the evidence he had evaluated in Blue Book supported the theory that UFOs were real, developed a classification system for UFO contact, which he termed "close encounters."

Hynek originally had three initial categories, categories to which UFO researchers subsequently added so that there are now five categories of contact:

Close Encounters of the First Kind are sightings from a distance of six hundred feet or less of strange craft or lights that cannot be attributed to any known or conventional craft or to any human technology.

Close Encounters of the Second Kind are events that involve physical effects from the encounter such as heat, disorientation from a heavy electrical field, sickness, temporary paralysis, or radiation. This category also includes interference with television or radio signals. Thus, the interference with police radios in the Xilitla incident in Mexico was a Close Encounter of the Second Kind.

Close Encounters of the Third Kind, as we remember from the feature film of the same name, involves seeing an alien or otherworldly being at close range.

Close Encounters of the Fourth Kind, added to the list after Hynek passed away, involves an actual abduction of a human being by an otherworldly creature. The Betty and Barney Hill abduction fits into this category.

Close Encounters of the Fifth Kind involve reciprocal communication between an alien intelligence and a human being. The difference between the fourth and fifth kinds of close encounters involves the issue of reciprocity, where the encounter is not just a one-way channel from the alien to the abductee, but full-on communication with an alien being.

The Close Encounter of the Fourth Kind was suggested by UFO researcher and Hynek associate Jacques Vallee, who suggested that there were cases of contact where the witness experienced a change in consciousness or in his or her concept of reality as a result of that encounter.

The Close Encounter of the Fifth Kind was suggested by CSETI founder Dr. Steven M. Greer, who, based upon his own self-described experience when he was a young man, described an encounter with extraterrestrial entities in which there was a consciously deliberate sharing of information between ET and the contactee.

As we researched our two guest contactees for this episode, we discovered that we were dealing with two separate Close Encounters of the Fifth Kind, encounters that have continued right through today.

CLOSE ENCOUNTERS AND CONTACTS

Close encounters are not new. George Washington's vision of a spiritual entity at Valley Forge, who lifted his spirits and showed him the victory in the war against Britain, was not a worldly entity. Whether it was a life-form from another planet or an angel or a manifestation of an interdimensional being is not as relevant as the message it gave, lifting Washington's spirits and inspiring him at a moment of desolation to rally himself and his troops.

Even before Washington at Valley Forge, however, the Swedish philosopher and theologian Emanuel Swedenborg described his contact with aliens in his 1758 Latin treatise *Earths in Our Solar System*, in which he described the beings he had seen. He claimed to have journeyed throughout the entire solar system, meeting beings on Mars, Venus, and Saturn, the furthest known planet from the sun at that time.

In 1900, University of Geneva psychology professor Théodore Flournoy wrote about the travels to Mars undertaken by spiritualist Élise Müller, also known as Hélène Smith. While Müller believed her travels to be real, as was her interpretation of the Martian language, Professor Flournoy saw this as a case in psychology, in which his subject's fantasies captivated her mind. Müller broke with Flournoy over his refusal to believe her visions were anything more than a psychological aberration; she said she continued to have visions about alien contact throughout the rest of her life.

By the 1950s, self-described contactees Frank Stranges, Howard Menger, George Van Tassel, and George Adamski were describing their experiences with extraterrestrials, writing books, making public appearances, revealing sketches and photographs of alien craft and of humanoid extraterrestrials, and inviting their friends to meet these visitors from the planet Venus. On October 28, 1983, at 2:15 A.M., as reported in Allen Hynek and Phil Imbrogno's *Night Siege*, engineer Jim Cooke was driving along lonely Croton Falls Road in New York's Hudson Valley when he spotted a formation of lights in the sky. He followed the lights to the Croton Falls Reservoir, where he stopped and got out to observe them. He said the lights, now hovering about fifteen feet above the water, were actually a structured craft made of a material this former airplane repair specialist could not identify. The craft seemed to be sending a red laserlike beam of light into the water as if probing it. When the craft seemed to notice Cooke, it emanated a blinding flash, and the next thing Cooke realized was that he had lost track of the time he spent watching it.

In 1997, at the same time as the Phoenix lights appeared over parts of Nevada and Arizona, the infamous Heaven's Gate cult in Rancho

Santa Fe, California, claimed that they were in contact with an alien craft in the tail of the Hale-Bopp comet. Cult leader Marshall Applewhite said that to avoid the destruction of the earth, cult members would have to commit suicide so their souls could ascend to the craft in the comet's tale. The resulting mass suicide, similar to the suicides at Jonestown in Guyana, made international headlines.

Alien contact, therefore, has both benevolent and malevolent aspects to it.

THE CONTACTEES

The two contactees we met came from different backgrounds, lived in different states, and were as diverse as any two young men could be. Yet both had sent us very compelling videos of strange lights in the sky and images of structured craft that they said were not only appearing in the skies over their cities but seemingly stalking them. In one case, after the contactee saw a craft hovering over his house, he then saw—and videotaped—a darkly camouflaged helicopter hovering right outside his window. Our other contactee-guest said that UFOs were hovering over his boat on Lake Erie at night. We began simply exploring their sightings and asking why they felt these constituted alien contact. However, by the end of our meetings with both young men, two very, very different stories emerged.

TERRELL COPELAND

We traveled to Suffolk, Virginia, to meet with Terrell Copeland, a twenty-five-year-old ex-marine who, we found out, was separated from the service for medical reasons. Terrell had reported and videotaped orbs that were appearing to him at close range, in increasingly greater numbers and with more and more frequent occurrences. It was almost like a swarm, and Copeland didn't know why.

We ascertained from Copeland's story of his having seen a huge

UFO at Northwest Naval Base in Chesapeake when he was a marine and at his parents' house as well as at his own apartment that he was probably correct in believing that the UFOs were looking at him. He said they seemed to be shadowing him, keeping him in sight, and that then military helicopters would show up to keep him in sight as well. It all sounded paranoid at first, but as Terrell told us his story, it sounded very convincing.

His encounter at Northwest Naval Base, for example, was unlike what most people report as typical sightings. One night, between 3 and 4 A.M., Copeland saw a ball of light in the sky that descended over the base. At first, he said, he thought it was a helicopter. But it made no noise and came within a hundred feet of him. Then it changed color. "It went from being a yellow light to a lime color," he said, right before his eyes. Then, Copeland said, he could make out a structured shape to the craft. "It was oval," he told us, adding that it was a solid object. Then the object began shining a beam of light across the naval base. It was as if the craft were surveilling the base or looking for something specific. It was a classic Close Encounter of the First Kind, an observation of an unidentified craft at less than six hundred feet.

Chesapeake Bay was the site of one of the first UFO sightings in American history, this one involving Thomas Jefferson. On July 31, 1813, Edward Hansford, owner of the Washington Tavern in Portsmouth, Virginia, had a terrifying sighting that he described to Jefferson in a letter as a flying "bright ball of light as large as the sun," which "assumed different forms as it ascended and descended." Whether President Jefferson ever received this letter is a matter of conjecture. But the existence of the letter dating back to the early nineteenth century is evidence that at least one person saw something that, unless otherwise identified, seemed to be a UFO.

Between 2004 and 2006, there were twelve sightings of UFOs over the Chesapeake Bay area. In 2006, the *Virginian Pilot* newspaper reported formations of unidentifiable lights over Virginia Beach that switched directions on a dime. These were massive glowing shapes and large triangles over Suffolk. These sightings were made at far-off distances. Terrell's sighting was made at a close distance of less than six hundred feet.

"What made you think you were seeing some kind of unconventional, or otherworldly, technology?" Pat asked.

It was his second sighting in 2005, Terrell told us. Even though he was convinced that his sighting over Northwest Naval Base was an oval, his 2005 sighting told him that he was looking at a flying saucer. During this sighting, on October 27 at 7 P.M. outside of his parents' home in Suffolk, Terrell said he saw a bluish orb moving across the sky. He could tell that it was not a planet or a star. When it appeared two nights later on October 29, he said he was determined to follow it as it floated toward the local shopping center.

"I tried to chase it in my car," he said. "But it was gone before I could follow it."

On the third night, however, October 31, soon after 11 P.M., on a very dark night, it appeared again. This time, Terrell was ready. He followed the object in his car down Constance Road, where it led him to a local shopping plaza. As he watched it, he was shocked at what the object did.

"The orb becomes two orbs," he said. "And as the craft moved over my head, I could see that it was a structured triangle and larger than the shopping center lot that I was in. At first I thought the triangle was a Stealth Bomber, but I had seen those before, and we don't have anything this big in the military."

I believed that the multiple sightings that Terrell had was like a path opening up, a path leading him down the road to contact, a close encounter of a different kind. It turned out that I was right, because on March 5, 2007, Terrell had another encounter, this one different from any that he had had before. At 8:05 P.M., in total darkness, Terrell felt that something was outside his apartment. He grabbed his video camera and headed outside, where he saw two objects hovering near him at a distance of about forty feet, but staying in place. Then one of the objects began spinning like a sphere and started to change colors very violently. It emitted a series of pulsating colored lights. It looked to him as if the one pulsating orb was communicating with the other orb. However, then he noticed that as he moved, the pulsating orb seemed to mirror his movements.

"Many people have said that a sequence of an unidentified object's changing colors was actually a process of communication," I suggested to him.

"At that time," Terrell said, "I knew that one hundred percent."

Terrell was filming this object the entire time. But then he saw a military helicopter approaching, and the objects flew away.

If Terrell thought that he was only seeing objects that were changing colors, his life was about to get even more weird, because shortly after his 2007 sighting, he received a visit from a very strange individual. Terrell had already begun posting his videos on the Internet when this individual contacted him, ostensibly about the video. But during the conversation, the individual identified herself as a military contractor and seemed more interested in Terrell than in his videos. She asked him if he was ready for the "truth."

"I said, 'Sure, let's hear it.'" Terrell told us. "And the person said she had a close and direct relationship with the extraterrestrials." Terrell and this stranger had a long conversation. Later that afternoon, back at his apartment, he dozed off while reading a book. But he was awakened by the sound of someone trying to enter his apartment. He could hear someone outside trying to jiggle the lock, moving the door knob. His first instinct was to get off the couch and grab his firearm. But then, in his mind, he heard a voice inside the room telling him that he didn't need to grab that firearm.

"I could feel the book in my hands. I could feel myself sitting on the couch, but I could not move at all." For a frightening few seconds, Terrell was completely paralyzed, even though he was fully aware of his surroundings and, he said, completely awake. He explained that he knows what sleep paralysis is and also knows that he wasn't experiencing that.

"After I was able to get some movement in my limbs, I went to the door and opened it. No one was there." His experiences became even stranger because later that same night, he said, "I experienced missing time. On the night in question I awoke at 3 A.M. I thought I had had a nightmare. I sat there and looked around. I looked at the clock. Then the next thing I knew my alarm clock went off and it was 5:30. I had not fallen back to sleep. It was just as if I slipped forward in time by two and a half hours."

Temporary paralysis can be an indicator of a close encounter or it can be common sleep paralysis. It depends on the surrounding circumstances. In Terrell's case, he was asleep, but became alert when he heard his doorknob moving. He was a marine, trained to get to his feet immediately. Yet, not in a semi-dream state, he felt complete paralysis when he heard the voice in his head telling him not to get his firearm. Similarly, Terrell's missing-time experience could be explained by his waking up from a dream and then falling right back to sleep, only to be awakened by his alarm clock. But, again, Terrell said he had no memory of falling back to sleep, only of moving forward in time. We wondered, were Terrell's experiences Close Encounters of the Second Kind and, in the case of missing time, an abduction marking a Close Encounter of the Fourth Kind? Or were they natural experiences, which, in the context of his UFO sightings, could be misinterpreted? Terrell's further experiences, however, provided more of a context.

I had to probe for more information even at the risk of setting Pat—who was looking for a conventional explanation—completely off. Terrell kept referring to a training program that this mysterious individual, the alleged contactor, kept talking about, and I thought that if there was a government research program involving people who had repeated sightings or even reported close encounters with UFOs, its members would be scouring the Internet looking for self-described contactees. If that was the case, Terrell and his videos would make him a good candidate for this research project. However, there could be another agenda.

What if there was a group, hiding inside different government departments, that sought out contactees to determine whether their background or even their physiology indicated that they were something other than human, a combination of human and alien or, in terms used by the contactee community, a hybrid. I suggested to Terrell, to get his reaction, "You are a hybrid between ET and human."

As Pat went into shock and then gave me a withering look, Terrell said, "That's surprising, but at the same time not so surprising, because the reason I'm not in the military today is that I have an unknown blood disorder."

Terrell's disorder is a rare elevation of the enzyme creatine kinase—damaged muscles release the CK enzyme into the bloodstream. The navy's medical report on Terrell indicated that he had a very high level of the enzyme creatine kinase in his bloodstream, a level ten times higher than normal. As far as Terrell was concerned, he was perfectly healthy and certainly fit for duty. But because the navy couldn't find a reason for the elevated enzyme, Terrell was discharged for medical reasons after only two years of active service in the marines.

Pat believed that I was jumping to conclusions, but I was only making a suggestion based on Terrell's stated experiences. Terrell also said that he was born dead, completely cyanotic because of lack of oxygen, and had to be resuscitated. His grandmother, he said, called him "the devil's child." In addition, he explained that from the time he was a child, he had psychic abilities and could predict not only when the phone would ring but who was calling. These powers frightened his parents to some extent, and when his UFO sightings began, especially at his parents' house, they became even more nervous. They have since settled down and have come to a level of acceptance, albeit lightheartedly.

After Terrell's segment aired, Terrell said that he pursued the course of study that his advisor said was intended to connect him with the star people. Terrell revealed that not only has he stayed in communication with the craft that seems to be tracking him, but his close-encounter experiences increased. Finally, three years ago,

Terrell says, he came into direct contact with extraterrestrials. He wrote,

> I was finally taken up into the ship sometime in February of 2008. It was the last Saturday of that month. I was in my sleepwear and felt a little embarrassed because everyone there was dressed in crisp white. But no one noticed and I actually felt at home. There were so many people up there in this large white "banquet room" as I would describe it; because everyone was eating. I was introduced to a Caucasian looking woman who was bald and had an elongated skull. Her eyes were black—that's all I remember from that. The next memory is me waving goodbye to a small cylindrical ship.

MICHAEL LEE HILL

As did Terrell Copeland, Michael Lee Hill pursued what he told us were his extraterrestrial contacts after we aired his segment in the "Alien Contacts" episode. We met Michael outside Cleveland, where he lives and from where he visits the shores of Lake Erie, where he video-taped strange objects over the water. As with Terrell, the more we talked about Michael's sightings and videos, the more we became intrigued that there was something else, something bigger, behind his sighting stories. By the end of our visit, our suspicions were proved correct.

His UFO sighting on August 18, 2006, over the lake was one of the events that, he said, wound up changing his life. For the next few months, he kept visiting the lake, where he saw a multitude of orbs and continued to film them, posting these videos on the Internet. Although lights in the sky that look like orbs have been explained away as conventional aircraft, Michael said they didn't behave in a conventional manner. Moreover, he added, where he saw the lights and the location he photographed the lights from was right next to Perry nuclear power plant. "Since 9-11," he said, "you can't fly planes or helicopters over a nuclear power plant. It's restricted airspace." He was correct. Since September 11, 2001, the FAA put what are called temporary flight restrictions around nuclear power plants. In the Code of Federal Regulations, the CFR, which is published every day, section 99.7 directs pilots to avoid the airspace over nuclear power plants.

Also, lights near the horizon over the opposite shore of Lake Erie have been explained as police or emergency vehicles. But, Michael told us, this explanation makes little sense because, just as Pat Uskert videotaped a UFO over Venice Beach in 2004, Michael videotaped UFOs over Lake Erie. As a test to see if lights on the Canadian side of the lake could be mistaken for UFOS, Michael specifically tried to videotape emergency vehicles and car lights across the lake, and he said, "You can't even see the other side of the lake."

As Michael Lee described these objects, he could only see "one solid sphere of pulsating light" whenever he spotted them individually. He also suggested that the lights seem to be aware of him, appearing on a consistent basis whenever he visited the lakeshore.

We wondered whether Michael's sightings were unique to him or whether objects over Lake Erie had been spotted before. We found out that similar lights over the lake had been spotted by a witness in 1988, when she described not only lights, but lights "descending out of a huge metallic gray object," and that the event was witnessed by the United States Coast Guard, which filed a written report about it. They said that the "smaller objects began hovering in the area where the large object appeared. They appeared to be scouting the area." The Coast Guard was never able to resolve this event fully.

Similarities notwithstanding, we also needed to get Ted and Jeff to analyze the images we were comparing from Terrell and Michael, specifically with respect to whether the splitting of the lights at close range could be due to defocus, a camera's inability to hold an object in focus at extreme close range, and chromatic aberration, the splitting of a single white light into colors based on the camera's defocus. A lower-quality lens in a consumer-grade video camera cannot focus on more than one color when the envelope of focus is pushed at extreme digital telephoto. When that happens, the inherent colors bleed and show up separately. Ted also pointed out that the different colors were pulsating separately. He said that if this were a single coherent object, the colors would all be pulsating at the same time. They were not. Therefore, he called the images a camera aberration.

Then, at long distance, Ted and Jeff analyzed the aerodynamic performance of the lights. They hovered. They moved not in conventional aircraft patterns but zigzagged at constant speeds. "I've never seen anything like that in imagery," Ted said. "I can't explain where that would be from." The lights did not move like conventional aircraft, and they did not have the requisite navigation lights that airplanes or helicopters have. Also, even assuming for the sake of argument that the lights were from police or emergency vehicles on the other side of the lake, they did not pulse or flash like emergency lights. Ted said that nothing he could do would enable him to tell exactly what these lights were, and so he categorized them as "unknown" primarily because the tools weren't there at that level of video to pull apart the images successfully.

In comparing Terrell's and Michael's videos side by side, Ted said they both looked like single points of light. However, because of the nature of the cameras, "the information contained in the footage is so low, I'm not sure that we'll be able to extract enough information to tell definitely what these are," Ted said. The conditions under which the videos from Michael and Terrell were shot were simply not conducive to capturing distant objects in the sky and were too harsh for cameras of that grade to produce clearly focused images at extreme digital zoom.

Moving on to the next level of similarities, we wanted to compare Michael's story to Terrell's to find out what, if any, commonalities there were between the stories and to get a timeline for Michael's experiences. Michael Lee and Terrell lived five hundred miles apart, did not know each other, were from different backgrounds and of different ethnicities, and yet they both filmed similar aerial phenomena and both felt a strange bond with the objects they were filming. Pat Uskert's admonition to me notwithstanding, I believed I was on to something and had to find out if my hunch about Michael Lee was correct.

Michael's story was that he had contact with creatures he described as otherworldly his entire life. He said that as a child, he would sometimes wake up in the middle of the night for no reason except that he saw blood on the floor. He had no cuts or scrapes and couldn't explain it. Sometimes when he was older he would walk to his bathroom sink and see blood. But again, unless it was from his nose or mouth, which he could not tell, he could see no incisions. Then, Michael told us, one night he awoke and saw creatures "working on me." He said that he was in his bed, strapped down, looked over to his right, and saw a "being." He said to the entity he saw, "Look, I'm awake. I'm right here and know what you're doing. And it hurts."

We asked Michael Lee if he had any other types of strange experiences, other types of sightings, or things he would characterize as contact subsequent to his childhood experiences. He said that one night he walked out to his music studio and saw what he called a "plasma device" hovering in the air. He said that the device was a small cylinder connected to two balls, which he said looked like plasma balls, at either end. This, Pat Uskert suggested, was similar to something Terrell Copeland said about his seeing a floating orb, walking up to it, and watching the orb split into two orbs.

Could it be, if Michael Lee Hill's experiences were similar to Terrell's, that the objects were showing up to guide Michael Lee along to some greater truth, perhaps about himself? "I know," Michael Lee told us, "that they know that I'm filming them. I am in contact with something higher. If you were in contact with something higher and you didn't listen, wouldn't that be the stupidest thing?"

It was time to get Michael Lee's blood tested as well, and he agreed to do it. Both Michael and Terrell were tested at Massachusetts General Hospital in Boston. As Michael put it, "It looks like what you were looking for, you found." Indeed, both Terrell Copeland and Michael Lee Hill tested positive for higher than normal levels of the enzyme creatine kinase. This enzyme is produced by a number of factors, including, but not limited to, the breakdown of muscle and skeletal tissue. It is usually indicative of muscle damage. Hence, when the navy found that Terrell's CK levels were too high and that it was accompanied by muscular stress and his tiring easily, they deemed it medically significant because it affected his ability to perform his duties as a marine.

When Terrell's blood was tested, seven years after his separation from the service, the results revealed that he still had elevated levels of CK, a result that was most unusual. For the enzyme elevation to have persisted this long means that there is a cause other than simple muscular stress as a result of his military service. Also, because Michael Lee Hill, who had an entirely different background, had an elevated creatine kinase level as well, there had to be some reason for the two similar anomalies. Maybe, as both Terrell and Michael suggested, and Ted Acworth agreed, using a blood test to determine the CK levels of self-described abductees and contactees would be very revealing.

Another interesting correlation that medical research picked up regarding elevated CK levels in individuals was that the higher the CK level, the less likely a male subject's sperm level was to be mature enough to conceive. Could it be, admittedly going way out on this, that if there are alien-human hybrids, the males of the culture cannot conceive on their own because their sperm is less adequate because of lack of maturity? Pure speculation.

The story of Michael Lee Hill became even more interesting after he and Terrell shared their experiences with one another. Michael confided to Pat and me, after we asked him about his parents and any extraterrestrial experiences they might have had, that he was an adopted child. We asked him if he would make any attempts to learn the identities of his biological parents and find out whether they had any strange experiences. He agreed and eventually told us:

For the first time in my life I contacted my biological mother, and I also got to meet my two half sisters as well. It has been great to be in touch with them all, and I feel I should have done it sooner I guess but the timing wasn't right until recently. Well the point of this is I also found out who my biological father is. My biological mother told me it's Eric Clapton and has plenty of facts and info to back up that claim. My mother did tell me Eric has a blood anomaly as well.

This was the story that Michael told as he learned it, he said, from his mother, whom he contacted after his meeting with Terrell. Although neither Michael's mother nor his half sisters have had any ET experiences, it would be interesting if Michael could contact his biological father to see what the nature of the alleged blood anomaly is and whether his biological father had any ET experiences.

BILL'S BLOG

In the years since this episode was broadcast, I have received all kinds of communication and responses on radio shows to my comment that Terrell Copeland was a hybrid and that Pat Uskert was right in calling me out on that. Here's how that went down. First of all, nobody heard the conversation that Terrell and I had off camera about his strange feelings of some kind of alien presence in his life. His story of the woman who had approached him under the guise of being a government agent and who then began urging him to explore his star seed was eerie. Similarly, Terrell's story of someone outside his apartment door trying the lock and then being able to perceive that Terrell was reaching for his handgun, ordering him to put it down, and then rendering him unable to rise up from his couch, which story he related to us, was an astounding story. Granted, the events in his story could have been caused by sleep paralysis, how that paralysis prevented him from getting his firearm because he heard someone trying to break into his apartment. But that sleep paralysis, because he might have been in a hypnogogic state between waking and sleeping, might have rendered him unable to move until he shook it off. Was the person at the door part of a dream so real that he believed it was reality? It wasn't until he was finally released from his paralysis, he said, that he was finally able to get up and go to the door, and he found no one there. His psychic abilities and the history of his birth led to his compelling out-of-the-ordinary background.

I wanted to get as much of this story on camera as possible because I thought it was right on point and germane to the subject of alien contact. It added a whole new dimension to real close encounters. I did think that the story of Terrell's being urged to explore his star seed was important. What did that mean? How do you explore a star seed, and why Terrell? Maybe that was part of his search. That's why I made the suggestion to Terrell Copeland that these events surrounding him were more than just coincidental, that they had a relationship and that relationship had to be explored, even if it meant going out on a limb to do so.

Pat, for his part, wanted to be more centrist in his interpretation of the story. He felt that someone might have been playing with Terrell because of the images on Terrell's Web site. That was why, as we were leaving Terrell's house, Pat told me that he thought I was out of line in making the suggestion that Terrell was a hybrid. Our coexecutive producer and show runner, Alan LaGarde, heard what Pat said and asked him to save it for the camera. This was part of the discussion he felt belonged out there publicly instead of remaining private. So Pat agreed and Alan set up the shot right in front of Terrell's parents' house.

When the time came for editing that episode, the first editor wanted to cut out the entire exchange between Pat and me. However, our new story editor, Stu Chait, had just come on board and was watching the raw video in the editing bay when that scene came up. As the editor moved to cut it, Stu told him to leave it in. He said he liked the interplay, which was a real moment between Pat and me in which Pat expressed an honest view that I had gone too far. That was the great part about working with Pat and Ted during the first two seasons. Pat would always be a balance, saying I was going too far. And Ted would always ask, "Where's the proof or what's the evidence?" Stu Chait correctly saw that this was honest debate and, as story editor, felt that the show had to be about reality, not just narrative Q&A like the old *UFO Files*. He prevailed, and the interchange between Pat and me stayed in past the first cut.

At Stu's insistence, our executive producers left the scene in as well. Then, when our original network executive at History, Dolores Gavin, who had green-lighted the series based on the pilot History had ordered but never broadcast, moved up the corporate ladder, our new network exec Mike Stiller paid a visit to our production offices in Santa Monica, California. *UFO Hunters* was up for renewal, and the network wasn't sure whether our format would work as they began retooling their programming. Mike's concept for programming was that the new series had to be organic and feature the interaction of personalities as well as the narrative of a specific story line. Thus, when Mike was reviewing the proposed final cut for this episode and saw the interchange between Pat and me and Pat's honesty in confronting me about going over the top, he said that the scene stayed and that the show was renewed for a second season. Stu Chait's instincts were right on. Mike Stiller liked what he saw: real personalities being honest with each other on camera, and he reupped us. It was vindication for Stu, who made the right call, and a boost for Mike Stiller, as it would have been for any network executive producer, because the show's ratings climbed for the next two and a half seasons, but most of all it was vindication for Alan LaGarde and Pat Uskert, who believed that honesty was television's best policy.

This episode on alien contact, along with our second season's "Area 51" and our third season's alien-intervention and Dulce episodes, were among my personal favorites because they explored areas of what I believe is an ongoing conspiracy to cover up the truth about human evolution. At the same time, I really believe that our RAF Bentwaters and "First Contact," Aurora, Texas, Airship Mystery segments were just about the best from a scientific perspective because they used detailed forensic techniques to substantiate what might have really taken place in those cases. However, I think the larger picture is that there was, and still is, an element of intelligent design about the development of human beings and that it's not all pure chance and happenstance. Too many coincidences smack of synchronicity, and synchronicity, if you talk with those in the field of remote viewing and remote influencing, bespeaks a larger causality. If somebody can show me scientifically how the primum mobile or prime mover for Big Bang was pure chance, I would like to see it. If someone can show me what the matrix or form was for the less than microdot singularity before the Big Bang, before time began, I would like to see that as well. And if everything was compressed into a micropoint of reality in which all pretime and all matter were entangled, then why would that entanglement not exist today and why can't the future coexist with the past and the present in order to control it as well?

If there is one species of sapient life-form, us, then there can be millions, and not just in the farthest reaches of the universe. They can be right here, Don Juan's allies and enemies, orbs and grays, surveilling us, intervening in our lives just below our ability to perceive them, sometimes breaking the surface tension of our consciousnesses, and even hybridizing us with them for a purpose we may only discover within ourselves.

INVASION TEXAS, 2008

W e shot an episode in early 2008 in Stephenville, Texas, which is located in the middle of the state in Erath County. The first stories about strangle lights flying over Stephenville began in late 2007. By 2008, the first stories about these strange lights in the sky began appearing on the AP wire. We received reports of the activity from people living in the area and, of course, saw the stories in the local newspaper, written by reporter Angelia Joiner. At the time, we had just come back from the United Kingdom and had a full schedule of episodes, but the Stephenville story was a happening event with current witnesses and lots of activity in the area. MUFON was holding witness meetings, Angelia was still writing, and the national media was covering the story. This would be our chance to get on the ground in the midst of a story instead of following up on a story that was years or decades old. More important, the witnesses were still reporting having seen lights and the air force was caught in the midst of a story change. Add to all of this that the events taking place were close enough to President Bush's Crawford ranch to make one wonder whether the president had been alerted to it. After all, it was his father, George H. W. Bush, who, as CIA director at the time, had told the president-elect, Jimmy Carter, that he had no need to know what the CIA knew about UFOs. Thus, UFO conspiracy theorists believe there is a UFO insider legacy among the Bush family members.

We had already changed our travel schedule once to accommodate the National Press Club UFO conference in November 2007. Now we had to convince our bosses of a way to change the schedule again to accommodate our traveling to Texas. This was no small task, but our senior producer, Dave Pavoni, and our coexecutive producer, Al LaGarde, both wanted a current, breaking UFO story to slide into the schedule. They were able to swap out a trip back to Los Angeles, where we were to film the NASA UFO episode, moving that to the end of the shooting schedule, for a trip to Texas in February, and they came up with the plan for an entirely new type of episode.

Because we were going to be meeting those who were currently having sightings, interviewing them on camera, we decided to create a new format for those interviews. This new format was called the white box and featured a stark white background that focused attention on a witness talking directly into the camera and telling his or her story as if giving personal testimony. We also knew that because the Stephenville story was so fresh, there were probably witnesses who had not gone public with their stories but who might like to tell them on camera. For that reason, we also opened up a *UFO Hunters* office right in downtown Stephenville on the courthouse square. It was a brand new concept in inviting and encouraging witnesses to come in to tell their stories and a novel way of conducting interviews. This format was so successful that we used it, in one form or another, for the next two and a half seasons.

THE STEPHENVILLE LIGHTS STORY

From late 2007 to early 2008, one of the most exciting UFO flaps took place over Stephenville, Texas. This case, of a strange object hovering in the sky and then shooting off at lightning speed while being chased by a pair of F-16s from nearby Carswell Air Force Base, was

publicized by major news organizations and talked about on CNN's
Larry King Live.

Stephenville has had a long history of UFO-related events since
one of the first airships landed in the center of town back in 1897, on
its way to Cuba to fight the Spanish on the eve of the Spanish-
American War. The sightings continue to this day. But the 2007–2008
flap, like many UFO flaps, began with a series of disconnected, strange
sightings that only became public after the news surrounding the
sightings hit the national wires of the Associated Press.

The first anomaly, not a UFO sighting, actually, took place over
Thanksgiving 2007, when a Margie Galvez was trying to figure out
what kind of animal was carrying off the chickens she was raising on
her property. Night after night, she would notice that some of her
birds were missing, until she finally decided to launch her own investigation. She installed a night-vision camera in her backyard, set to
start recording at around midnight. In the morning she inspected the
tapes and, in almost every case, found nothing. But over Thanksgiving in 2007, Margie discovered some very strange images in a tape she
reviewed from that camera.

In the eerie gray-scale images measuring the differential between
the background ambient temperature and anything generating a heat
signature, Margie saw her animals pecking the ground. Then she saw
two eyes peering through the darkness. Probably a deer. But then, from
out of frame at the top of her screen, she could see a cone of white. It
was a sharp-edged cone that suddenly appeared as if it were being
fired by something hovering above the ground and scanning the
ground beneath it, swinging back and forth like a pendulum. But,
Margie noticed, if this were simply a light beam, giving off some requisite heat, why didn't the beam hit the ground? In fact, the beam was
sharply cut off before it hit the ground. The beam made three or four
sweeps and then snapped up as if it were suddenly shut off. And the
scene of a pastoral night returned to normal.

Margie saved the video to a DVD and tucked it away. It was strange,
to be sure, but she had no explanation for the anomaly. It would not

be until spring in 2008, when *UFO Hunters* came to Stephenville to investigate the Stephenville lights, that Margie would show that DVD for the first time and the anomaly would appear on national television. Also, it would not be for another six months that another witness stepped forward, albeit anonymously, to reveal that she had seen what Margie had seen. Only this witness saw it firsthand with a group of teenagers in her truck as she was driving them home from cheerleading practice. And this witness not only observed what seemed like the same type of beam but also saw a flat, huge craft with lights and portholes along the side hovering above the railroad tracks outside Stephenville. It was a traumatic sight that she only grudgingly revealed off camera.

While Margie's video of November 2007 was still sitting securely on a DVD, on the evening of January 8, 2008, Steve Allen, a pilot from Selden, Texas, south of Stephenville, noticed a group of flashing white lights about 3,500 feet above his home. As reported in *UFO Magazine* by Jim Marrs, national bestselling author of *Crossfire* (Carroll and Graf, 1990), Steve Allen said that the red, yellow, and green lights formed a rectangular pattern and traveled toward Stephenville at about five thousand miles an hour. As a pilot, Allen was a very credible witness both in terms of what he said he saw and how he analyzed the direction and speed of the light pattern. Jim Marrs, who lives in Texas and covered the story extensively, said that more than two hundred other witnesses saw the lights and described them as brighter than a "welder's torch." The lights danced around each other, sometimes in pairs, witnesses said, forming patterns themselves as they moved across the sky, and then they would disappear. Perhaps, Marrs speculates, they didn't disappear, only became dim so that the witnesses only saw the brightest lights.

Steve Allen said that he thought the object might be as large as a mile long and a half mile wide. Much too large for any conventional aircraft. He also said that he could make out two F-16 fighters from the nearby airbase following the object after it had passed. Other witnesses who saw the object said that they called it a "mothership" because it was so large. Steve Allen's sighting also raised the question of why two air force fighter jets were chasing a formation of lights observed not only by Steve Allen but by two hundred other people.

Steve Allen's description of what he saw and the descriptions of the other witnesses about lights in the sky that they saw indicated to us that something strange did happen in Stephenville. Two days after Steve Allen's sighting, Angelia Joiner, a staff writer for the *Stephenville Empire-Tribune*, wrote her first article on what the witnesses had seen. Her article on January 10, 2008, described the sightings by Steve Allen, Mike Odom, and Lance Jones, who, she wrote, were out admiring the evening sunset when they saw the formations of lights. This was a multiple-witness sighting that Joiner took seriously as a journalist and that caught the attention of folks outside Stephenville. As bestselling author Jim Marrs wrote in *UFO Magazine*, after more than sixty years of derisive reporting, local and national media suddenly treated the Stephenville sighting with a "modicum of respect." Thus, he concluded, it may not have been the nature of the actual sighting that caught the nation's attention at the very first but the reaction of the media.

Angelia Joiner's early articles, spread through January and into February of 2008, described sightings that more Stephenville-area residents were having, and these articles were picked up by Angela K. Brown of the Associated Press. The early coverage was journalistically matter-of-fact. No sensationalism, no derision toward or snickering at the witnesses, no side comments from debunkers or skeptics to dampen the media interest. Instead, once the AP got a hold of the story, their reporter investigated it as well, and from there the story was carried in a headline in the *Washington Post* and by the Canadian Broadcasting Company.

Like the O'Hare Airport sighting in Chicago in 2006, newspapers suddenly found out that a very sober UFO-sighting story had legs. And the U.S. national media began running with it. When reporter Angelia Joiner and some of the early witnesses to the Stephenville lights, as they were coming to be called, appeared on CNN's *Larry King*

Live in February, the entire nation seemed to wake up to an ongoing and evolving UFO story in a small Texas town, the town that proclaims itself the Cowboy Capital of the World.

As in the O'Hare case, people became so interested in the UFO story that they hit the newspaper Web sites again and again, ringing up the page visits as they constantly sought updates on the story. And from Texas, the updates kept making the news. For example, Steve Allen's assertion that he saw F-16s chasing the formation of lights prompted AP reporter Angela Brown to contact the 301st Fighter Wing at the Naval Air Station Fort Worth Joint Reserve Base to find out if they had any F-16s in the air that night. The spokesman for the Fort Worth 301st Fighter Wing, Major Karl Lewis, said in a statement reported in the *Stephenville Empire-Tribune,* "no F-16s or other aircraft from this base were in the area the night of January 8, 2008, when most people reported the light sightings."

Major Lewis said he believed that what people saw were two commercial airliners whose paths were crossing. To folks on the ground, he said, it might seem as though the two sets of navigation and running lights would look like one set of lights on a huge craft. The fact that the lights were moving in one direction also might indicate that a large craft was moving across the sky. But people in Stephenville quickly dismissed that suggestion because, first, the lights were observed over the course of many nights. And, second, different people in different locations saw the same exact set of lights, which seemed to be moving separately with respect to each other, not simply in a tight formation. It was only Steve Allen who said he was able to perceive a rigid structure to the light formation, even though all the witnesses agreed that the lights seemed to be able to move in pairs. Thus, Major Lewis's speculation was not readily accepted by the witnesses.

One of the most dramatic sightings was reported by local resident Rick Sorrells in an interview with UFO investigator and author Linda Moulton Howe. Sorrells, also interviewed by *UFO Hunters,* said not only that his sighting was stunning in itself but also that the aftermath, when official attempts to silence him took place, impressed an inconvenient truth on him.

As quoted by Jim Marrs in his article on the Stephenville lights in *UFO Magazine* (March 2008), Sorrells had this to say:

> For some reason, I don't know what, I look up and look back down. I don't know what made me look up, but then I realized what I had seen with my eyes and immediately looked back up. There was this thing. It covered from—I could not see the edges in my tree canopy. I couldn't see the front of it. I didn't think about looking behind me to see if I could see an edge that way. . . . How far underneath it I was, I'm not for sure [Sorrells later estimated about three hundred feet], but apparently I walked underneath this thing. When I first realized it and looked up, I thought: "What in the world is this?" I raised my rifle up and because I was in such a hurry to go deer hunting and knew I was going into the woods. I did not turn it [hunting scope] down from 9X to 3X. So when I raised my rifle up it's still on 9X. It was real blurry.
>
> I immediately turned down my rifle scope power to 3X and I looked back up there at it, and I can see what I would call a "mirage" coming off of it. It wasn't steam.
>
> I don't know, really—I've seen it like on a hot highway how the heat waves come up. And this was coming down. I really didn't know what to think. I was not scared, so I dropped my gun. And then I really started noticing how big this thing was. I also noticed that it had these round indentations. They were in a grid pattern all running left to right and front to back. They were all placed about 40 feet apart. They were deep, like maybe 4 to 6 feet deep into this craft.
>
> It basically looked like a piece of sheet iron that had been pressed. I couldn't see any nuts; no bolts, no rivets, no welds, no seams. I was really studying the structure of this trying to get an idea about how it was built. It is huge!
>
> I've actually been back into the woods and looked. In my mind, I did the football field measurement. I know it was longer than 3 foot-

ball fields. . . . While I was looking at this [craft], it drifted to the right by about 100 feet. And I remember looking to my left to see if I could see the edge of this thing. And I could not see the edge of it. I turned back to my right, and I was like, Wow, this is crazy!

And now, I'm rushed with emotion as far as, what is it? What is it going to do next? Do I need to get out of here? I still haven't formed a conclusion. I really don't know. I hope it's our military. I hope we have something that is this advanced.

If it's not ours, then we're in trouble. I don't know the capabilities of this thing to move at such speed that it has and as big as it is. Does it have the capability of weapons? I don't know. But if they can build this, I'd sure hate to see if they got mad at us! You know what I'm saying?

What had Sorrells seen? Although one explanation advanced by a number of science experts was that the early-evening sightings people had were only "sundogs," the reflection of the sun on ice crystals in the sky, Jim Marrs speculates that this doesn't account for either the light sightings or Steve Allen's and Rick Sorrells's sighting of a rigid object.

Another explanation that some people put forward was that the lights were easily explained away by a training exercise out of Fort Worth in which jet fighters were dropping either ground-illumination flares or phosphorescent chaff, a countermeasure that generates a heat signature so intense it lures heat-seeking missiles away from the jet. These were the same explanations advanced a decade earlier to account for the dramatic Phoenix lights that captured the world's media's attention in 1997. But now, as then, the flare explanation couldn't account for the strict formation of lights, their ability to move independently with respect to each other, and their ability to move in one direction without descending to the ground. And still another military explanation argued that what folks saw was a jet guarding President Bush's ranch at Crawford. That, too, would have made sense on the surface, except for the fact that Crawford was seventy-five miles away and President Bush was not at the ranch that night.

While the explanations and counterexplanations were flying back and forth, the 301st Fighter Wing added another twist to the story. They made an announcement that their original press release saying that there were no jets in the Stephenville area on the night of January 8, 2008, was in error. In fact, they said, they had made a mistake because there were actually ten F-16s in the air that night on a training mission. This time, for the first time in a long time, it was the news media that was skeptical of the official air force statement. At first, reporters commented, the air force outright denied that they had any planes out that night. But, after the story began to gain traction in the media, the air force, needing an explanation, suddenly reversed themselves and said there were not just two or three planes in the air but ten planes. As area residents also said, that much nighttime activity for ten planes would have involved so many personnel and so much money that they doubted the air force could have pulled it off without lots of ancillary activity around the training exercise. Also, because many of the personnel lived in the Stephenville and Dublin areas, there would have been activity in many of the families and the story of the upcoming training exercise would have been widely circulated. Moreover, the pilots themselves would have been talking about it. What made the story even more implausible, however, was the silence of the object that witnesses saw. Ten jets, they said, would have made an incredible noise overhead. But light was completely silent. It could not have been a formation of jets. Therefore, people claimed, the air force story was a hoax upon the public, a lie becauses it supported the claims of the witnesses from January 8 that the lights were not conventional commercial aircraft crossing flight paths in the night.

With newspapers buzzing around the state with UFO stories and commentators on the local news carrying interviews with Stephenville lights witnesses, the Mutual UFO Network decided to catalog witness interviews to establish a careful record of the sightings. State MUFON chairman Ken Cherry and Texas chief investigator and assistant state chairman Steve Hudgeons brought eight additional investigators along with them to Stephenville to interview as many witnesses as chose to come forward. As Jim Marrs and Angelia Joiner reported, Cherry said that the number of sightings in the Stephenville area was well beyond the normal few sightings a month for that area of Texas. In fact, Cherry said, the number of sightings was well over a hundred. That told him, after he had eliminated the conventional possibilities, that witnesses were probably seeing similar things in the sky and that the sighting reports had formed a pattern. It was time to collect all the sighting reports and correlate the common elements.

On January 18, Ken Cherry, Steve Hudgeons, and their team of MUFON investigators assembled the witnesses in Dublin, Texas, a small town south of Stephenville, to begin the process of sifting through all the sighting data. What startled them was the overwhelming presence of the media. In fact, the gathering of witnesses had turned into a media event as much as a data-collection event, because the media, seventy-five members of it, overshadowed the hundreds of witnesses who showed up. Moreover, because six hundred people flooded into Dublin to hear the reports, the small town had one of the worst traffic jams in its history. At the meeting, Ken Cherry and Steve Hudgeons not only collected two hundred witness reports, both in writing and verbally, but also secured many videos and photographs of the lights as well.

What made the media and the rest of the towns take these sightings so seriously? Ken Cherry said that he believed it was the nature of the witnesses themselves even more than the nature of the sightings that caused the media and the public at large to sit up and take notice. This was "middle-class America coming forward," Cherry said. "Not just some jokesters coming out of the woodwork." The witnesses, he told the newspapers, were actually pillars of their respective communities. They were pilots, flight attendants, peace officers, farmers, ranchers, and generally very sober people who are not given to flights of fancy or to hyperbole. The other major piece of information that came out of the meeting, Cherry said, was the public's misinterpretation of what had happened, which, Cherry added, was partly attributable to the media, who narrowed the entire event down to the

January 8 sighting. But, as Angelia Joiner had meticulously reported in the *Stephenville Empire-Tribune*, there were actually many different sightings from different parts of the area. In fact, Cherry had collected hundreds of sighting reports, which, he said, the major media simply ignored, in part because the witnesses, out of fear of public ridicule, had chosen to remain anonymous.

Ken Cherry was right. Over the course of sixty years of UFO investigations, witnesses were generally regarded as kooks or malcontents. The level of ridicule was often so intense in the media that many legitimate and credible sighting reports never made it into the public arena. Pilots and flight attendants, for example, who routinely see strange things in the sky, keep quiet for fear of being cast as unreliable by the FAA and the media. Police, both in the United States and in the United Kingdom, have often been ridiculed by their colleagues for turning in reports of their sightings. In two cases investigated by *UFO Hunters*, constables in the United Kingdom were actually driven off the force by higher-ups in their departments responding to pressure from official agencies and, in turn, making the constables' lives intolerable on the force.

Ken Cherry, collecting reports in the context of these sixty years of derision and ridicule, was gratified by the number of people who came forward with their descriptions of what they saw. Cherry, who developed a database of the history of UFO sightings in the areas of Dallas, Fort Worth, Stephenville, and Dublin, Texas, said that the history of these types of sightings, and even encounters with strange objects, goes all the way back to the late nineteenth century. These sightings were not a one-time event in Stephenville, he said. In fact, Texas MUFON pointed to newspaper articles from Dallas and other local papers describing reports from residents, including judges and politicians, of objects shaped like cigars, some with wings and others with hanging gondolas, that slowly hovered over the area. One object, most likely a metal-clad balloon, actually landed in Stephenville in 1897, prompting the entire town to gather around it before the craft's pilot got his engine working again and took off. Sarah Canady, the

Stephenville historian, suggested that this might have been the same object that crashed into a windmill in Aurora, Texas, a day or so later and exploded into a thousand pieces.

Ken Cherry told *UFO Magazine* and the *Stephenville Empire-Tribune* that, from his experience in investigating UFO sightings, the Stephenville lights marked a turning point because of the interest of the national media. Maybe the actual identity of whatever people saw that night would never be discovered, he speculated, but, at the very least, the multitude of sightings and the reaction of the air force stirred up the media to the extent that it was the government that was seen as covering up the truth and not UFO witnesses that were seen as distorting the truth.

THE EPISODE

On February 25, 2008, we arrived in Stephenville to set up headquarters in a two-story office building across the street from the courthouse. We coordinated our activities with Ken Cherry and Steve Hudgeons of MUFON and set up interview facilities downstairs to greet witnesses and process videos and assembled a more formal studio upstairs for the white-box direct-to-camera interviews. The town had made headlines across the country on January 10, for a series of UFO sightings and stunning descriptions of a craft by Steve Allen, a pilot, who said he saw an object with lights, flying low, that was about a mile long and half a mile wide. Constable Leroy Gaton described it as one red and white glowing light moving very fast.

Even before we met witnesses, Ted suggested the kinds of parameters we should look for in our questioning. First of all, he said, we needed to find out such basics as the condition of the sky, the weather, the exact position of each witness, the time of day, and the direction the object people said they saw was moving. Then, we needed to compare the geographic positions and directions of the object to look for commonalities and to triangulate the positions. Next, we went on the radio station, 98.5 KCUB in Stephenville, to put out a call for witnesses to come in to talk to us. This was also a first for us, something we would repeat in seasons 2 and 3 for ongoing sightings.

Our call for witnesses, photos, and videos brought an immediate response. Working the phones, Pat, Ted, Jeff Tomlinson, and I gathered as much information as we could from callers, noting names, locations, and descriptions of the sighting in a log that Pat kept. We invited callers to stop by the office and took face-to-face reports, most of which corroborated what other witnesses stated in newspaper interviews. We were particularly impressed with the descriptions of a low-flying object that didn't have any wings. Witness after witness told us that, contrary to some reports on national media, the town hadn't gone crazy and the folks who saw the lights weren't, in the words of one witness, "a bunch of space aliens." In the words of another witness, these were "upstanding citizens who were coming forward."

A police officer who was riding with Constable Leroy Gaton said that he saw a bright light hovering in the sky west of the highway. He saw it through the windshield of his police cruiser and said that it appeared to be spinning and changing colors. From his perception of what he said he saw, there was no way this object could have been a conventional aircraft.

The descriptions were very fascinating, but we had to find some more solid evidence, because when we diagrammed the locations of the witnesses and noted the different times of the sightings, we couldn't be sure if the people were seeing different objects. The times did not match up. Finally, we located one witness who said that he videotaped the object. His name was David Caron, a local mechanic. He told us that he was alerted by his grandson, who was startled by lightning in the sky on January 19, that there was an object overhead and coming toward their house. His grandson said there were bright-colored lights that seemed very close. He said the lights flashed like lightning. He told his grandfather, David, who ran to retrieve his camera from inside the house.

David Caron stood on his porch, braced his camera hand up

against the porch column, and started filming with his JVC 32X optical-zoom camcorder, recording the object for fourteen minutes. The object was round and had bright lights and red rays coming off of it. He could see the object with his naked eye as well as through his view-finder. As the object spun, he could see it changing colors, going from red to green to blue. He said that through the viewfinder, the object seemed to be streaming ribbons of light, something that would be very telling when Ted Acworth later analyzed the footage. He also said that it was noiseless and could not have been an F-16.

David Caron's footage provided some interesting images. As Pat pointed out, the image seemed to jump from place to place across the frame. This, he suggested, was a result of the camera's being on night shutter, which made the image stutter and look blurry. Ted also pointed out that the image was almost completely defocused at extreme close-up because the camera itself was struggling to accomplish three things: keep the object in view clearly, bring the object in close, and admit as much light as possible through the lens. These were impossible for a consumer-grade camera to accomplish at the same time and at this distance, and as a result the image became defocused.

Could this image, the changing colors and the ribbon-of-light effect, be reproduced in a lab? To test this out, Ted Acworth, Jeff Tomlinson, and special-effects expert John Tindall headed over to Tarleton State University to put Caron's camera through its paces. They tried to reproduce the camera shaking to see if they could duplicate the stuttering effect of the image. First, they rigged the camera on the base of a spinning drill. It rocked the camera left and right, mimicking David Caron's hand movements. Even though Caron said that he kept his hand steady, Ted theorized that even a small movement of his hand against the pole might make for a shaky image, especially with a camera set at extreme zoom for a close-up. Ted and John Tindall set up a light source at the other end of the lab, the focus point and object the camera was looking at. What he got was a ribbon-of-light effect not exactly like the image Caron captured but similar enough that Ted thought a shaky camera on night shutter could have been responsible for the ribbon, or streak, of light.

The next step was to see if it was remotely possible that the image that Caron captured could have been a plane. Ted theorized that an aircraft far enough in the distance and heading either toward or away from the camera might look stationary in a two-dimensional field of vision. If the camera were defocused and the object had conventional navigation lights, the lights would show up as different colors in the image. To reproduce this, John Tindall set up colored lights near the point of light. This time the camera recorded traces of the colored lights in streaks, which were similar, but not an exact match to, David Caron's footage. Therefore, John Tindall and Ted Acworth could not eliminate the possibility that the image in David's camera was a conventional aircraft. Tindall said it was likely that Caron was photographing an airplane. I wasn't so sure because the images were different.

While Ted, Jeff, and Tindall tested out the camera, MUFON state director Ken Cherry told Pat and me that the media was misreporting the sightings by saying that folks saw the swarm of UFOs on January 8. Actually, he showed us in the sighting reports, the sightings began over a month earlier. Throughout December 2007, the sighting reports grew, indicating to Cherry that this was a mass sighting, building over the course of two months. Cherry said that his reports and sightings log showed that critics who argued that people in Stephenville were simply imagining things in the sky because of the January 10 media reports of sightings were mistaken. Because the sightings began a month earlier than the first media reports and built in numbers and intensity, this could not have been a case of the media influencing the witnesses.

The sightings also moved south toward Houston throughout January and February and were still coming in even while we were covering the story in Stephenville. This suggested to the MUFON investigators that it was a swarm of UFOs that were flying over the area. What they wanted or what they were looking for, no one knew.

Investigators only knew that witness reports indicated that the sightings of objects were moving south toward the Gulf.

We were still looking for some definitive video, something out of the ordinary with a good witness story behind it. And we got our wish when Margie Galvez walked in with her DVD of something that had taken place in her backyard around late November 2007, in Brownwood, Texas, right in the area where the sighting swarm first started. Margie said that because her animals—ducks, chickens— were slowly disappearing from her property, she had to figure out a way to find the culprit. Were coyotes or other predators taking her animals? She devised a plan to find out. She placed a night-vision camera in her backyard and turned it on at night. On November 22, when she replayed the tape, she saw the truncated beam of cone-shaped white light snap on from above the frame, scan the ground, and then snap off. It was something she had never seen before, something that Pat and I had both heard about but were now seeing on a video. It was very chilling.

As Ted Acworth mentioned, there could be other explanations for the source of the beam that did not involve UFOs, perhaps a helicopter with a sunspot light shining down along the ground looking for predatory animals. The heat from the lamp beam would have shown up on an infrared camera as well as a night-vision light-collecting camera. However, if Margie had heard the thwap-thwap of rotor blades at night, then it would have meant that somehow her property was the object of a black, silent-rotor helicopter search. Highly unlikely.

We wanted to find out if anyone else in town had seen a beam like the one on Margie's camera. Once again, we caught a break. A woman, who begged that her name not be used in the episode or her face on camera, called us to tell us of a frightening encounter she had with a UFO just outside town when she was driving her daughter and some friends home from cheerleading practice.

She didn't want her identity revealed and asked that I meet her at a remote location and drive with her in her pickup to where she saw the

UFO. She said she was terrified and so were the girls in her truck, but because her sightings were part of the goings-on in Stephenville, she felt she had to let us know about it.

The witness drove me to the spot where she saw the object and, on the way, said that it was January 19, 2008, at ten in the evening, just hours after David Caron filmed the object he saw and only three miles away. Here, she and the girls pulled up to a railroad trestle and saw the circular object overhead, spinning slowly as its ring of lights gave off different colors. They followed the slow-moving object for a couple of minutes before the object simply, in the words of the witness, "zapped out." The object emitted a cone-shaped beam, the witness said, visible to her and her passengers. "The beam," she said, "was strange because it did not hit the ground."

I asked our witness about the air force's changing its story about the presence of F-16s in the air on the night of January 8. She, too, said the story made no sense for two reasons. One, why were the witnesses on January 8 saying that the objects they saw in the air were totally silent? Jets aren't silent. Two, more important to the witness, she saw an object on January 19 and other witnesses saw things in the sky at the end of December. These were not accounted for by the air force. Regarding the circular object she saw, she said that it was definitely not an F-16 or any other kind of jet. It was noiseless, hovered and floated, shot a beam of light that did not hit the ground, and then simply turned itself off and disappeared. "The military is definitely hiding something," she said.

Ken Cherry was also deeply suspicious of the military's story. He is familiar with how military air operations work and told us that it would have been a major undertaking to get ten F-16 fighters in the air on a training mission that night. Just the fuel alone would have been enormously expensive for a simple training mission, not to mention the large amount of personnel to service the planes and ready them for takeoff. However, if we assume the air force did launch F-16s that night, might they have done so not for training purposes but to scramble them because an unidentified object was flying less than seventy miles away from President George W. Bush's Crawford Ranch, sometimes referred to as the "Western White House"?

Ted and Jeff looked at the possibility of some of the sightings of objects having originated from surrounding airbases. Could witnesses have seen objects over military operations areas, or MOAs? Stephenville is surrounded by the Naval Air Station Fort Worth Joint Reserve Base, the Clark Field Municipal Airport, and the Dallas/Fort Worth International Airport. Stephenville is also twelve miles to the northeast of the Brownwood Military Operations Area, a restricted-air-traffic zone where only military flights are allowed. Pat followed up on this possibility by calling military officials at the 457th Fighter Wing and the 301st's Major Karl Lewis to see if they could confirm any strange activity in the skies over Stephenville in January or to talk about the possibility that fighters on a training exercise ventured out of the MOA. However, no one at any of the bases was willing to talk about the UFO sightings.

Ted and Jeff also suggested an experiment in which they would position witnesses, who say they saw something at the same time, in the same locations where they were on January 8, the night of the most sightings, and triangulate where in the sky the object would have been. In that way, they believed, they could fix the position of the object to determine whether it was in a MOA or directly over Stephenville. All of us fanned out to find witnesses, log in the times of their sightings, and get GPS coordinates of their locations where they had the sightings. If the position of the object they sighted was not in or very near to a MOA, then it was more than likely that the object was not a flight of F-16s.

Our first witness was Bill Hensley, who saw an object on January 8 from his front porch. It was a bright light moving noiselessly and slowly at an angle of inclination of eighty-one degrees. Half a mile away from Bill Hensley lived James Huse, a retired U.S. Air Force technician, who reported seeing a bright object moving slowly at the same time and on the same date as Hensley. He told Pat that he saw two bright red orbs traveling from northwest to southeast flying as low as fifteen hundred feet. MUFON took us to our third witness, a man who said that he saw the object from his car on Interstate 67.

While Ted, John Tindall, and Jeff Tomlinson set up the triangulation experiment, Pat and I interviewed witnesses who said they'd been seeing strange objects in the sky over Erath County for decades before the January 2008 swarm. One witness said that he saw a football-shaped object back in 1964. It was very bright and had a lot of lights on it. Others said they saw a cigar-shaped object, possibly a disk flying on its side, an object similar to the one reported over Dennison, Texas, in 1981. On May 25, 1995, Captain Eugene Tollefson of America West Airlines flight 564 called into air traffic control his sighting of a flying "cigar shape" over Bovina, Texas.

We wondered, how far back do UFO sightings go in this area? Pat and I had to do some background research. We found that there are reported unidentified craft in the north Texas area dating all the way back to the nineteenth century. From the look of the sketches contemporary residents made and gave to local newspapers, it seemed clear that many of these well-decked-out cigar-shaped craft were lighter than airships and were balloons clad in metal and propelled by internal combustion engines. The 1897 crash in Aurora, Texas, seemed suspiciously like a balloon. Balloons as military assets had been in service in the United States military in the Civil War for the purposes of surveillance of enemy positions.

There was at least one other nineteenth-century event that seemed far less explainable. In 1881, residents in the Stephenville area saw a flaming round object floating in the air that they described as a "flaming ball of cotton." Town historian Sarah Canady walked us through the UFO history of Erath County. In the 1970s, residents saw a large cigar-shaped craft with huge red lights. Craft had been turning up in the skies over Stephenville for well over a hundred years, Sarah Canady told us, and for a hundred years these sightings had been covered in local newspapers. This current sighting in Stephenville would have been much like the others had it not been for the U.S. Air Force changing their story about F-16s flying over the Stephenville area on the nights in question. They first denied having any planes in the air and then released information that no one in the town could believe about a large-scale training mission. After hearing about the history of UFOs in the area from Canady, Pat and I had to get back to Ted and Jeff, who were conducting the witness-triangulation experiment.

As Ted explained it, this would be the first full-scale U.S. geographic-triangulation experiment that attempted to verify a multiple-witness UFO sighting. We were focusing on just one of the sightings, the January 8 sighting in Stephenville between 8 and 9 P.M. The theory was that if the team could confirm that the three witnesses saw the same object at the same time from their respective locations, even without knowing what the object was, we would at least know there was an object in a location that we could determine. We could then figure out whether that location was over a MOA or over someplace else. That would help us ascertain whether the object was likely to be an air force plane.

Jeff, John, and Ted took the locations of the three witnesses and, with laser emitters, pointed a laser in the direction and at the angle of inclination of the sighting. If the laser beams converged at the same spot, it would show that something was there where the witnesses said it was. We had the support of the Stephenville Fire Department as well as a number of local residents, one of whom took John Tindall's witness position because John was working the weather balloon as the target for the lasers. It is against FAA regulations to point lasers directly into the sky. However, we were floating a balloon into the position in the sky where the witnesses reported seeing an object. The balloon would be the target of the lasers if the witness reports were accurate.

With the three team members at their locations, Tindall gave the OK to fire the lasers. At that moment, he launched the weather balloon, which, in a matter of minutes, floated right into the three converged laser beams. The experiment successfully showed that there was something in the sky on the night of January 8, 2008, between 8 and 9 P.M., just as witnesses claimed. The experiment showed that it was likely that if different witnesses in different locations said they saw a strange object in the sky at the same time—they said it was about 8 P.M. that night—that they would have been able to see the same object. Our experiment demonstrated the likelihood of a multiple witness sighting of the same object. It was an object approximately two miles southeast of Stephenville near Clark Field Municipal Airport, and it hovered at an altitude of about one thousand feet in an area outside, not inside, of an authorized military operations area, also referred to as a "MOA." The closest MOA border is nine miles to the southwest. Moreover, according to FAA data that was released to the public, no known aircraft were in the air that night, thus belying the air force press release of an F-16 training mission. But what did the residents see that night?

Stephenville city councilman Mark Murphy said that he heard at least one attempt at an explanation from a friend who was in the air force. He said the air force was working on a cloaking device—something we would see at Dugway Proving Ground the following year—that could account for a craft's being mistaken for a UFO. The device made the craft invisible unless it was painted with a laser. But even though the story had gained traction in town as a rumor, residents familiar with aircraft said that anything flying at a thousand feet, cloaked or not, would still generate lots of noise. Therefore, they said, lights without noise were most likely not a cloaked conventional aircraft.

The sightings of unidentified objects continued even after the team left Stephenville with reports coming in from Corpus Christi just weeks later that witnesses had seen a configuration of lights moving slowly and noiselessly through the sky at a low altitude. Many residents said that they thought it was something not from this world.

THE AFTERMATH OF THE STORY

MUFON reported that even after the initial UFO flap, residents in the area kept on seeing strange lights. Whether they were top-secret air force or intelligence-agency craft or whether they were truly otherworldly, no one knows. One conjecture by military analysts and reporters was that these objects were top-secret observation platforms that were capable of neutral buoyancy or even antigravity. Platforms such as these can scan an area with infrared—which is what showed up on the Margie Galvez video—or with electron beams to scrub for any electronic data or heat signatures. The government, in these instances, would rather folks believe them to be extraterrestrial craft than military weapons because it helps keep the technology secret. As one CIA agent was reported to have said, "Even the CIA likes UFOs because they were cited in the past as ways to cover up real classified aircraft."

Also, in July 2008, the MUFON research director in Texas, Robert Powell, worked with radar expert Glen Schultze to investigate the radar tapes from various air traffic control locations, which revealed two things. First, Schultze and Powell correlated the witness reports with radar tapes on the nights in question to determine that there were radar targets in the sky that were most likely the sightings that the witnesses reported. In other words, these sightings were not mere delusions or fanciful, wishful thinking; they were real. What they were, the radar tapes did not reveal. But the radar revealed that they were something.

The other interesting aspect to the radar report was that the object or objects witnesses saw were indeed heading toward President George W. Bush's Crawford ranch, also known as the Western White House. The information lends itself to a lot of speculation about what type of object would be heading over to the Crawford ranch, but given the size of the object and the indications that this was not a plane—there were no transponder returns that the radar tapes reported—one can only wonder what it was. An air force or intelligence-agency top-secret aircraft flying stealth might not return a friend or foe transponder reading. But one would think that any type of aircraft flying near a restricted zone such as a presidential residence would have to identify itself or be intercepted. Might that have been the reason that the object was chased by two F-16s? In the absence of any documentation, one can only speculate.

The Stephenville sightings continue off and on to this day, but now they're being taken almost in stride by Stephenville residents, who know they're there even if they don't know whose they are.

BILL'S BLOG

Admittedly, it took a lot for me to convince the production company to change the shooting schedule midstream and head down to Texas when we were supposed to be in California. We had already changed the schedule once to make it to the National Press Club conference run by Leslie Kean and James Fox. Here it was a little over two months later and we were changing the schedule again. But it was worth it.

The story was important because we arrived on the heels of massive media coverage of the event and got one of the city councilmen to go on camera talking about what had happened. In terms of the series, we also launched an entirely new format for the show because we had current witnesses willing to go on camera. We also performed scientific experiments on ongoing phenomena and were able to set up a headquarters to run a live investigation on camera with real people. It was to be the model for future episodes in Tinley Park and Kokomo, Indiana, in the following season.

We also discovered something about UFO investigations that said a lot about how the media cover the phenomena. UFO stories have become so hot in the media that local people who began the investigation sometimes worried that the national media would distort the story by coopting it for their own purposes, either to sensationalize it or debunk it. But either way, as the story moved from the local newspaper to the national newswire, it captured the imagination of a national audience on the twenty-four-hour cable news cycle. How the Stephenville lights story played in the national media told us that UFO stories weren't just for fringe elements anymore. UFOs were big news, and they were being taken seriously.

I learned something else about the power of television as well during the Stephenville episode. By the time we arrive in Stephenville, *UFO Hunters* had been on the air for almost a month, premiered on Wednesday nights and rerun during the week. The show and its impact preceded us into town, which enabled us to talk to local witnesses, who knew that we weren't going to distort their words or edit them in ways that made them look less than credible. This enabled us to conduct very candid interviews with people who were not afraid to speak out about what they saw. We were also able to get lots of cooperation for our science experiments, both with David Caron's video footage and the geographic laser and balloon triangulation.

Most exciting for me in this episode, though, were the appearances of Margie Galvez and her mysterious beam-of-light video as well as of our anonymous witness who saw a beam of light like the one in Margie's video, this one emanating from a circular craft with colored lights slowly rotating in the sky over a set of railroad tracks. And her daughter and friends were in the vehicle and saw the same thing. To me, this was real corroboration of a sighting of a structured object, one that hovered noiselessly in such a way as to indicate that it was using some kind of exotic levitation and propulsion system and that was doing something active by emitting a mysterious beam of an unknown frequency at the earth. We don't know what it is or what it was doing or looking for. But we know that it looked like it was doing something.

The Stephenville case, and the follow-up radar analyses showing that something was there that night, also marked a high point for MUFON and the way they were able to assemble witnesses and get their statements even in the midst of a media firestorm, where stories could easily become inflated, confabulated, and completely distorted as they were told, retold, shared, edited, and broadcast.

Through it all we were also impressed with the initial reporting that Angelia Joiner did for the *Stephenville Empire-Tribune*, because, were it not for her consistent following up and courage in interviewing of witnesses, the story might well have died before it had even begun.

We were really lucky to have worked with all parties in Stephenville: Angelia, Ken Cherry, Steve Hudgeons and MUFON, Sarah Canady, and the local media.

AREA 51 REVEALED

This was our highest-rated episode in season 2 and the second-highest-rated episode in the history of the History Channel. It was dangerous to film, thrilling to film, rewarding to film, and the repercussions of our filming haunted us through the third and final season of the show as debunkers, perhaps operating as an off-the-books MIB stunt, tried to make us look silly. But, best of all, we got to film a UFO.

WHAT IS AREA 51?

Officially, except for references in some CIA memos, there is no such place as Area 51. Informally, the name Area 51 was given to the location in southern Nevada, in part because it was located on a tax map as grid block number 51.

The facility was originally an Army Air Force gunnery range in the 1940s but was abandoned after the war. It was restarted in the 1950s under an arrangement between Lockheed's Kelly Johnson and the CIA because Johnson needed a secure and secret facility with the capacity for long enough runways to test a new craft the CIA and air force had asked him to develop: a spy plane that could observe what nuclear- and missile-facilities construction the Soviet Union was up to during what was becoming an increasingly intense cold war. The intelligence agencies and the military had to have some idea of the advances the Soviets were making. Also, in the early 1950s, according to Lieutenant Colonel Philip Corso, the United States needed a plane that could test the Soviet antiaircraft missile defenses. Not only did we want to spy on the Soviets, just like they wanted to spy on us, but we also wanted to know the capabilities of their antiaircraft missiles. How high could they reach, how vulnerable would our bombers be, and could we outfly them? To accomplish a mission like this, the intelligence services and the air force needed a plane that could fly high over the missile's ceiling while photographing the facilities on the ground below. The plane had to have a uniquely advanced design but must be developed and tested in secrecy. The old Army Air Force gunner range that would ultimately become popularly known as Area 51 was the perfect place. Now they had to build out the runways and the hangars.

In 1955 Johnson; his chief test pilot, Tony LeVier; and a CIA representative traveled to the old gunnery range in Nevada and found it perfect for a secret development base. With President Eisenhower's approval and his order turning the airspace over the new base into a restricted zone, the base management was taken over by the CIA and the Atomic Energy Commission, with management of the development taken over by Lockheed. In August 1955, the first U-2 spy plane was launched from the dry lake bed on the new facility at Groom Lake, soon to be dubbed, informally but not officially, Area 51.

The base became a top-secret facility. Pilots flying near, but not over, the base reported sightings of strange craft. They could see long runways and the building of large hangars. Indeed, there was something very secret going on at the base. The CIA, knowing that they had to have a cover story for what was being developed under wraps at what was now called Groom Lake, had been feeding popular fiction writers and motion picture producers and their studios stories, claiming they were fiction, about flying saucers and extraterrestrials. The agency was trying to find a way to turn the stories that were popular in the 1950s about flying-saucer sightings into fiction in order to marginalize them and make them harmless. At the same time, they were trying to marginalize those who were calling on the government to admit the truth about the intrusions by flying saucers into U.S. airspace. Making flying saucers fiction, not real, was the best way to do it. There was an added benefit. When people began to speculate that the strange craft at Groom Lake were flying saucers, the CIA actively fed those rumors. As one agent was reported to have said to one of our guests on *UFO Hunters*, a guest who shall remain nameless, "It's a good thing for UFOs because if they weren't real we would have had to invent them."

The base today is heavily guarded, ringed by motion sensors and hidden microphones, and guarded along its perimeter by snipers, some of whom had been members of Delta Force, an elite joint special operations command team of commandos. Armed with night-vision telescopic scopes, Delta Force snipers could pick off intruders onto the base with a single lethal shot. In fact, signs warning potential intruders that any trespasser onto the base is subject to lethal force are ringed around the base. Even if no sniper shoots you immediately if you stick your toe over the base perimeter, there is no mistaking the intent of the government to prosecute anyone who enters onto the base even if it's only for criminal trespass upon a top-secret facility. We found out just how serious the government was when we visited the perimeter of the base in 2009 and saw base security—camo dudes, as they have been called—go on alert when they saw and heard us.

THE BOB LAZAR STORY

The association between what was being called Area 51 and flying saucers was advanced to intensity by the revelations of a young man named Robert Scott Lazar, who claimed to have been an MIT physicist hired by the air force to work at the Groom Lake S-4 facility on the propulsion systems of extraterrestrial craft. He claimed his job was to figure out how to reverse engineer them. His story is shrouded in controversy, with some ufologists saying there's not a single shred of evidence to support his claims and supporters such as George Knapp of KLAS-TV in Las Vegas and *Coast to Coast AM*, along with retired CIA pilot and test pilot John Lear, saying that they were out in the desert at the perimeter of S-4 with Bob Lazar watching reverse engineered UFOs being tested. And they have the video as evidence.

Bob Lazar's story, which on the surface seems almost like an American comedy of errors had he not been, he says, at the very cutting edge of technology, involved his being recruited to S-4 from Los Alamos, where, George Knapp says, records prove that he once worked. At S-4 he had very odd work hours, leaving sometimes at two in the morning to work for extended periods. He says that his research involved trying to determine how and whether very exotic propulsion systems could be fitted into craft developed here on Earth. At first he thought he was working on terrestrial designs, but he soon found out that the craft were extraterrestrial in origin with propulsion mechanisms that even the engineers at S-4 couldn't figure out.

In one story, Lazar said that he was escorted into a hangar where he saw alien spacecraft, craft that he was told were in the process of being reverse engineered so that the military could develop propulsion systems for homegrown aircraft based on those designs. In another story, Lazar told friends that he was walked past a door with a window in it. Looking through the window, as he was told to do, he saw a flickering candle. The person he was with told him to watch the candle carefully and tell him what he saw. Suddenly, the candle stopped flickering and seemed to freeze. Lazar, at a loss to explain what he was seeing, just said that the candle had stopped flickering. The person he was with explained that the candle was still burning just as it was before, but what Lazar was seeing was that the candle had stopped, that time, itself, inside that chamber seemed to be frozen. The candle, Bob Lazar said he was told, was in a slipstream of an energy field generated by an element called 115, which had sucked time, and space, around the generator in a way that made time seem to stand still to anyone viewing the phenomenon from outside the slipstream. That was how the story of element 115 got into the popular culture of UFOs, and it is what former CIA pilot John Lear explained to us on *UFO Hunters*. He said that a beam of energy generated by element 115, when focused from the extraterrestrial craft at a particular point in space, is so powerful that it doesn't propel the craft through space, it draws space and time around the craft and in so doing creates a temporal distortion field. That's why the candle seemed to be frozen. Time itself was frozen and drawn past the element-115 generator that made the candle look like it was not flickering.

Bob Lazar said that when the government pulled his security clearance and fired him from his job, it also erased his former employment records so that, if he spoke out, no one would be able to verify what he said, and he would look as if he were fabricating his story. How he got into this mess is a story in itself.

Former workers at Area 51 confirmed that activities at the base were so secret that workers would many times be called into work at odd hours, sometimes in the middle of the night. They were not allowed to discuss what they did or compromise base security by announcing their whereabouts. Their wives and family would have to trust them. In Lazar's case, he would be called to report to McCarran International Airport at 2 A.M., from where he would be flown to the base, where he would stay for twelve or more hours at a time before being flown back to Las Vegas. His wife believed that her husband was meeting someone, having an affair, and using his work at a top-secret facility as his alibi. As things in his relationship got more tense, Lazar finally broke down and told his wife what he was doing. That only made it worse. Imagine telling your spouse, who is accusing you of having romantic trysts with another, that you are actually being flown to a top-secret research facility in the dead of night because you're the expert on reverse engineering the propulsion system of an extraterrestrial spacecraft, a flying saucer, into a mechanism the air force can use as a weapon. What kind of an explanation is that? Nevertheless, to prove that he was telling the truth, he brought his wife and their friend Gene Huff out to the perimeter of the base to watch a UFO being tested in the night sky. It was so thrilling that he brought them out again. Although he was able to show his wife what he was working on at odd hours, the base learned of his breach of security and pulled his clearance, and he was fired.

He told his story to KLAS-TV newscaster George Knapp, who was able to verify some of Lazar's claims of having worked at Los Alamos. He also told retired CIA pilot John Lear, and brought Knapp and Lear out to the base perimeter, a spot in the desert, where they could observe activities in the restricted air space, to see alien craft being tested. Lear videotaped their outings. George Knapp reported the story on KLAS-TV, and by 1989, the Lazar story was breaking news.

It was the story of Bob Lazar and the reverse engineering of extraterrestrial craft at the mysterious Area 51 that brought the *UFO Hunters* team out to Nevada for the final episode of season 2, an episode in which the crew not only climbed up Tikaboo Peak to film inside the base itself with a powerful telephoto lens, but also, by setting up surveillance cameras around the perimeter of the base, cameras aimed skyward, was able to capture a UFO over the base. We also tracked Janet Airline planes, Janet being the name of the airline that shuttles workers and personnel for Area 51, by running their tail numbers from a hotel room over the airport to see who the planes' registered owners were. Guess what? These were not commercial planes as most people understand the term.

THE EPISODE

We traveled to Las Vegas at the end of our filming schedule in 2008, where Ted, Pat, and I went in different directions to research background on the base. Pat was going to the base itself to film as much as we could of the facilities on the base; Ted was meeting with UFO researcher, Area 51 expert, and historical fact finder Peter Merlin out in the Nevada desert for background on the technology underpinning the goings-on at the base; and I was off to meet with the very famous CIA pilot John Lear, who had visited the area with Bob Lazar to talk about what Lazar learned, what happened to him, and what Lazar was reverse engineering. We would all reconvene at the base perimeter to meet with Pat and guest Susan Wright, who had written a book about trying to enter Area 51.

Peter Merlin is one of the foremost unofficial experts on Area 51, having studied satellite photos of the base, interviewed former workers there, and studied declassified files describing activities at the facility. While Peter Merlin and Ted were talking about Area 51 history and the likelihood that the air force and CIA were developing drone technology at the base, Pat and another Area 51 expert, former combat photographer Mark Farmer, took a trip out into the desert to observe craft over the flight paths leading to and from the Area 51 runways. They went to a location twenty miles north of Area 51 in an old plutonium-dispersal field to see what aircraft were being tested. But, to their surprise, they were the ones being observed when a pair of F-15s flew overhead, circling Pat and Mark Farmer, surveilling them electronically.

Mark Farmer explained that, in addition to whatever the jets could see as they flew over the location, ground-based sensors were picking up electronic emanations from any visitors to the area. Even if hikers approached the base without crossing the perimeter, very sophisticated electronic sensors would pick up their presence and register a heightened electrical activity on a screen somewhere in a security facility monitoring the base fence line. For example, Mark explained, since most people carry cell phones and their cars have GPS devices, there is a constant signal to and from satellites. These signals easily register on the base security computers. In fact, because cell phones send a unique signal, which is how the satellite recognizes them when they make phone calls, the base security can determine who owns the cell phone and probably identify those approaching the base. As one

CIA officer once told me, if you want to be electronically invisible to intelligence agencies and police forces, simply take the battery out of your phone so that it will stop sending a signal. Just turning it off won't work.

After the F-15s circled Pat and Mark a few times, they flew off, and the area was quiet again. By now it was obvious that the base security was aware of the presence of *UFO Hunters* and simply shut down whatever it was about to do so we could not capture anything on camera.

With Pat and Mark Farmer trekking around the desert to observe the skies over Area 51 and Ted and Peter Merlin going over satellite images of the base, I headed over to the studios of KLAS-TV in Las Vegas to talk to my old friend, on-air news reporter and *Coast to Coast AM* host George Knapp, the person who broke the story of Bob Lazar and Area 51 in November 1989 about what Lazar was working on, how he blew his security clearance, and how the government erased his identity. This was a story many UFO researchers would not buy.

Bob Lazar went public with his claims. Veteran investigative re- porter George Knapp, UFO conspiracy theories and skeptics' counter- claims notwithstanding, smelled a real story. Knapp uncovered actual evidence of Lazar's background. As he explained it to me, when he called Los Alamos to check on Lazar's employment there, the office he spoke to said there were no records of a Bob Lazar. However, Knapp said that he checked an old Los Alamos personnel phone book and found Lazar's name in there. He called Los Alamos back and told them he had found Lazar's name in their employee phone book, and they still said that they had no records of his employment. You have to wonder, was the government trying to hide that Lazar had ever worked at Los Alamos or Area 51?

Knapp also said that he found an old *Los Alamos Monitor*, the news- paper of the facility, on whose front page was a photo of Lazar and a car he was working on. The paper noted that Lazar was a physicist at the lab. Again Knapp called Los Alamos, and again they said they had no records of him despite two official notices that Lazar worked there.

George Knapp followed up on the story and interviewed a number of people who worked at Los Alamos who confirmed to him that they knew Lazar worked there. "The key for me," Knapp explained, "is if he worked at Los Alamos in classified jobs, then it was conceivable that he could have worked at Area 51." I asked George flat out, "Do you believe Bob Lazar's story?"

"I do," George said unequivocally.

Knapp said that in his ongoing interviews with Lazar he learned about Lazar's discovery of the work that was being done at S-4 on the energy source known as element 115. "He speculated," Knapp said, "that it came from some other planet or some other solar system and [Lazar] would take it apart to find out how it works." Lazar said that it was element 115 that was used to power flying saucers, which is what John Lear explained, too.

PAT AND SUSAN WRIGHT AT AREA 51

We wondered, how close could Pat Uskert approach the perimeter of Area 51 without alerting security? We didn't have to wonder long because Pat and author Susan Wright (UFO Headquarters: Investigations on Current Extraterrestrial Activity in Area 51 [St. Martin's, 1999]) pulled right up to one of the gates to see what would happen. When Susan was writing her book back in 1997, she tried the same gambit and had a very scary experience when security personnel, whom she referred to as "camo dudes," intercepted her. Susan said, "They were blocking the road so we couldn't get in any further." Susan and her team pulled back to the next series of buttes, and "a helicopter just rose out of nowhere. It was like no sound, no warning. Suddenly the helicopter was, boom, right there in front of us, forty feet away."

She said that the group jumped into the car to protect themselves. "It was very frightening, very intimidating. It was obvious that's just what they wanted to do, to scare us away from the area."

With Susan's story as a caveat, Pat and Susan continued on toward the main gate of Area 51 to see what would happen as they approached. Would they be challenged again? Did the folks at Area 51 know *UFO Hunters* was on the way to film them? Apparently, as I would find out during our third season on the road from a retired officer in our clandestine services, they did.

At the intersection of Highway 375 and Groom Lake Road, Pat turned his SUV onto the dirt road that leads directly up to the front entrance of Area 51.

JOHN LEAR, BOB LAZAR, AND S-4

The mysterious John Lear, whose CIA background has become legend, probably knows as much about what Bob Lazar discovered at S-4 as Lazar himself, because he, along with George Knapp and Gene Huff, was Lazar's confidant. While Pat and Susan slowly made their way along the dusty Groom Lake Road, I met with John at his home in Las Vegas. John's father invented the Learjet, and John was literally born in the pilot's seat. Working for the CIA for decades as a pilot, John has been flying all types of planes all over the world. He admitted to us that he was the famous October Surprise pilot, carrying the messages from George H. W. Bush to keep the U.S. diplomats hostage in Tehran until Jimmy Carter was out of office and Ronald Reagan sworn in. A stunt pilot by the time he was seventeen years old, Lear retired with over nineteen thousand hours of flight time. He holds the most FAA certificates ever earned by a single pilot. But his entire life changed when he developed a close personal relationship with Bob Lazar back in the late 1980s.

John Lear said that Bob Lazar would take him on late-night excursions to the outskirts of Area 51 to see the test flights of reverse-engineered flying saucers. "There is no doubt about it," John told me. "I saw a flying saucer at Area 51. It was radiating yellow, blue, and gold. Bob Lazar told me when it was going to be there. And it was there."

John played a video for me, a video shot by Bob Lazar, in which

Lear, standing on the perimeter of Groom Lake, says that just a few minutes earlier he was an eyewitness to a flyover of a government-reverse-engineered UFO. "We watched it for seven or eight minutes," Lear says against a dark a spooky night sky. "The mission was organized by Bob Lazar, who is a theoretical physicist who works at Groom Lake." Bob Lazar's voice from off camera, amid laughter, says, "Who is also a dead man at this point."

Lear also said that Bob Lazar gave him detailed accounts and descriptions of the work he was doing at S-4. "He was trying to reverse engineer the exact same system that propelled these craft hundreds of thousands of light years away." To illustrate how Lazar explained it to him, Lear displayed a model of the propulsion-generating system the craft used that Lazar worked on. He took the domed cap off the model to show what looked like an upside-down water spigot. Inside the cap covering the spigot was a piece of fuel called element 115. "Bob said that we have five hundred pounds of this stuff at Los Alamos," Lear revealed.

John explained that the generator shoots protons into the tip of the element 115 fuel source, bumping the 115 up to element 116, at which point, because it is highly unstable, it instantly decays, releasing enormous amounts of energy. This incredible release of energy, according to what Lazar told Lear, allows the craft to violate the conventional laws of physics and travel at unheard-of speeds. In harnessing the energy, the speed of the craft is actually an illusion, because the craft doesn't move through space in conventional ways, as an aircraft does, but moves space through and around it.

"What they do," Lear said, "is to pull space around them and wrap it around them and that's what allows them to travel so quickly across the vast distances of space. They are not traveling through space, but pulling it towards them." He also explained that in pulling space, slipping it around the craft like a stream, the propulsion system also warped time inside the slipstream itself. It would give the perception that time was standing still—hence Bob Lazar's observation of the candle that looked like it had been frozen or, more to the point, the experiences of many UFO witnesses close enough to the objects, who said that it seemed as though they could not accurately account for the passage of time.

PAT AND SUSAN ARRIVE AT THE MAIN GATE OF AREA 51

With clouds of dust churning from the wheels of their SUV, Pat and Susan arrived at the northeast corner of Area 51. As they pulled up to the fence, Susan pointed out that, high on a hill overlooking the approach road, there was a vehicle with security personnel in camouflage uniforms. Pat and Susan could see through their binoculars that the security detail was watching them in a kind of a standoff. Then the guards turned on their vehicle's lights, almost in response to Pat's and Susan's spying on them. In the distance, Pat could see cameras buried in the tall scrub brush, cameras aimed at them. Despite being tracked, however, Pat and Susan marched on toward the actual fence line. At the orange posts along the border of the base, the pair, keeping just inches outside the base, walked along the orange boundary markers. As they walked, the security vehicle began to move along with them, keeping them in constant sight, waiting to see what they were going to do. Then, watching security across the perimeter and seeing that security was watching them, Pat and Susan turned around and headed back toward the Jeep, got in, and drove away. Next stop, Tikaboo Peak.

THE CLIMB AND THE SURVEILLANCE

Twenty-two miles off the edge of the base, Pat met up with experienced Area 51 researcher Glen Campbell. Their challenge: an eight-thousand-foot climb, sometimes on their hands and knees over a twenty-degree incline, to reach the summit of Tikaboo Peak to look inside the base with a high-definition video camera mounted with an extreme telephoto lens. This would be a treacherous climb because, even though they were starting out in daylight, they had to set up a base camp partway up the hill so they could make the rest of the trek in darkness. Their plan was to arrive at the peak before dawn and capture the base in the first rays of the rising sun from a mile-and-half-high vantage point. The sun would illuminate the features of the base in stark relief, allowing them to get photos more accurate and with greater resolution than any Google Earth satellite could capture.

At the same time that Pat and Glen were setting up their base camp, Ted Acworth was setting up a series of surveillance cameras midway between Rachel and Alamo, Nevada, along a stretch of road where UFO sightings are frequently reported in the airspace above Area 51. Ted's plan was clear. Because so many amateur videographers had claimed to have captured images of UFOs over Area 51 on a regular basis, Ted contracted with a surveillance company, Southwest Surveillance out of Las Vegas, to bring in three high-res video cameras and orient them toward Area 51 to see if they could capture anything on tape. Maybe the cameras would confirm some of Lazar's accounts of reverse-engineered alien craft being tested in the skies over the base.

The three cameras were set up one hundred feet apart and were set to record a panoramic portion of the sky above Area 51 for three days and nights. We hoped they would capture any strange aerial activity over the base.

Meanwhile, with the coming of night, Pat Uskert and Glen Campbell doused their campfire at their base camp and prepared for the long hike to the top of Tikaboo Peak along with the camera and other gear. In dry and chilly night air, the climbers got set for the hardest part of the climb after midnight to enable them to arrive before dawn at the summit, where the camera would be set up and the lens fitted on and pointed into the base, approximately twenty-five miles away. Tikaboo Peak was the only spot from where someone could legally observe the activities at Area 51. Finally, three hours after they began their final ascent, they crossed the last ridge, and the full scope of Area 51 came into view. "This place is huge," Pat said as he saw the full array of lights across the expansive runways and long hangars. The base, Glen Campbell explained, was about ten miles by six miles, marked by the very long runways necessary to accommodate the planes that were initially developed there. The military, however, had acquired all the land surrounding the base, making the area itself much larger than the actual working base. As a result, the entire military complex, according to Campbell, was the size of the states of Connecticut and Rhode Island combined.

It took Pat and his crew over an hour to set up the camera, and by that time, as the first rays of the sun began to illuminate the valley below, the camera was able to capture and record views of Area 51 never before seen on television. The close-ups of hangars and other buildings were very revealing, far more revealing than any satellite imagery of the base had shown thus far. But as Pat peered into the base, he saw something else that few people other than the personnel there had ever seen. He saw flights of unmarked jets, white with red stripes along their sides, making their landing approach and touching down on the runways. Were these the fabled Janet Airline flights rumored to transport workers in secret to the base from McCarran International Airport in Las Vegas, jets that also shuttled Area 51 workers and military personnel to other locations in secret? Campbell said, yes, the Janet Airline 737 jets at dawn would be ferrying workers into the base every half hour.

The images captured on camera were so clear that, Pat explained, it made it worthwhile that the ultra-long-range telephoto lens was brought along. It had to be lugged up separately, which had made the climb up the peak especially arduous. But this lens was particularly special. A normal camera has a 50-millimeter lens, but the lens carried up the mountainside was 1,140 millimeters, a huge and heavy device. The lens, once mounted, aimed, and focused, revealed rows of buildings in the middle of the nowhere of Area 51 and long runways. But the biggest mystery of all, Pat found, was a very long hangar building that had only recently been constructed.

Peter Merlin later explained to Ted that the recent buildings' construction at the base, from an initial expanse of a runway and trailers for living and working in the 1950s to today's complex, began in the 1970s. By the 1980s, the area had been completely transformed into a city with dormitories as well as a munitions storage area and a hardened explosion-proof structure. Extralong runways and taxiways were added just before Bob Lazar started working at the base. But the new hangar that Pat and Glen Campbell found, in addition to the twenty-three other hangars, posed the question, why would the base need a hangar that large? What was going on inside there? Was this hangar the home of the giant triangles seen over the Hudson Valley in New York in 1989; over Phoenix in 1997, as reported by former Arizona governor Fife Symington III; over Tinley Park, Illinois, in 2004; and over Wales in the United Kingdom in 2008?

Retired Rocky Mountain bureau chief of *Aviation Week,* Bill Scott (*Space Wars* [Forge, 2008]), said that there might be a completely conventional explanation for the triangular craft; it might be a stealth blimp whose existence might never be revealed because its mission will be forever classified by the military. It could well be that Pat's camera and satellite imagery captured the hangar, the home of the craft, whether terrestrial or extraterrestrial, that had been responsible for UFO sightings over the past twenty years. The next step in the investigation into Area 51 would be to speak directly to former Area 51 employees to get a sense of what they worked on and how that might have fed into the lore or the reality of flying saucers at Area 51.

THE JANET FLIGHTS

We focused on the Janet planes, the white 737s with red stripes along the side, to see if we could determine their origin. Whoever the contractor is, the flights themselves were a mystery because no one talked about them. They depart on a half-hourly basis from McCarran and fly directly into Area 51. While Pat and Glen spotted the Janet flights from the ground outside McCarran, Mark Farmer and I tried to track them from a Tropicana Hotel high-floor room overlooking the Mc-

Carran runways, picking out their tail numbers and running them through the FAA database. We found that every registration number we ran showed that Janet planes were registered to the United States government as owners.

"What does all this mean?" I asked Mark. He explained, "If you went to the Janet terminal, you would not see any markings on the planes. You would, however, see a nondescript building, a barbed-wire protected area, maybe some security guards who wouldn't stand out. Nothing would be out of the ordinary because the most classified airline in the United States is hiding in plain sight."

We confirmed that employees were ferried into Area 51 from Mc-Carran, as Bob Lazar said they were, on unmarked planes. We confirmed that these were called Janet flights and that the registration numbers on the 737s flown by Janet were registered to the United States government according to the FAA's own Web site. Detective work proved this. Now it was time to talk to a former employee and get him on the record.

T. D. BARNES

Bob Lazar's public statements notwithstanding, it was almost impossible to get former employees at Area 51 to speak publicly about their work there. However, we were fortunate in meeting up with retired electrical engineer T. D. Barnes, who agreed to describe his years working at the base from 1968 to 1972, years before Bob Lazar said he went to work there. During his years at Area 51, top-secret craft such as the A-12 and the F-117 Stealth Fighter were under development there.

Barnes told us that the identity of every engineer at the base was kept secret while they were employed there. "We had code names," he said, "pseudo names so, while we were working there, there was no record of our actual identities that circulated." This supports Lazar's claim that there were no records at the base of his employment.

Further, Barnes explained, if you weren't working on a specific project, you were given no knowledge of it. You only knew about what you worked on and nothing else. Therefore, anything could be going on in another department, and if you had no need to know, you simply weren't told and you certainly would not ask about it if you wanted to keep your job.

Barnes remembered that there were times when things were going on outside on the base that the majority of noninvolved employees weren't allowed to see. "They gathered us all in the mess hall," he said, "dropped down the black shades over the windows, and we'd sit there for three or so hours until whatever was going on was over." If any strange technology, for example, were being tested and you weren't a part of the program, you didn't see it.

I asked him whether he knew anything about UFOs at the base or reverse engineering going on. As expected, he said that he knew nothing he wasn't supposed to know. He couldn't deny there were any UFOs at Area 51, because, since he didn't work on them, he wouldn't have known about them even if they were being worked on there. There could have been any number of strange projects going on there, but the work was so compartmentalized that there was no cross-pollination among the projects even in the same work groups.

The T. D. Barnes interview was instructive, not because of what he did or didn't say about Bob Lazar but because his description of some of the working conditions at Area 51 comported with Bob Lazar's descriptions. Barnes made it clear that the modus operandi at the base was don't ask and don't tell. If you were too curious, it would be considered a problem because the very structure of the work environment there was to keep work groups separated from each other so that no one group knew the entire picture unless it had to. Reverse engineering did go on at the base, he explained, but from his perspective, it was reverse engineering of Soviet technology to find out what they were working on. Barnes said that among the projects he personally worked on were the A-12, an early model of advanced reconnaissance aircraft that was the prototype of the SR-71.

TED ACWORTH'S SURVEILLANCE CAMERAS

After three days of recording, Ted recovered the videos and took them to photo analyst Terrence Masson for his evaluation of any images the cameras caught. On the first night, October 7, 2008, at 10:39, the camera picked up a strange bright light over Area 51 that descended behind the mountains. "For it to be that bright," Ted said, "I think it has to be some sort of propulsion system or a jet." In other words, Ted suggested, the light was artificial.

For more perspective on where the light was going, Ted asked Terrence to overlay a daylight shot of that same area with the nighttime image. Terrence combined the two images. As he cross-faded between the nighttime and daylight image, tracking the circular light as it descended, Terrence said that the object grew dim and disappeared "a good deal before it went behind the mountain." This surprised him because it was blinking off on its own as it approached the beginning of the runway at Area 51.

Ted was equally intrigued by the image and said they should try to calculate the object's possible speed. Ted used the known distance between the camera lens and Area 51, about fifteen miles, to estimate the object's speed. Then he got from Terrence an estimate of where the object was when it winked out, about twice the height of the mountain range. Ted estimated that the object was traversing about 10,000 feet in about 2.2 seconds of camera time, which translated to about 3,600 miles an hour. "Pretty fast," Ted and Terrence agreed. However, if the object were farther away from the camera, say twenty-five or thirty miles, then it would be traveling at extremely high speeds, only consistent with a falling meteorite. Yet, Terrence suggested, the image wasn't consistent with a meteorite because he said it was traveling way too slowly. And besides, it blinked out before it fell behind the mountain, as if it were turned off. The only craft that was able to achieve speeds in excess of this object was the X-15, which broke speeds of 4,500 miles an hour. But that aircraft's final flight was on October 4, 1968, over forty years earlier. No known aircraft has achieved these speeds since. This image, Ted said, was a mystery. "Something descended at high speed into Area 51 and we're not sure what it is." In other words, it was a flying object neither Ted nor Terrence could identify.

What we were left with were the facts that recent construction of a huge hangar indicated that Area 51 was still active. Pat and Susan ascertained that the base was still high security and that personnel were clearly on alert to their presence and ready to respond were they to have done something foolhardy and crossed the perimeter. Pat and I showed that the mysterious Janet flights were still going into Area 51 from McCarran International Airport on a daily schedule and that the 737s flown, as Mark Farmer helped us determine, were owned by the federal government. Thus, Area 51 was at the time an active base staffed by personnel flown in by federally owned, but unmarked, jets. Finally, Ted and Terrence Masson determined that the surveillance cameras had captured an artificial, unidentifiable object, not a meteorite, that turned itself off before it descended into Area 51. They had captured on camera, by definition, a UFO. Whether the craft was ours, meaning the government's, or theirs, meaning an extraterrestrial's, was something they couldn't determine. But if some agency were jealously guarding the base's secrets to keep UFO investigators from digging out any facts about the place, we showed them that their efforts were futile.

And in the end, we did what UFO Hunters does best. We caught a UFO on camera over Area 51.

BILL'S BLOG:
AREA 51, THE MONSTERS, THE CRITICS,
THE DEBUNKERS, AND THE MYTH

Over the course of three seasons of production, we visited four sensitive military installations, all of which were rumored to be bases where there was involvement with UFOs: Area 51, Utah's Dugway Proving Ground, New Mexico's Dulce, and AUTEC (Atlantic Undersea Test and Evaluation Center, which is the top-secret U.S. naval base at Andros Island in the Bahamas). Of all of them, Area 51 has attracted the greatest amount of interest from UFO researchers because of its long history of UFO involvement and, of course, the Bob Lazar story.

Ever since the "Area 51 Revealed" episode was first broadcast on February 25, 2009, there has been lots of new theory concerning the base, and one former worker at Papoose Lake contacted us to say that we had been barking up the wrong trail. Calling himself Viper, not his real name, of course, this person said he was a retired air force sergeant who worked as a repair technician for the cooling and heating system at Papoose Lake, a facility at the corner of Groom Lake, where, he said, the real reverse engineering of UFOs took place. He said that he was personally ordered on at least eight UFO-crash-retrieval expeditions during the course of his work at Papoose Lake, one of which was in New Mexico and another near Dakota during an operation "Red Flag" exercise, when an F-4 Phantom jet collided with a UFO. These are the kinds of stories that keep on circulating about the Area 51 complex, which, Viper said, officially does not exist except in the minds of UFO hunters.

There is no doubt that the Nevada facilities around Groom Lake and Nellis Air Force Base are home to secret operations. T. D. Barnes told us that, and we saw the facilities from Tikaboo Peak with our own eyes and photographed them. But it is the nature of those secret operations that has been so fascinating to UFO researchers over the decades, especially since George Knapp broke the Bob Lazar story on KLAS-TV almost twenty-five years ago.

Just recently, however, in what at least one of my friends who've described their background as being in the U.S. clandestine services has said was a deliberately inspired disinformation gambit, a 2011 New York Times bestselling book on Area 51, by Los Angeles Times contributor Annie Jacobsen (Area 51: An Uncensored History of America's Top Secret Military Base [Little, Brown, 2011]), spent lots of time going over the reverse-engineering story of Oxcart and other projects at Area 51, material already out there as a result of our "Area 51 Revealed" episode. However, the book took a sharp detour from established facts by linking Area 51 (incorrectly saying the base was established in 1951) with the story of the crash at Roswell, saying that, according to an unnamed source, the crash at Roswell was connected to the future Area 51 because the craft that crashed in the New Mexico desert in 1947 was actually a Horten Brothers flying wing dispatched to the United States by Joseph Stalin with the help of Dr. Josef Mengele.

How anyone could come up with a crazy story like this, crazier than a UFO story, is beyond me because not only does it smack of a cover story rife with disinformation, just like a Project Mogul story, but also the facts are wrong on their face. Let's take the first basic fact Jacobsen states about Area 51, that it was founded in 1951. Not to criticize any fact-checkers at the publishing company, the New York Times, who reviewed her book, or any one of the numerous television shows where she appeared to talk about her book, but Area 51 was opened in 1955. Is anybody out there?

Incorrect dates regarding Area 51 aside, what about the Horten Brothers flying wing? Would it have fooled the Roswell Army Airfield base intelligence officer, Major Jesse Marcel, who had just graduated from radar school? Answer: No. Why? Because not only was the Horten Brothers flying wing made of wood, a substance not at all exotic and something even an eight-year-old would have recognized, but also the latest version was powered by a jet engine. No element 115 here. The United States Army Air Force already had jet engines by 1947 and had seen jet-powered fighters in the war in 1945. There could have been no mistake about a jet or even a rocket, which we were launching at White Sands just down the road. Any officer at the Roswell Army Airfield would have recognized the flying wing for exactly what it was, especially since the United States had developed its own flying wing before World War II.

Let's keep going. How would the flying wing have gotten to New Mexico? Would it have flown? Yes, if it had been able to fly. The problem not only with the Horten Brothers designs—which began in the late 1920s with a flying-wing glider because the Germans weren't allowed under the terms of the Versailles Treaty to develop warplanes—was that the advanced powered versions couldn't fly any distances. They had no range. Indeed, one of the desperate developments the Germans were trying to facilitate toward the end of the war was an intercontinental bomber to attack the United States. They didn't have one by the war's end in 1945, and they certainly didn't have one by 1947. Accordingly, even if Stalin had gotten his hands on a flying wing, he couldn't have gotten it to New Mexico.

Clearly, without going into the reams of facts and solid evidence about the Roswell crash, the Horten Brothers flying wing / Area 51 cover story is simply that, a cover story. It was disinformation, the kind of stuff pumped out all the way back in the 1950s that was wacky enough to identify the Area 51 scientist who revealed it. Mention Mengele to someone and a monitor in security might be able to pinpoint the source and take appropriate disciplinary action to curb further leaks. And this is most likely why there was such a crazy cover story about Area 51 told to some of the contract workers at the base.

By the way, Dr. Mengele was in South America after the war, fleeing for his very life and more afraid of the Soviets than he was of the Allies, and he would have been incommunicado with any Stalin agents asking him to create physically deformed pilots to pilot an unflyable craft to the New Mexico desert to frighten the United States at the outset of the Cold War.

Given the real facts surrounding this story, one has to wonder why talk show hosts, in particular Jon Stewart, and even the revered *New York Times*, declined to comment on the obvious disconnect between Jacobsen's book and verifiable facts. I remember when *The Day After Roswell* was published in 1997. During that week, the air force released its Project Mogul story and the *New York Times* not only gave it a front-page coverage, it also went out of its way to mention *The Day After Roswell* as another one of those Roswell stories, which the air force was now disposing of. Again, the skeptics doing their job for the flag, motherland, and the American way didn't bother to check any facts about Project Mogul. But Stan Friedman did, and he established that in 1947, high-altitude strings of balloons, which would have been what the Mogul project managers would have used that year, were made of the same rubber as the standard weather balloons already in use. Again, Jesse Marcel would have recognized the neoprene rubber in a weather balloon, regardless of the number of balloons strung together.

Getting to the facts about Area 51, in much the same way as we got to the facts about Roswell earlier in season 2, was one of the most thrilling parts of filming this episode. Whether you believe Bob Lazar or John Lear, the simple fact that a reputable, credible news correspondent like George Knapp said he was able to verify Lazar's employment at Los Alamos and report it on camera was a high point of our show. Similarly, seeing the John Lear videotapes of his excursions into the desert outside Area 51's perimeter at night with Bob Lazar behind the camera proved that their relationship was verifiable. And finally, Ted's setting up an array of cameras to surveil the skies over Area 51, where he caught an object that seemed to defy the aeronautical characteristics of a conventional craft, an object he could not identify from the surveillance tapes, was almost too good to contemplate.

You see, at the end of season 2, *UFO Hunters* actually achieved what it had set out to achieve. Sifting through lots of legend and lore, talking to witnesses about everything from alien implants to underwater USO bases, we found the one item, the one object that marked a milestone on the way to discovering something true about UFOs.

We found the UFO.

INDEX

William J. Birnes is the *New York Times* bestselling coauthor of *The Day After Roswell* and *The Haunting of America*. He was the lead host and consulting producer of History Channel's *UFO Hunters* and guest host of History's *Ancient Aliens*. Birnes is also the guest expert on UFOs and American history on the History Channel series *America's Book of Secrets*.